UNDER THE BUS

UNDER THE BUS

HOW WORKING WOMEN
ARE BEING RUN OVER

CAROLINE FREDRICKSON

THE NEW PRESS

NEW YORK
LONDON

To my beloved mother who taught me to believe in the intrinsic dignity of all people

Requests for permission to reproduce selections from this book should be mailed to: Permissions Department, The New Press, 120 Wall Street, 31st floor, New York, NY 10005.

Published in the United States by The New Press, New York, 2015
Distributed by Perseus Distribution

LIBRARY OF CONGRESS CATALOGING-IN-PUBLICATION DATA

Fredrickson, Caroline.
 Under the bus : how working women are being run over / Caroline Fredrickson.
     pages cm
  Includes bibliographical references and index.
 ISBN 978-1-62097-010-2 (hardback) -- ISBN 978-1-62097-080-5 (e-book) 1. Sex dis-
crimination in employment--United States. 2. Women--United States--Employment.
3. Household employees--United States. 4. Part-time employees--United States. I. Title.
 HD6060.5.U5F74 2015
 331.40973--dc23
                    2014041282

The New Press publishes books that promote and enrich public discussion and understanding of the issues vital to our democracy and to a more equitable world. These books
are made possible by the enthusiasm of our readers; the support of a committed group of
donors, large and small; the collaboration of our many partners in the independent media
and the not-for-profit sector; booksellers, who often hand-sell New Press books; librarians;
and above all by our authors.

www.thenewpress.com

Composition by Bookbright Media
This book was set in Goudy Oldstyle and Futura

Printed in the United States of America

10 9 8 7 6 5 4 3 2 1

CONTENTS

ACKNOWLEDGMENTS

Thanks first to Diane Wachtell, Jed Bickman, Sarah Fan, and The New Press for being interested in publishing this book and helping me to shape it; it has been a wonderful partnership, and without their support the book would not have come into being.

I am eternally grateful to Peter Edelman, who has been a magnificent mentor and friend, as well as a sounding board for the ideas in this book (and who gave me the occasional hug when I needed encouragement). And of course I would be remiss if I did not thank my colleagues and the board of the American Constitution Society for Law and Policy, which works every day to ensure the law is a force for good in the lives of *all* people.

I am very much in debt to the many, many people and organizations who offered me suggestions, invaluable insights, and areas for further exploration, including Sheena Wadhawan and Gustavo Torres of Casa de Maryland; Darrah Sipe, Rebekah Christie, Dolly Martinez, and Nala Toussaint of the Retail Action Project; Myrla Maldonado, Marietta Toboso, Eric Rodriguez, and Lisa Thomas of Latino Union; Ai-jen Poo, Patricia Francois, Andrea Cristina Mercado, and Rosana Reyes of the National Domestic Workers Alliance; Andrea Lee and Katie Joaquin of

Mujeres Unidas; Sarita Gupta of Jobs with Justice; Kimi Lee of the United Workers Congress; Saru Jayaraman of the Restaurant Opportunities Center; Haeyoung Yoon and Christine Owens of the National Employment Law Project; Terisa Chaw of the National Employment Lawyers Association; Joe Sellers of Cohen Milstein; Lynn Rhinehart of the AFL-CIO; and Judy Scott at SEIU, who provides me with ongoing good counsel as a member of the ACS Board. I know I have not captured all of those who have helped me shape this book and my thinking—please forgive me.

I must of course thank my darling husband, Sean Dobson, who read the drafts and gave me tough but constructive criticism with a hug and a smile and the occasional shoulder rub.

INTRODUCTION

Mathilda Olafsson was only eighteen when she left Sweden at the end of the nineteenth century. At home in the fishing village of Nogersund, she had helped her widowed father raise her younger siblings, but when they died one by one, she became just an extra mouth to feed and was forced to set out on her own. Sweden was so poor that her only hope for survival was to come to America. She gathered up her few possessions and sailed steerage to Boston, with no family to meet her and no savings to sustain her. Though she was lucky to land a job as a scullery maid on Beacon Hill, her days were full of backbreaking labor; she ate the scraps from her employers' plates when they were done with their meals, and she hoarded her small earnings. Immigrant women were subject to sexual harassment, underpayment, abusively long hours, and no hope of overtime, health care, or retirement security. Mathilda was my great-grandmother.

I found Mathilda's bravery very inspirational when I was young. I even used it as the basis for my college application essay. It was so cinematic—in my mind's eye, I could picture her taking her bedroll and a few coins and setting off by herself across the sea, the wind in her hair and her eyes on the horizon. I never thought about the cramped and fetid quarters belowdecks, about the likelihood of her facing physical danger or enduring sexual assault, or about her actual experience once she arrived in Boston. Least of all did I focus on the harsh reality of her life downstairs, scrubbing pots until her fingers bled, eating food scraps, suffering abuse—and having no legal rights at all. There was no romance in that story, and it seemed far from today's world.

Well over a century later, Ephese, another domestic worker trying to escape poverty, arrived from Port-au-Prince, Haiti, to find abusive conditions similar to those Mathilda faced. After ten years as a caregiver in New York, Ephese still cries every day before going to work. Her first job was caring for three children part-time in Brooklyn, where she lived. Her employers paid her incredibly poorly, and the $75 she earned for three very long days per week did not come near to covering her bills. Moving to a full-time job as a home health aide, Ephese was not allowed to take any breaks during her shifts, and when she moved back to a child care job, she wasn't allowed any days off at all, even on occasions when she was so sick she needed to see a doctor.[1]

And there's Sonia Soares, who has toiled as a home health aide and housekeeper for more than thirty years, suffering similar abuses. Testifying in front of the Massachusetts legislature, she painted a bleak picture of her conditions of work: "My colleagues and I clean up to 14 houses a day and still struggle to make ends meet. . . . I personally have been slapped in the face, pushed, yelled at and sexually harassed." Other nannies and health aides told legislators stories of eighteen-hour days, employers who subtract money from their wages, who refuse to allow them to see a doctor when sick, who have no legal obligation to pay overtime.[2] What is shocking is that, in the twenty-first century, domestic workers and workers in certain other professions dominated by women have little more legal protection than women like

Mathilda had, doing those same jobs in the late nineteenth and early twentieth centuries.[3]

Over the past one hundred years, America has adopted a variety of progressive laws meant to improve wages and working conditions, but these laws have left many behind. During the New Deal, President Franklin D. Roosevelt and his allies, forced to bargain with the Dixiecrats, traded off the rights of certain African American and women workers in order to get votes for bills providing a minimum wage, overtime, and the right to join a union for other workers. Subsequently, legislation barring discrimination in employment, requiring family leave, and providing health insurance, among other features, has excluded many women through different mechanisms but with similar consequences. Not just nannies, home health aides, and housekeepers, but also farmworkers, small business employees, independent contractors, temporary workers, and others have almost no protections under the law. The numbers add up fast.

Few of us are aware of how the labor and employment laws leave out so many women. Indeed, even I, who practiced labor law and have long been involved in legislative and policy efforts in this area, must admit how blind I have been. Working as a congressional aide to then Senate Democratic leader Tom Daschle (D-SD), I drafted a pair of bills, one of which has become law, designed to address discrimination (one dealing with genetic issues and the other, the Paycheck Fairness Act, with women's pay). With nary a thought about the merits of doing so, I used the provisions from those same labor and employment laws as a model, picking up the same built-in exclusions.

Reading the stories of Ephese, Sonia, and other domestic workers forced me to reconsider what I really knew about Mathilda. How did she escape from the "downstairs" of Back Bay, and how did she manage to raise nine children? But the stories also made me reconsider what I knew about the real state of our laws for working women. Since I had not known that domestic workers had been cut out of most of our labor laws, what else did I not know? And I began to wonder what a nanny does with her children when she works late or when one of them is sick, and how many women get by without paid family leave, affordable child care, and access to good jobs, each of these not a separate but a simultaneous problem. Unfortunately, most of those engaging in our national conversation about women and work wear similar blinders, failing to see what is evident all around us.

"Opting out" or "leaning in." These seem to be the only two options now under discussion for women in America, as pronounced most recently by former high-level State Department official Anne-Marie Slaughter, stating definitively that women "can't have it all," and by Facebook executive Sheryl Sandberg, arguing that what women really need is to change themselves to be successful. Most of the time, in both elite media and popular publications, when we talk about women and the struggle to combine work and family, our discussion is implicitly limited to white-collar (and white) professional women and their efforts to succeed in the corporate world and simultaneously have a family.[4] And even that discussion is hobbled by two peculiarly American cultural blinders: our tendency to avoid collective solutions to collective problems in favor of self-help approaches, and a separation of so-called identity issues from the discussion on economic justice. Together these tendencies allow us to blame women for their status: we say that they aren't tough enough in the workplace or that they have a biological need to be with their children that can't be overcome.

Rarely, if ever, do we ask how those women without high

wages, paid leave, affordable child care, or flexible schedules, who don't have the choice to "balance" work and family—that is, most women—juggle their desperate need to earn money with caring for their children. But this is the big question that we all should be asking, because it turns out that there are real consequences for all of us.

Charlene Fletcher shares the one bedroom in her tiny apartment in Duarte, California, with her husband and two kids, one an infant. Charlene is employed by Walmart, where she is not accorded even the basic dignity of knowing her work schedule in advance. Instead, she has to call in to her supervisors every day to find out if she's on the rotation and how long her workday will be. She's often away from her family on weekends and holidays unexpectedly, making it really hard to plan for child care and to know how much money might be coming in each pay period—and whether they can pay their bills. Her pay, at $9.40 an hour, is so meager that she is officially poor. Putting a brave face on it, she said to a reporter, "We all stay in one bedroom. . . . We managed to get all three beds in there—the crib, the twin, and my grandmother's old-fashioned bed frame."[5] Even with her husband's full-time job, they earn so little that they are eligible for California's medical welfare program, the tarnished silver lining of poverty that ensures that at least their basic medical needs can be addressed. And she qualifies for the federal Women, Infants, and Children program, allowing her to get subsidized food. She doesn't want to depend on government assistance, but her children need to eat.

Sheryl Sandberg, Ann-Marie Slaughter, and I have had the luxury of considering whether we want to "lean in" or "opt out." Unfortunately, Charlene Fletcher has not. Her story is a reality check on the superficial picture we normally get of a working woman, briefcase in hand, trying to decide whether to use her high-priced education to make money or to homeschool her kids,

and provides a much truer depiction of what too many women experience. Charlene doesn't have the luxury of "opting out" to stay
home with her kids, and if she pushes for higher wages at work,
especially if she does so by organizing with her co-workers to demand a collective raise, "leaning in" might just result in getting
canned. Another Walmart worker, Betty Dukes, did try to argue
for a raise and a promotion and suffered the consequences—a
demotion and a pay cut.[6] A mere request for a vacation day is
enough for some women to lose their jobs. Beatriz Garayalde, a
nanny in New York, had put up with harsh working conditions
at her workplace for a long time, forced to work from 7 a.m. until
late at night. An immigrant from Uruguay, she had hopes that
she could make a better life for herself after her employers promised her a good work situation. Instead, they demanded she work
days and nights, gave her no privacy, and denied her days off. She
told researchers,

> I don't think I slept at all during the first three months. I
> stayed in the room with the children. My only real sleep
> was between 7 a.m., when the parents came to my room for
> the children, until 9 a.m., when I went back to work. After
> getting up, I'd wet my head and stick it out of the window
> in the dead of winter so I could stay awake. And if I man-
> aged to sleep some at night, my brain would still be alert,
> listening to the children's breathing. During the day, I'd
> do my chores, cook, clean and take care of the children—
> months passed like this, working day and night—I forgot
> that I was a person, only looking after the children and the
> housework.

She reached her limit, but when she finally asked to take a day
off, she was fired.[7] And there was nothing she could do about it.

Betty Dukes sued and lost, and Beatriz Garayalde had no legal rights to sue over. Be careful of "leaning in."

As for "opting out," few can do that either. For women like Sumer Spika, a home health aide in Minnesota, there is no such thing as time off to have a baby. Her job gives her no benefits and no vacation, let alone paid leave. When she delivered her child by cesarean, she had to be back at work in only a week.[8] She loves Jayla, the little girl she cares for, but the challenges of a low-paying job with no benefits make it hard for her to care for her own family.[9] Shaquonica Johnson, also a Minnesotan, went back to work even sooner—within a day—after a hysterectomy, because, as she said, "missing work means my children do not eat."[10] Johnson's concerns are not limited to her wages; she also worries that poor working conditions mean such high turnover among home care aides that she and her family members will not get quality care when they might need it themselves.[11] And many women are in the same situation as Olivia, who had left Mexico to escape an abusive relationship there. An undocumented immigrant working in an Iowa meatpacking plant, she was brutally raped by a supervisor. Left bloody and beaten, she did get to see a doctor but could not go to the police: "No, I was scared of the police. . . . And I was scared of [the attacker]." Afraid of being deported and afraid of losing her job, she kept her mouth shut. "I had a lot of need, and if I didn't go to work, what would I do? I had to pay a lot of rent, many bills, my sick daughter, and my sick parents who depend on me."[12]

After she had children, Chandra Benitez of Alameda, California, would have liked to "opt out." But needing two incomes to cover her husband's school loans and pay off debt on their credit card, Benitez went back to work as a bus driver for elderly and disabled people. Like Fletcher at Walmart, she's an on-call employee; she doesn't know her shifts until the night before when she checks in with her supervisors. Some of the shifts start early, others go late, but she never knows until a short time beforehand, making her constantly worry that, if she has a sick kid and has to stay home, she could lose her job. Even when her children are healthy, she worries. She has been able to enlist her mother and sister in child care, but her sister is also looking for work. Knowing her ailing mother could not care for the kids alone, she worries, "If my sister finds a job . . . it might put me out of a job."[13] She doesn't know how they would make ends meet without her salary.

When many women exit the workforce to care for their kids, it could be described not as "opting out" as much as getting kicked out. Rhiannon Broschat lost her job when a snow day closed schools in Chicago and she had no other option but to stay home to care for her son, who has special needs. The single mother had nowhere to turn and hoped her employer, Whole Foods, would be flexible and humane enough to let her stay home. No such luck. She had used up her unpaid leave days and was told by her boss not to come back.[14] Yvette Nunez, a single mother from Bay Ridge, Brooklyn, had to quit her grocery store job when her boss scheduled her to work weekends, adding $75 to her weekly child care bill. A single mother with three children, Nunez got some government support, but even with the subsidies, almost half of her weekly salary went to child care. In the end, she decided to quit and stay home. As much as she wants to return to work, she doesn't because the cost of child care makes it barely worthwhile.[15] Sunah Hwang didn't want to "opt out" either. A public school teacher, she loved her job, but since her salary hardly covered day care bills, the family budget dictated that she should stay home because her husband earned more. Hwang had not thought she would be forced to make this decision: "I always wanted to be a teacher. I thought I could spend time with my kids and have the best of both worlds."[16]

Overall, American workers are not doing well. Incomes have flattened, even for couples with two salaries, and people are working longer hours than ever. Organized labor has sharply contracted in the United States, and globalization, with increased outsourcing and offshoring of jobs, has pushed down wages for most Americans. Good jobs are more and more scarce. A recent study estimates that midwage jobs constituted 60 percent of the jobs lost during the recession that began in 2008 but only a little more than 20 percent of those created during the subsequent recovery; by contrast, low-wage jobs were 21 percent of the jobs lost during the recession but have been close to 60 percent of the new jobs created post-recession.[17] Because of how little these jobs pay, Americans work dramatically longer hours per employee than workers in any other developed country. This is true even though more and more workers are able to get only part-time work, despite their need for full-time hours—meaning the longer hours actually reflect people who work two or even three jobs. And since the 1970s, there has been a precipitous decline in the number of jobs with benefits; fewer workers have a pension or health insurance.[18] Lowest wages, longest hours, loss of benefits. This is not the "American exceptionalism" we have been promised.

Workers in dead-end jobs, no matter how hard they work and scrimp and save, have a nearly impossible task in raising themselves out of poverty. Yet conservative economists deplore social programs and still peddle the false hopes raised by the Horatio Alger story and the persistent myth of the American Dream.[19] In his book on the lives of the working poor, David K. Shipler, Pulitzer Prize–winning *New York Times* bureau chief, punctured a hole in the myth of mobility:

> While the United States has enjoyed unprecedented afflu-
> ence, low-wage employees have been testing the American
> doctrine that hard work cures poverty. . . . Some have
> found that work works. Others have learned that it doesn't.
> Moving in and out of jobs that demand much and pay lit-
> tle, many people tread just above the official poverty line,
> dangerously close to the edge of destitution. An inconve-
> nience for an affluent family—minor car trouble, a brief
> illness, disrupted child care—is a crisis to them, for it can
> threaten their ability to stay employed.[20]

Unrelenting attacks from free market advocates who can't stomach government programs, even when—or perhaps espe-cially when—they are helping people, have shrunken eligibility and funding for critical antipoverty efforts and killed efforts to provide child care and sick leave. These changes have helped propel the stunning growth of inequality in America, which poses a truly moral dilemma for our nation, and challenges us to do better . . . or else.[21]

And who has borne the brunt of these changes? Women. By and large, women, and particularly women of color, have been the canary in the coal mine signaling the growing insecurity of work in America. Although the United States had a higher per-centage of men than women in the early 1950s, women are now the majority, making up close to 51 percent.[22] Overall, the work-ing population has grown significantly more female, diverse in race and ethnicity, and older.[23] In sheer number, whites are the largest group in poverty, but women of color, especially those with children, are grossly overrepresented.[24]

It will be no surprise to anyone that women make up the vast majority of nannies and manicurists, or that they fill most of the jobs as home health care aides and maids who clean houses for a living. What is less well-known is that these extremely poorly paid service sector jobs dominate the low-wage economy, and women make up 53 percent of the low-wage workforce.[25] (The low-wage workforce, or "working poor," is defined as persons who spent at least twenty-seven weeks in the labor force but whose incomes fell below the official poverty level.) They are domestic workers, caring for children and the elderly, cleaning houses, or otherwise serving in someone's home; they wait tables or act as hostesses in restaurants; they are "independent contractors," cutting hair and doing makeup and nails, cleaning offices and homes, and taking care of lawns and gardens. They work for small businesses as receptionists and secretaries. Many of them work part-time jobs.

An overview of the statistics helps put these facts in perspective.

- Women are now 63.9 percent of breadwinners or co-breadwinners (co-breadwinners are those who earn at least one-quarter of their families' income).[26]
- Women are 63 percent of minimum-wage workers.[27] (Minimum-wage workers are approximately 5 percent of all workers, and their numbers are growing.)[28] In 2013, 16.8 million women earned less than $11 per hour.[29]
- Women are 73 percent of tipped employees, including waiters, manicurists, and hairdressers. These workers make only $2.13 per hour before tips.[30]
- Women are 86 percent of personal care aides, a profession expected to grow 49 percent from 2012 to 2022. Within that category, they are 94 percent of child care workers and 88 percent of home health aides.[31]
- Women are 35 percent of the 10.3 million independent contractors.[32]
- Women are 63 percent of part-time workers.[33]

Women occupy jobs that are excluded from legal protections, making the workers very easy to exploit and underpay. Even when there are protective laws, they are easy for employers to ignore, because there is very little enforcement. So, in addition to dominating the low-wage workforce, women, particularly women of color, dominate the unregulated or minimally regulated workforce. These facts have a growing relevance because not only is this group already surprisingly large, but these jobs are also the ones more and more people will hold in coming years. Projections for job growth forecast that, in the future, we will see the biggest increase in job categories that are low paid and currently dominated by women.[34] As more and more men are shut out of manufacturing jobs with decent wages, men are facing these same conditions. Stephanie Coontz, a frequent commentator on women and work, wrote in the *New York Times* that "millions of men face working conditions that traditionally characterized women's lives: low wages, minimal benefits, part-time or temporary jobs, and periods of joblessness. Poverty is becoming defeminized because the working conditions of many men are becoming more feminized."[35]

Families are changing and women's wages have become necessary for families to stay afloat. So the fact that women dominate sectors of the workforce covered by few, if any, protective laws means that their families suffer as well. If we ever had an *Ozzie and Harriet* family structure, it is surely gone now. A lifestyle that used to require one man's salary now takes two incomes to meet expenses. For poorer families, those in the lower 20 percent of income, the importance of women's wages is even greater, with more than 66 percent of women bringing in as much as or more than their husbands.[36]

Not surprisingly, the challenges for single mothers are even more substantial. While more than three-quarters of high-income working women are married or have a partner who works full-time, only 14 percent of low-income women workers are in such relationships.[37] In a growing number of families, women are the sole earners; these households are our economy's poorest segment.[38] Between 1970 and 2009, the percentage of single working mothers with children under eighteen doubled, and right now almost four in ten American mothers serve as the only breadwinners for their families.[39] This increase has been accompanied by a corresponding growth in the number of children of single mothers who are poor. In 1959, 24 percent of such children were below the poverty line; in 2010, 55 percent of children living with a single mother were poor.[40] To look at it another way, in 2009, 28 percent of unmarried working women with children earned less than the poverty level, compared to only 8 percent of all women workers.[41] The adverse impact on these children, and our nation's future, is substantial.

Even for women and families who do have some job protections and have two incomes, many do not have family leave, either paid or unpaid. Most families find the cost of child care staggering, with far too few slots in Head Start and other early education programs, and private child care taking up a third or more of many families' budgets. The cost of child care rivals that of college tuition, and the quality of the facilities and teachers is often suspect. A professor at Baruch College in Manhattan with a PhD in anthropology, Carla Bellamy brings in $74,000 per year, putting her in the group of higher earners, but even with her composer husband's income bringing them up to $110,000 per year, they struggle to pay for child care for their two children. There's nothing left over for anything nonessential. She said, "Our entire disposable income goes to child care. . . . It's not a tragic story, but is tiring and tiresome. I have a career, I work really hard, and yet I get no break." She was even tempted to take a second job waiting tables during her summers off but needed the time to do the writing and research essential to keeping her teaching job—publish or perish is a truism in academe.[42]

So how did we get into this sad state of affairs? We tend to think things are not so bad—maybe not in Sweden's league in gender equality, but not in the Stone Age either. After all, we have banned discrimination against women, required equal pay for equal work, and adopted family leave legislation. But most people do not know that we allow discrimination by small employers and leave more than half of women out of the family leave law. Or that we cut certain workers out of the wage and hour laws. Or that part-time workers are rarely entitled to benefits. Child care breaks the bank for many families, and very few workers have paid family leave. A confluence of factors, including race, ethnicity, immigration status, and gender, has put an array of workers beyond the protections of the law. Domestic workers, farmworkers, day laborers, tipped employees, minimum-wage workers, guest workers, workers in so-called right-to-work states, independent contractors, and temps are all thrown under the bus. And over the years this contingent of workers has grown as more women enter the workforce, unions decline, industrial jobs disappear, and our population becomes browner.

Beneath all this is a history of racism and sexism upon which the structure of our labor protections was built.[43] Through both direct and intentional efforts spearheaded by legislators during the New Deal to exclude workers based on their race and sex, and the statutory limitations built into later laws, certain workers have slipped through the holes in our porous system of labor protections. In each case, vulnerable groups were the bargaining chips for the policy's enactment. This is not to blame the leaders, women and men, who fought so hard to achieve the protections we have. At every step in the process, some of those seated at the table were trying their best to create good policy, but to do so they felt they had to give something up. Over and over it was women—especially women of color—who were left out. In the case of the New Deal legislation protecting workers' rights to join a union and to earn overtime after forty hours of work in a week, Senate Dixiecrats conditioned their votes on the exclusion of household workers and field hands so wealthy southeners could continue to benefit from these workers' cheap labor. Charles Hamilton Houston, the head of the National Association for the Advancement of Colored People (NAACP), described the Social Security Act when it passed in the 1930s "as a sieve with the holes just big enough for the majority of Negroes to fall through."[44] Unfortunately the holes in the sieve have not been filled, and many, particularly women of color, are still falling through.

When you layer the Family and Medical Leave Act on top of the Fair Labor Standards Act and the Civil Rights Act of 1964, you can see that each time political compromises were made to get legislation passed, certain women, often the same women, got shut out—and by design. Over time, as the United States developed and augmented its labor protections, the poor, the immigrant, and African American and Latino workers have been left out—and a disproportionate number of these are women. A nanny, for example, faces legally acceptable discrimination—it is absolutely legal for an employer to fire a woman because of her sex or refuse to hire a nanny because she is black—has no provisions for leave if she is having a child of her own, and can be forced to work long hours without overtime, all because of the size and type of her employer.

Right now, the path to prosperity is steep for most families. They struggle to get by on two incomes (if they are lucky), with few benefits, unpredictable work schedules, limited sick leave, and unaffordable child care. It is clear that Americans want change—all races at all levels of the income scale. We work too hard, our families suffer from neglect, and we have little time to pursue the intangible good things in life allowed by a bit of time for oneself. Wages, hours, leave, and child care—each demands a new way of thinking, where we abandon our traditional assumptions about how the workplace should be structured. We can no longer relegate the fight for a fair and equal workplace to a discussion at the "women's caucus" or describe policies addressing child care and family leave as "women's issues." And we cannot allow the conversation to be dominated by the issues facing corporate CEOs and high-level bureaucrats.

With respect to wages, for our nation's fiscal health, as well as for women and their families, eliminating the gap between men's and women's wages would have a significant and positive impact. Economists estimate that bringing women's wages up to a level equal to that of men would raise women's earnings by more than 17 percent, and family incomes would climb yearly by almost $7,000 per family, or $245.3 billion nationwide.[45] A key element of lifting women's wages is combating occupational segregation and improving enforcement of discrimination laws, which will enable more women to earn higher wages and expand the opportunities available to both sexes. We have to stop treating workers like machine parts and we have to end on-call and just-in-time staffing, where workers' schedules are arbitrarily changed, creating havoc in child care arrangements and financial plans. Benefits need to be decoupled from full-time status to ensure that employers are not encouraged to drop workers' hours to avoid providing health care or family leave. And we must finally adopt a paid sick leave and family leave policy. Our current laissez-faire approach means that many mothers, and not only those who are low income, are forced to give birth and immediately come back to work, with negative consequences for both mother and child. And a country without a child care system disserves working parents, their children, and our nation's future. Our current expensive, and mostly private, system provides decent care to few families and affordable care to almost none. We should provide universal, affordable child care. Most important, we need to expand the labor protections we do provide to *all* workers and not exclude certain workers because of their job titles or employer size or because they have been designated as a temp or a contractor. In essence, we need to consider whether the "system" as a whole works or not—and make systemic and not narrowly targeted changes so that we can all benefit, and no one is left out, intentionally or otherwise.

Many authors have examined the plight of these different types of workers; lots of historians have noted the separate instances when loopholes in the safety net were created; everybody now knows that median living standards are stagnating or declining in America. This book puts it all together, explaining how this huge and growing segment of the workforce—overwhelmingly female and of color—was created, how and why it is growing, and how if we don't fix this problem, all American workers will be swallowed by this trend.

So while the media debate "opt out" and "lean in," the real focus should be those who are "left out." Women work, and increasingly they are filling jobs with few benefits, low wages, and unpredictable schedules. Even middle-class Americans are suffering from the consequences of the changes in our workplaces and the need for two incomes. Our workplace laws threw women of color under the bus from the beginning, but we will all get run over if we don't reinvent our system to get everyone on board.

1

THE TEST OF OUR PROGRESS:
A BRIEF HISTORY OF RACE, GENDER, AND WORKER PROTECTIONS IN THE TWENTIETH CENTURY

I see a great nation, upon a great continent, blessed with a great wealth of natural resources. . . . In this nation I see tens of millions of its citizens—a substantial part of its whole population—who at this very moment are denied the greater part of what the very lowest standards of today call the necessities of life.

I see millions of families trying to live on incomes so meager that the pall of family disaster hangs over them day by day.

I see millions whose daily lives in city and on farm continue under conditions labeled indecent by a so-called polite society half a century ago.

I see millions denied education, recreation, and the opportunity to better their lot and the lot of their children.

I see millions lacking the means to buy the products of farm and factory and by their poverty denying work and productiveness to many other millions.

I see one-third of a nation ill-housed, ill-clad, ill-nourished.

But it is not in despair that I paint you that picture. I

paint it for you in hope—because the nation, seeing and understanding the injustice in it, proposes to paint it out. . . . The test of our progress is not whether we add more to the abundance of those who have much; it is whether we provide enough for those who have too little.

—*Franklin D. Roosevelt, Inaugural Address, January 20, 1937*

One of the great achievements of the New Deal was guaranteeing workers a minimum wage and a forty-hour workweek, enforced by the requirement of overtime pay for extra hours worked. Workers fought successfully for the right to join unions and bargain collectively with their employers. As the New Deal gave way to the civil rights movement, workers were able to win protections against job discrimination based on race, national origin, religion, and gender. Subsequent legislation added prohibitions on age and disability discrimination—and some states, and hopefully soon the federal government, have made it illegal to discriminate on the basis of sexual orientation and gender identity. The twentieth century would seem to have been a linear march forward for workers' rights—but only if we ignore those workers who did not seem to merit protection or were explicitly thrown under the bus by the lawmakers who drafted the bills.

It is typical in the legislative process for legislators to cut deals to get laws passed, opting to give less to one group in order to get more for another. During the New Deal, even those elected officials who thought they had the best interests of low-wage workers at heart saw fit to exclude certain people to accommodate hostile legislators predominantly from the South. As President Franklin D. Roosevelt explained rather forthrightly when pressed about his failure to support antilynching legislation—which, like providing job protections for African American workers, was anathema to southern congressmen—"If I come out for the anti-lynching bill now, they will block every bill I ask Congress to pass to keep America from collapsing. I just can't take that risk."[1]

Thus, in spite of the advances, the history of the adoption of our progressive labor laws tells a story that sometimes shows overt racism and sexism on the part of the statutes' authors; that sometimes demonstrates unconscious—or at least unspoken— prejudices; and that often reflects a vision of a workplace that no longer exists (and for many, never did), when men worked in factories and women stayed home and raised the children. Who was left out tells as much as does who was put in.

WOMEN'S WORK: MISOGYNY AND MIXED MESSAGES

In the twentieth century, workers fought for job protections, re- sulting in some phenomenal victories—the Fair Labor Standards Act, the National Labor Relations Act, and later the Equal Pay Act, Title VII of the Civil Rights Act of 1964, the Pregnancy Discrimination Act of 1978, and the Family and Medical Leave Act of 1993. Workers gained the right to earn a minimum wage and work a limited number of hours per week or get paid over- time; they were allowed to join unions and bargain for wages and benefits; they were protected from job discrimination on the basis of race, ethnicity, gender, religion, and disability; they won the right to take time off when having a child or caring for a sick family member; and women would no longer face adverse job consequences when they got pregnant. Well, sort of.

It is important to put all this legislative activity in context, not just in the familiar frame of economic hardship that was the Great Depression and the response that was the New Deal, but in the mind-set of the cultural milieu, and in particular that pe- riod's entrenched racism, visceral anti-immigrant paranoia, and deep-seated hostility to women's emancipation. This context is not just scene setting but goes a long way to explain how our laws came to omit certain workers from their embrace.   •

During the Great Depression, working women were frequently criticized for allegedly taking jobs away from men, who were assumed to be the primary breadwinners in their families. The media disparaged working women, who had allegedly abandoned their true calling of motherhood and housework for shallow and silly reasons.[2] They were accused of working simply because they desired a little extra money for frivolities or wanted to fulfill themselves rather than focusing on their proper roles in the home of wife and mother. Writer Frank Hopkins asked, "Would we not all be happier . . . if we could return to the philosophy of my grandmother's day when the average woman took it for granted that she must content herself with the best lot provided by her husband?"[3] Working women were blamed for many social ills, from undermining the strength of family ties to contributing to the delinquency of their children.[4] Not surprisingly—because while emancipated white women were viewed with hostility, commentators blithely ignored the fact that black women were continuing to work in high numbers—the great angst about working women and their dereliction of their duties of hearth and home focused on white women. As the historian Jacqueline Jones notes in her book *Labor of Love, Labor of Sorrow*, "Working wives became a public issue to the extent that they encroached upon the prerogatives of white men at home and on the job."[5] Black housekeepers and nannies did not take men's jobs away or challenge men's role as family patriarchs and thus could be ignored.

Although newspaper reporters and commentators characterized working women as silly and shallow, the sad reality was that many women desperately needed a job to keep their families from falling off the cliff.[6] By 1931, 2 million women who had been employed before the Depression found themselves out of work. Between 20 and 50 percent of the newly unemployed women had been the family's sole breadwinner, making the loss of employment existential and plunging their families not just into poverty but into destitution.[7] But with high unemployment, notes historian Philip Foner, "some legislators and employers sought to deny work to married women whose husbands had jobs. Section 213 of the 1932 Federal Economy Act, for example, required that one spouse resign if both husband and wife worked for the federal government. This meant, technically, that it was up to both marriage partners to decide which one should resign. But a Women's Bureau analysis of the results of Section 213 showed that more than 75 percent of the spouses who did resign were women. Section 213 remained on the books until 1937."[8]

State legislatures around the country also debated legislation that would have directly barred married women from certain jobs. Although many bills did not pass and others were found unconstitutional, women were still excluded from state jobs by executive order in several states. And, according to a survey done by the National Education Association in 1931, more than three-quarters of the fifteen hundred school systems in the survey would not hire women as teachers if they were married and two-thirds of the schools had fired married women.[9] Married women were also pushed out of jobs in banks, insurance companies, utilities, and public transportation.[10] African American women suffered even more from unemployment in the Great Depression. Some white families fired their black housekeepers, cooks, and nannies because they could no longer afford the help, while others did so because they could afford to replace their black employees with higher-status white servants—more white women were seeking domestic work to support their families and bumped African American women out of these jobs. For African American women, the impact was devastating.

In such urgent need of work, African American women in urban areas would gather at specific street corners to wait for the white women who would drive in to hire them for day labor. Similar in nature to the parking lots where landscapers and construction firms hire day laborers today, these street corner labor exchanges were known as "slave markets."[11] In a 1935 article for *The Crisis*, the magazine of the National Association for the Advancement of Colored People, Ella Baker and Marvel Cooke described how these "slave markets" could be found all over the Bronx, catering mostly to white women who came in from Westchester, Long Island, and the Upper East Side to purchase a few hours or a full day of a black woman's time for between 15 and 30 cents per hour. "The lower middle-class housewife, . . . having dreamed of the luxury of a maid, found opportunity staring her in the face in the form of Negro women pressed to the wall by poverty, starvation and discrimination," they wrote.[12]

The busiest markets, those with the highest "bids" and the most "buyers," were the two at 167th Street and Jerome Avenue and at Simpson Street and Westchester Avenue. The black women started to gather early in the morning and stayed until they were hired or the white housewives had stopped coming. Sometimes white men came "shopping" for a different kind of labor from the women. Leaning against walls, crouching, or, if lucky, sitting on a box or a bench, the "slaves" came in foul weather and fair, braving bitter cold and enervating heat to earn a bit of money to keep their lives together. Many of these women had once worked as servants for upper-class families, before the Great Depression made white maids more affordable. The large pool of unemployed and desperate women made it easy for white families to mistreat them by forcing long hours and extra duties for no extra money, lowering wages, or failing to pay wages at all. A contemporary account captures the mind-set of those white employers taking advantage of the destitution of African American women: "A southern white man . . . admitted as a matter of course that his cook was underpaid, but explained that this was necessary, since, if he gave her more money, she might soon have so much that she would no longer be willing to work for him."[13]

The "slave market" was more than metaphorical. In many southern states, legislators attempted to bind African American workers to low wages and penury by enacting a web of laws that amounted to slavery by other means. Prohibitions on leaving work and debt laws subjected workers in the fields and in the plantation homes to nearly insurmountable restraints on their ability to pursue better opportunities. Despite Supreme Court decisions starting in 1911, declaring these laws unconstitutional under the Thirteenth Amendment, states did not cease to enforce them until the early 1940s.[14]

Pervasive attitudes about race, women, and work played an enormous role in shaping and limiting what work would be considered deserving of protection by members of Congress during the New Deal. The belief that so-called women's work, consisting of caregiving, housekeeping, and similar occupations, was women's natural role helped justify legislation that gave rights only to those engaged in real "work," mostly white men. With much of the work in the home having been done by African American women, it was particularly devalued as a legacy of slavery and racial oppression. Domestic labor was known as "niggers' work," and, two legal scholars observe, "Not surprisingly, the mammy image—a large, maternal figure with a headscarf and almost always a wide-toothed grin—persists as the most enduring racial caricature of African-American women."[15] Such attitudes made it easy to throw these women and these jobs over the side. Historian Susan Ware writes that "while the New Deal pushed the federal government in new directions, the coverage of these new programs was never complete. Many workers were left outside of the scope of the relief programs and social security. In the case of blacks, the exclusion was often the result of deliberate discrimination. But for women, who likewise did not always receive their full share of benefits, the discrimination was less calculated. Unless reminded, policymakers simply forgot that women, too, were hurt by the Depression."[16] This deliberate discrimination and less-than-benign neglect characterize not only the New Deal laws but much of what came after, continuing to shape our laws and their application today.

PROTECTING THE JIM CROW ECONOMY

Even with the omissions, a broad swath of workers was helped significantly by the reforms pushed through by President Franklin D. Roosevelt, including the National Industrial Recovery Act, which set up minimum standards for wages and hours in certain industries through the National Recovery Administration, the jobs program run by the Works Progress Administration (WPA), financial help for single mothers, retirement security, and the Fair Labor Standards Act. Despite the wage discrimination built into these statutes, they did serve to raise women's wages because women had been in such low-paying jobs before the legislation was adopted. Overall, women's wages increased by 3 percent, to equal 63 percent of men's wages by the mid-1930s.[17]

But women and people of color were certainly not granted the same protections as other workers and unquestionably were not seen as entitled to equal wages or an equal chance to get a job. In the work projects created by the government, women and

African Americans were considered less worthy of a job than men—very few women overall, and an extremely small number of women of color, were hired to do WPA jobs.[18] These jobs went to the most "deserving" workers—white men were assumed to be breadwinners and were at the head of the line for any openings. African American women were at the bottom of this hierarchy. From 1935 to 1941, only one-fifth of WPA workers were women. African American women made up only 3 percent of the workforce, despite their overwhelming need—a much higher proportion of black women, especially in the South, were sole breadwinners for their families.[19] Complicating the efforts of black families to stay afloat, southern whites worked assiduously to prevent both black men and black women from getting WPA jobs because the attraction of better pay and working conditions would deny employers domestic help and farm laborers.[20]

So while women's wages went up because of some of these programs, they stayed well below what men were earning, and the National Recovery Administration explicitly pegged women's wages below men's, even when they were doing exactly the same work. For example, men in the garment industry coded as "Jacket, Coat, Reefer and Dress Operators, Male," earned $1 per hour, while the code "Jacket, Coat, Reefer and Dress Operators, Female" paid only 90 cents per hour. The National Recovery Administration code also gave higher wages to certain job categories that were filled by men despite requiring no higher skill level than the job categories filled by women.[21] The segregation of women into certain types of jobs, which, though equal in skill, experience, and training, pay less than those held by men, is a pervasive element of our current economy, even though no longer mandated by statute.

Southern members of Congress had also tried to set lower wages for African American men, in addition to the lower wage rate for women. Unlike the efforts to pay women less, the racially based wage distinction was not adopted, but that was only because legislators chose superficially race-neutral means such as geography and occupational distinctions to achieve the same end.[22] By using these categories, the statute implicitly reaffirmed the preexisting discrimination in the South against women, blacks, and rural workers; at the very bottom of the wage scale were southern black women employed by laundries and tobacco-processing plants.[23] The National Industrial Recovery Act also strengthened prevailing inequalities by putting the implementation of the programs under local control, which meant, particularly in the South, that they were not administered fairly, to put it mildly.

The Social Security Act went further: it directly excluded farmworkers and domestic servants from old-age benefits and unemployment insurance, clearly targeting the African Americans who filled these jobs. While not specifically exempting black workers, excluding these particular workers had the same effect—and the architects of the act knew that to be the case. And like the National Industrial Recovery Act, the law put administration under local control, allowing local officials to limit access even further, so that any blacks technically eligible for benefits could still be cut out.[24] Between the job exclusions and the local administration, African American workers in the South got lower benefits than white workers, or—even more likely—they got none at all. Southern whites were thus able to use New Deal programs to build their prejudices into the law, infusing a large amount of federal spending into efforts to maintain what historian Jacqueline Jones describes as "the fundamental racial and sexual inequalities in the former Confederate states."[25]

In a colloquy discussing an early draft of the Social Security Act, which at this point still covered all workers, Representative

Howard Smith of Virginia alluded to how domestic and agricultural workers could be excised without violating the Fourteenth Amendment, which requires equal protection under the law: "It just so happens, that *that* race is in our state very much of the laboring class and farm laboring class. But you will find no suggestion in my remarks of any suggested amendment that would be unconstitutional if I can use that expression." Smith and his southern colleagues abandoned their efforts to use explicit racial exclusions in favor of the fig leaf of occupational carve-outs, where they found success. Opponents of the subterfuge called it out for what it was. Charles Hamilton Houston, the leader of the National Association for the Advancement of Colored People, testified that "in these States, where your Negro population is heaviest, you will find the majority of Negroes engaged either in farming or else in domestic service, so that, unless we have some provisions which will expressly extend the provisions of this bill to include domestic servants and agricultural workers, I submit the bill is inadequate."[26] At the time, 90 percent of African American women who worked were domestic or farm laborers, and a very large percentage of all women workers were servants, with at least half of them women of color.[27]

This sad refrain repeated itself in other New Deal legislation. In 1935, Congress adopted the National Labor Relations Act (NLRA) to help pull the United States out of the Great Depression by giving workers the right to organize and bargain collectively, which was envisioned as a way to ensure a more level playing field for workers and, ultimately, higher wages. Senator Robert F. Wagner—the NLRA is often called the Wagner Act—originally attempted to cover all workers. His first draft was inclusive, relying on a broad definition of "employee" to capture the entire workforce.[28] But as the bill went through the committee process, the term "employee" came to include fewer workers.[29] The southern Democrats in Congress demanded a variety of concessions meant to leave in place the legacy of Jim Crow and to allow them to continue to mistreat black workers as conditions for their votes.[30] Thus, the NLRA disqualified "any individual employed as an agricultural laborer, or in the domestic service of any family or person at his home" from the provisions providing a right to join a union.[31] For Senator Wagner and President Roosevelt, the stakes were very high, and rather than risk the entire bill and any coverage at all, they capitulated to the racist southern congressmen and jettisoned agricultural and domestic workers.[32]

Along the way, Congress decided to drop another group of workers from the NLRA's protections, based on similar racist and sexist biases—hospital workers, who were primarily women, poor, and nonwhite, had few advocates. They had been excluded from much of the New Deal legislation, including the statutes providing unemployment insurance, disability benefits, and minimum-wage protection. The National Labor Relations Act, as enacted in 1935, did cover hospitals as employers, but when Congress adopted the Taft-Hartley Act, in 1947, legislation designed to limit the power of labor unions, it dropped out nonprofit hospitals.[33] While unions fought against Taft-Hartley, they were not focused on the hospital exemption—partly because many unions of the time did not see the value of organizing hospital workers and thus did not care whether they were excluded.[34] Low-skilled African American women did not seem likely candidates to join a union.[35] Congress changed the law only in 1974, bringing these workers under the NLRA when workers began to engage in illegal strikes to get a union and the industry had grown into a major player in the American economy.[36]

The NLRA did have an undeniable impact on the growth of

unions and women's participation in those organizations. With changes in manufacturing and the need for unions to organize by industry rather than by craft or trade—that is, all workers at an auto plant rather than pipefitters or carpenters—union leadership came to recognize the value of organizing women workers who held some of the jobs in these industries. Moreover, women's low wages served as a drag on men's wages and thus needed to be raised to avoid giving employers a low-cost alternative.[37] The number of women joining unions grew rapidly, reaching eight hundred thousand by 1940, three times as many as were union members in 1930. Just including women generally in the legislation was empowering—by recognizing their right to engage in collective bargaining, the law spurred women to seek better wages and working conditions by joining unions and gave impetus to labor organizations to include women workers in their efforts to unionize a workplace.[38]

But so many women were left out. Domestic workers alone, excluded from unions, equaled the number of those employed in the coal mines, railroads, and the automobile industry combined.[39] Little has changed. Today, only California protects domestic workers' right to organize; the other states adopted the approach of the federal law and explicitly excluded them.[40] And the same is true for those who pick strawberries or lettuce. Only four states prohibit employers from firing farmworkers for trying to join a union.[41] So many years later, domestic and agricultural workers—millions of people—remain outside many of the law's protections.[42]

Two years later, the Fair Labor Standards Act (FLSA) entitled workers to a set number of hours per week, with overtime pay for excess hours. Secretary of Labor Frances Perkins lauded it as achieving "its principal objectives. . . . Shorter hours have made a more humane schedule."[43] It marked a significant step forward in workplace regulation and should rightly be celebrated. But there is much it did not do. And there are many it did not help.

The noble image of the FLSA from Roosevelt's 1937 inaugural speech, which led this chapter, is the one many of us have of this legislation. But despite these lofty words, the FLSA left many workers still subject to the "pall of family disaster." At a time of great social change, the legacy of slavery remained, if not constant, then at least an obvious impediment to forward progress for all Americans.[44] At the end of a lengthy battle that included a hostile Supreme Court ruling that invalidated many earlier attempts to enact wage and hour legislation, the act finally became law on Saturday, June 25, 1938. It was a victory, but one more limited in its impact than its proponents had initially hoped. The law as enacted covered only 20 percent of the workforce, setting 25 cents as the minimum hourly wage and forty-four as the maximum number of hours in the workweek.[45]

Unsurprisingly, the racism that was shared by so many legislators emerged as an ugly undercurrent of the congressional debate.[46] The act faced much opposition based on the fear, expressed forthrightly by southern Democrats, that regulating wages and hours would disrupt the southern economy, which benefited from low-wage labor by African Americans in the home and in the field. Representative James Mark Wilcox, a Florida Democrat, described the backlash that would engulf the region:

> There is another matter of great importance in the South, that is the problem of our Negro labor. There has always been a difference in the wage scale of white and colored labor. So long as Florida people are permitted to handle the matter, this delicate and perplexing problem can be adjusted; but the Federal Government knows no color line

and of necessity it cannot make any distinction between the races. We may rest assured, therefore, that . . . it will prescribe the same wage for the Negro that it prescribes for the white man. . . . Those of us who know the true situation know that it just will not work in the South. You cannot put the Negro and the white man on the same basis and get away with it. Not only would such a situation result in grave social and racial conflicts but it would also result in throwing the Negro out of employment and making him a public charge. There just is not any sense in intensifying this racial problem in the South, and this bill cannot help but produce such a result.[47]

Statements like these make it understandable why the civil rights leaders were pursuing antilynching legislation simultaneously with labor protections.

A southern senator, appropriately nicknamed "Cotton" Ed Smith, complained bitterly about the changes that had come to the South after the Reconstruction Amendments ended slavery and gave blacks the right to vote and to equal protection of the laws: "Antilynching, two-thirds rule, and, last of all, this unconscionable—I shall not attempt to use the proper adjective to designate, in my opinion, this bill [the FLSA]! Any man on this floor who has sense enough to read the English language, knows that the main object of this bill is, by human legislation, to overcome the splendid gifts of God to the South."[48] If this statement weren't in the *Congressional Record*, it would be hard to believe it didn't come straight out of *Gone with the Wind*. Said another congressman, Representative Edward E. Cox of Georgia, "The organized Negro groups of the country are supporting the [FLSA] because it will, in destroying State sovereignty and local self-determination, render easier the elimination and disappearance of racial and social distinctions, and by the concentration of this vast despotic power in a political board or administrator in Washington throw into the political field the determination of the standards and customs which shall determine the relationship of our various groups of people in the South."[49] It is so easy to see the forebears of the Tea Party in these legislators.

By the time it passed and was signed into law, the FLSA had been significantly watered down from President Roosevelt's ambitious draft. Going from an original 40 cents per hour and forty hours per week to 25 cents per hour and forty-four hours per week, the bill that passed was amended to add more exemptions and weaken the enforcement structure.[50] Agricultural workers, as in all previous New Deal laws (and for much the same reason) had also been left out.[51] Going further than the prior laws, the FLSA extended its exemption of these workers to capture those who were in any way involved with farming, from field to market, and was particularly designed to sweep in those mostly black workers who worked in the ginning or baling of cotton. Also left out, indirectly this time, were maids and other domestic workers because the statute defined a covered worker as one "engaged in commerce or in the production of goods for commerce."[52]

It wasn't just members of Congress from the South who wanted to make sure their housekeepers, cooks, and nannies would not have access to the law's benefits. Magazine advertisements addressed to white women trumpeted, "Housewives beware! If the Wages and Hours Bill goes through, you will have to pay your Negro girl eleven dollars a week." Making sure he could get enough southern votes to pass the bill, President Roosevelt declared that "domestic help" would not be covered by the bill.[53]

Despite all the concessions made to gain their votes, when the bill finally advanced through the House of Representatives on May 24, 1938, most of the no votes came from Democrats—fifty-six of the ninety-seven votes against the bill—and fifty-two of the no votes were from the South. When the House passed the conference report soon after, many of the negative votes again came from southern Democrats.[54] Now, it is easy to understand their strategy—it wasn't to make the bill palatable so they could support it but to make it weaker, and perhaps so weak that the bill's own advocates wouldn't support it because it was too watered down.

Ninety percent of black working women received no benefits from the new laws providing for a minimum wage, maximum hours, and assistance for the unemployed and elderly. By leaving out these workers, New Deal legislation actually ensured that, relative to other workers, African American women particularly, and domestic and agricultural workers generally, would be worse off than before.[55]

Today, the National Labor Relations Act still excludes domestic workers and farm laborers, and the Fair Labor Standards Act does not require overtime for farmworkers or even the minimum wage or overtime for many domestic workers.[56] The implications of these exclusions have been profound, denying a growing workforce the basic workplace protections most of us take for granted.[57]

TOO SMALL TO COVER: SMALL BUSINESS AND THE LAW

Beyond excluding those jobs everyone knew were held mostly by women and people of color, Congress left out many of these workers through other, less direct means. Powerful political forces worked to ensure that large employers, more likely to be found in the industrial North and to have a more white male workforce, were covered by all the labor laws. But in making the distinction between large and small employers and narrowly defining who are "real employees," the New Deal legislation set in motion two parallel and similarly harmful strategies: Congress left unprotected those who work for small employers, a workforce already suffering from little bargaining power and many abuses. At the same time, and perhaps more significant, it created a perverse incentive for a company to try to pass as a small employer, either by spinning off functions, outsourcing, setting up franchises, or designating a certain number of employees as independent contractors to bring the company under the threshold, which is based on either the number of employees or the size of the company's profits. Avoiding overtime liability or the minimum wage, not to mention a possible union drive, has bottom-line appeal for employers. But even if the company hit the threshold in terms of employees, its non-employee employees (temporary workers or independent contractors) are not covered by any of these New Deal laws.

Without a doubt, the exclusion of small employers in the Fair Labor Standards Act and other statutes has disfavored women and people of color. This type of size-based exemption has been incorporated in other statutes based on two somewhat contradictory and paternalistic arguments. First, proponents painted a romantic picture of the small workplace, claiming that such employers are like parents, benevolent toward their workers, and the relationship between them had a special quality that should not be interfered with. The other argument, less poetic, stated more directly that these entities, having consciences like individual people, should not be required to associate with people not of their own kind (just like some who argue today that corporations have political or religious beliefs and thus are not subject to certain laws). In sum, this position, declared quite forthrightly by members of Congress, explicitly accepts the right of certain employers to discriminate.[58]

Originally, the FLSA did not set a size limit for companies directly. Rather, it excluded those workers not personally "engaged in commerce or in the production of goods for commerce." Under the prevailing understanding of the time, however, the act was understood to apply to those who were engaged in *interstate* commerce and thus would not affect workers whose particular employment was only *intrastate*, with "intrastate" encompassing a larger swath of economic activity than it was later seen to include. In any case, many small and, in some cases, large companies could fall back on the exemption for "any employee engaged in any retail or service establishment the great part of whose selling or servicing is in intrastate commerce." Over time, courts and Congress broadened the understanding of what constitutes interstate commerce, but, nonetheless, small firms have been able to remain out of reach of the law. Business lobbyists ultimately prevailed in getting an explicit exemption in the FLSA based on the size of a firm. In 1989, as part of another Faustian bargain, legislators advocating for a minimum-wage increase agreed to carve out businesses that do less than $500,000 in business annually, essentially making it a zero-sum transaction, as just about as many workers were removed from minimum-wage protections as gained the new raise.[59]

The size-based exemption, with its underlying premise that small business owners are entitled to discriminate, has become a standard and more or less unquestioned element of all protective labor legislation. In 1964, Congress passed the landmark Civil Rights Act, which, among other things, outlawed job discrimination based on race, national origin, religion, and, ultimately, gender, but only for companies with more than fifteen employees. Some contend that the amendment adding sex as a protected category was designed as a poison pill to kill the bill, and one can certainly imagine that those forces that had been fighting civil rights at every turn would use any tactic to bring it down. But at the end of the day, the amendment passed, and so did the bill. Intended to bar the use of these characteristics from decision making on hiring, pay, and promotion, the act has had far-reaching consequences. It is a happy example of women being *added in* to a statute and gives us much to celebrate. Unfortunately, it has not done enough.

As with other regulatory regimes, opponents of the legislation decried the cost of compliance and worked to exempt as many companies as possible. Members of Congress lamented the "burden" that would be placed on the small employer and waxed poetic about the "personal relationships" that exist in such firms. Speaking on the floor of the Senate, Senator Cotton pronounced that "when a small businessman . . . selects an employee . . . he comes very close to selecting a partner; and when [he] selects a partner, he comes dangerously close to the situation he faces when he selects a wife."[60] We can only imagine what Senator Cotton thought about mixed-race marriages, but there is no doubt that the legislators debating Title VII knew full well the real basis for a small-business exemption. Senator Cotton himself made it crystal clear when he went on to explain his reasoning: "If I were a Negro, and by dint of education, training, and hard work I had amassed enough property as a Negro so that I had a business of my own . . . [if] I wanted to help people of my own race to step up as I had stepped up, I think I should have the right to do so. . . . [I] do not believe that anyone in Washington should be permitted to come in and say, 'You cannot employ all Negroes. You must have some Poles. You must have some Yankees.'"[61] That can only be described as "magical thinking." So many successful black entrepreneurs in the 1960s waiting eagerly to discriminate against Poles.

And just like the legislators who pushed through the New

Deal exclusions, those senators and House members who pushed for a carve out for larger companies in Title VII, which outlaws discrimination in employment, were southerners and segregationists. Amending the law was not meant to improve the Civil Rights Act of 1964 but rather to kill it—this was the true poison pill.[62] Opposing the size limit, one senator stripped the mask off the ugly face of racism behind the amendment, saying that this

> is a moral issue as well as a great legal issue. I am at a loss to understand how it can be immoral to have an employer of 100 or more employees denied the exercise and have it granted to an employer of fewer than 100 employees. I do not intend to take my eyes off the basic issue, and that is the immorality of discrimination based upon race or the color of one's skin. It is just as wrong for an employer who employs two people to have that right to discriminate as the basis of his employment as it is for an employer of 2,000 employees to have it.[63]

Debate over a similar exemption in the Fair Housing Act, the section of the Civil Rights Act pertaining to public accommodations, reinforces this history. It was described as "Mrs. Murphy's exemption," and supporters justified it by creating a fictional person, a sympathetic racist, if you will: "If 'Mrs. Murphy' sought to make a little money by offering the extra room in her home to a boarder, should the government tell her whom she must invite?"[64] Had they been speaking more honestly, the supporters would have said that they clearly did not think the government should force poor Mrs. Murphy to rent to a black person. When Senator Mondale described his grudging support for the Fair Housing Act, he said, "I want it clearly understood as well that I do not agree with the need for granting this exemption." Instead, he made it clear that he knew that the size limit was "politically necessary."[65]

While the size limits in the civil rights bills were designed to allow smaller white employers to maintain a segregated workforce and landlords to avoid renting to blacks, their impact extends to women and is particularly relevant for women of color, who can be legally discriminated against for both characteristics. A huge achievement, the Civil Rights Act nonetheless bears the scars of legislative deal making—known as "sausage making," in which some of the meat gets into the casing but some gets dropped on the floor.

The reasoning for keeping certain workers out has gotten obscured by the mists of time, but the idea that smaller employers should be free to structure their workforces without the interference of the government has shaped subsequent protections for workers. While Congress lowered the threshold of coverage to fifteen from twenty-five employees for Title VII, the accepted premise that race or gender distinctions can keep people from being protected by law has not been directly challenged and has served as the unspoken foundation of much of what has followed.[66] While the small-business lobbyists and employers know full well that they have a license to mistreat their employees, that fact is not well-known by the public. Some analysts estimate that the exclusion leaves close to one-fifth of the workforce without remedy under the Civil Rights Act. In other words, leaving small firms out means that somewhere around 19 million workers are subject to discrimination at work, even without counting the large numbers of temporary and contingent workers. Or they don't get hired at all—and despite what could be overt discrimination, they have no legal remedy. There are consequences: data make the point very clearly that small firms are much less likely to take on minority employees.[67]

I have unthinkingly worked to put these exclusions in other bills. As counsel to the Democratic leader, I worked on a bill, originally titled the Genetic Justice Act,[68] which became law as part of the Genetic Nondiscrimination Act. The law bars employers from discriminating against workers who have the genetic marker of a disease, adding to the protections already available under the Americans with Disabilities Act. I modeled the substance of the legislation on the preexisting language of Title VII of the Civil Rights Act of 1964 and thus incorporated its exclusion of small employers without actually contemplating why such a size limit existed or should be added to the new bill. The bill I drafted, and the law it became, did not challenge the assumption that smaller employers should be off the hook. I also helped draft the Paycheck Fairness Act, a bill still struggling its way into the statute books. The bill amends the Equal Pay Act, which is part of the FLSA, and thus builds on the structure of that statute and its lack of coverage for employers who do less than $500,000 per year in business. Again, while this legislation would help many women fight against pay discrimination, there are many it would not help. In both of the bills I drafted, I imported the size and other exclusions from previous bills. While I cannot speak for those involved in drafting the Americans with Disabilities Act, the Age Discrimination Act, the Affordable Care Act, or the Family and Medical Leave Act, it is now so much clearer to me how many vulnerable workers are left out of the successful efforts to make the workplace more just. I imagine if I had tried to eliminate the size and other exclusions or even to reduce their impact, the lobbyists for business would have come out of the woodwork and the pushback would have been fierce. But I didn't even think to try—that's what disappoints me the most.

Explicit statutory exclusions and indirect omissions have left a large and growing part of our society in a law-free zone, where their work is underpaid, their hours are unpredictable, and their existence is precarious at best. While many of us benefit from rules and rights, these women have been denied so much of what we take for granted. Today, the widening chasm between rich and poor and the growing lower caste of women of color are the illegitimate progeny of compromises, deal making, and Faustian bargains on the road to a better America—for some, but not for as many as we think.

2

THE WAGES OF DISCRIMINATION:
PAYCHECK UNFAIRNESS

The image of Rosie the Riveter is justifiably celebrated, not only because it captured a fabulous gesture of proud defiance, but also because it signaled the importance of women's contributions to the United States' World War II economy. But many also know the next chapter of Rosie's story: men came home from the war, and women were sent back to the kitchen.[1] Even for women whose paychecks were essential to their families' incomes, there was no protection against getting fired simply for being a woman. Women who were able to remain in the workforce were no longer welcome in the more lucrative manufacturing jobs they had during the war—white women returned to clerical work and retail sales and women of color returned to domestic positions. In fact, even more African American women worked as maids in 1950 than had in 1940.[2] In her history of women in the American workforce, historian Alice Kessler-Harris comments that "questions the war had brought to the fore—like equal pay, child care, and community centers for wage-earning women—lost immediacy as women faced the reality of poorly paid jobs or none at all."[3] Since that time, women's participation in the labor force has climbed steadily, despite the hurdles put in their path.[4] But a few things remain the same: affordable child care is nonexistent, discrimination endures, and women are often shunted into lower-paying and contingent work.

We have all heard the statistic: women earn only 77 percent of men's wages.[5] While this figure represents progress of sorts compared to past decades, much of the increase has come at the top, where high-earning professional women such as Sheryl Sandberg have narrowed the gap slightly.[6] And sadly, women's wages have gained relative to men's earnings in large part only because men's wages have declined. The median wage per hour for women in 1979 was 62.7 percent of men's wages. That grew to 82.8 percent in 2012, but 25 percent of that growth comes from men losing ground. In the past decade, women have not made any progress at all, with the wage gap overall remaining stubbornly at 77 percent, with women of color faring even worse.[7] African American women make only 71 percent of what all men make, Hispanic women 62 percent, white women 82 percent, and Asian women 95 percent.[8]

Why do women, particularly women of color, continue to earn less than men? Several factors account for the gap. First, direct discrimination is responsible for a large share of the wage discrepancy, with a little more than 40 percent of the difference in pay not attributable to work experience, education, or type of job—basically, employers are paying women less just because they are women.[9] No doubt, some employers believe women are innately less intelligent or talented than men. Others may hold old-fashioned ideas, assuming that men are the breadwinners and providing them with a higher salary accordingly. And perhaps, all of these employers think women are more exploitable and take advantage of this fact to keep more profits for themselves.

A second drag on women's wages, besides direct discrimination, is a sort of indirect discrimination that comes from our society undervaluing so-called women's work. Almost half of the wage gap is due to entrenched occupational segregation, with traditional women's jobs paying less than men's jobs, even with comparable education and skills.[10] Many women continue to work in fields dominated by women workers, which are categorically paid less than those dominated by men. In fact, many of the jobs women fill are minimum-wage and subminimum-wage jobs, where they are the majority of the workforce. This group of workers has so little political power that the minimum wage remains at historically low levels, and women who earn the subminimum wage paid to tipped employees have their pay stuck at $2.13 per hour, where it has been since the early 1990s.

Lastly, the shrinking of the labor movement has stalled progress in achieving pay parity for women. While unions have worked to fight wage discrepancies between job categories, organized labor has contracted sharply since its postwar strength and is constantly under attack, making it hard to organize workers and get a contract even when the workers are protected by the National Labor Relations Act. Unfortunately, many low-wage minority and immigrant women don't have the legal right to join a union in the first place, which has kept wages even lower.

BECAUSE YOU'RE A GIRL: DIRECT DISCRIMINATION AND THE WEAKNESS OF THE LAW

For Lilly Ledbetter's entire career, her bosses had sliced a percentage off her salary because she was a woman. She spent almost two decades working as a supervisor at Goodyear's Gadsden, Alabama, plant and was one of very few women in such a position. She had suffered through sexual harassment and a boss who told her a woman should not have the job she had, but she put up with it. She was unaware of her colleagues' salaries, so it was not until she was slipped an anonymous note that she learned—to her anger and mortification—that from the very start she had been paid 40 percent less than the men. She could not stomach the unfairness on top of everything else she had had to deal with. She sued, taking her case all the way up to the Supreme Court. In an outrageous miscarriage of justice, the conservative majority on the Court told Ledbetter "tough luck." They said she should have complained when she was first underpaid twenty years before. That she didn't know about the discrimination because her company kept salary information secret—those are the breaks.[11] It took several years for Congress to correct the Court's perverse reading of the law, making it clear that women like Ledbetter can sue when they find out they are underpaid, even if the secret discrimination began years before. The National Women's Law Center explains, "The [Lilly Ledbetter] Act enables individuals to challenge continuing pay discrimination, ensuring both that employees are not penalized if they are initially unaware of the discrimination and that they remain able to challenge pay discrimination that is compounded by raises, pensions, and other contributions over time."[12] But Ledbetter was still out of luck—because she lost her court case and never recovered her stolen wages.[13] And even the fix adopted by Congress is just a Band-Aid on a much bigger wound caused by weak laws, broad exemptions, and obstacles to enforcement.

Most Americans know we have a system of laws forbidding discrimination in the workplace. While this is true and the laws have done much good, few are aware of how weak the laws are. But if they knew that overt discrimination still accounts for 40 percent of the wage gap between men and women, people might realize that the law is not achieving its goals.[14] Despite the passage of Title VII of the Civil Rights Act of 1964, which bans discrimination in hiring, pay, promotion, and the conditions of employment on the basis of sex, race, color, national origin, and religion, as well as the Equal Pay Act of 1963, which protects equal pay for women, why do we have such a persistent problem with discrimination? The main substantive difference between the Equal Pay Act, passed in 1963, and Title VII of the Civil Rights Act of 1964 is that the Equal Pay Act applies only to wage discrimination based on sex, while Title VII prohibits all discrimination in employment, including wages, hiring, firing, and terms and conditions of employment, on the basis of race, color, religion, or national origin, in addition to sex. There are also procedural distinctions in bringing a case, and, significantly, the Equal Pay Act does not provide for compensatory or punitive damages, but only back pay and other direct losses.[15] But even with both statutes, the truth of the matter is that the law is simply deficient. Substantively, lawmakers and the courts have severely circumscribed what constitutes discrimination, and so the law does not address some of the most persistent problems that face women in the workplace. Congress has not adequately funded the agency meant to enforce the law, the Equal Employment Opportunity Commission (EEOC), and the courts have placed insurmountable hurdles in front of victims. Moreover, and perhaps most surprising to a great number of Americans, many women are not covered by the law at all.

Even for women who are covered by the antidiscrimination statutes, the law's toothlessness gives them an inadequate shield against mistreatment and lower wages based on their sex. In particular, Title VII and the Equal Pay Act are basically blind to some obvious differences between men and women: women bear children and men do not, and women are more often the primary or sole caregiver for children and elderly relatives. The theory behind the law is that so long as a woman is just like a man, she should be treated the same. But where she is different, there is no basis for a claim of discrimination. Those who fought for purely equal treatment had a strong case—prior to the law's adoption, women had been subject to all sorts of work limitations, including prohibitions on working at night or in certain types of jobs, that grew out of deep-seated stereotypes that women were too weak or delicate to do certain jobs. These advocates fought against rules that kept women out of many higher-paid jobs, rules that rested on a belief in women's innate difference. But a too-rigid view of equality means that where women are truly different—they do, after all, bear children—the law sometimes fails to protect them from discrimination.

In an op-ed for the *New York Times*, an employment lawyer paints a picture of how little the law does for pregnant women:

> Few people realize that getting pregnant can mean losing your job. Imagine a woman who, seven months into her pregnancy, is fired from her position as a cashier because she needed a few extra bathroom breaks. Or imagine another pregnant employee who was fired from her retail job after giving her supervisors a doctor's note requesting she be allowed to refrain from heavy lifting and climbing ladders during the month and a half before her maternity leave: that's what happened to Patricia Leahy. In 2008 a federal judge in Brooklyn ruled that her firing was fair because her employers were not obligated to accommodate her needs.[16]

One would think that the Pregnancy Discrimination Act would have changed this outcome. Adopted by Congress after several courts issued decisions finding that when an employer fires or demotes a woman because she is pregnant that is somehow not *sex* discrimination—it's true; I'm not making it up—

the Pregnancy Discrimination Act amended Title VII to clarify that, indeed, discriminating against pregnant women counts as discrimination. But subsequent courts have decided that all Congress meant to do was simply to reiterate the basic point of the civil rights law—treat women just like men, even when they are pregnant. To paraphrase Chief Justice John Roberts, "If we want to end gender discrimination, we have to stop discriminating on the basis of gender"—it is exactly this kind of thinking that shows the danger of strictly interpreting "equal treatment."

The Pregnancy Discrimination Act forbids bosses from refusing to hire, terminating, or otherwise disadvantaging a woman solely because she is pregnant. If an employer offers a disability leave or decent sick leave policy, it must allow pregnant women or new mothers access to these benefits, but there is no requirement that an employer have such benefits to begin with. Only if an employer "denies a pregnant employee a benefit generally available to temporarily disabled workers holding similar job positions" would it be engaging in discrimination on the basis of pregnancy.[17] What makes it so hard to win these cases is that the pregnant woman must be able to show both that her employer's explanation for her termination is false and that her *pregnancy* (and not the *accommodation*) is the *sole* basis for the discrimination. The employer could concede that it discriminated but still win by arguing that it had an additional reason for firing her—that accommodating her health restrictions was too costly, that the company doesn't allow employees to change duties for any reason, whether it be injury, illness, or pregnancy, or simply that the company was changing its business plan and needed an employee with different skills. The justifications are often ridiculous—but just because a reason is silly doesn't mean a court will find that the company engaged in discrimination. For example, a pregnant worker in Salina, Kansas, got canned by Walmart simply for carrying a water bottle contrary to store policy because she needed to stay hydrated to avoid bladder infections.[18] Peggy Young, a delivery driver for the United Parcel Service (UPS), asked for light duty when she got pregnant, something UPS did routinely for workers who had a job-related disability or injury. Instead, UPS put her on unpaid leave for an extended period of time and she lost her medical coverage as a result—just when she needed it most. UPS hid behind its collective bargaining agreement, saying it could not treat pregnant workers differently from other workers—our rules are "pregnancy-neutral," said the company. In essence, UPS argued that when employees need light duty, what matters is the cause of their disability, not the fact that they need an accommodation for their health. And the courts seem to agree—the federal trial and appellate courts ruled in favor of the company.[19]

In a welcome advance, in 2014, the EEOC issued updated guidance on what constitutes discrimination against pregnant women, saying that pregnancy should be treated like a disability under the Americans with Disabilities Act, requiring employers to make accommodations.[20] As one commentator noted, "if we can make work accommodations for men who have hernias or heart attacks, why not for pregnant women?"[21] But whether the courts will follow the EEOC remains to be seen. And with this Supreme Court, it is something to worry about.

There has been some progress, at least in a few states and localities. Floralba Fernandez Espinal's experience in New York shows the difference a good law can make. She had suffered a miscarriage in a previous pregnancy and was experiencing complications from her pregnancy, so she asked her employer, a thrift store, to allow her to avoid lifting heavy piles of clothing, which she otherwise did regularly. She requested reassignment to light duties with a doctor's note, as required by her supervisor—instead, she was told that she would be put on unpaid leave. All of a sudden, Floralba was pushed out and lost her income, just when she had a new baby to take care of. "How do they expect me to pay rent, to buy food?" she asked.[22] In most places, this story would have ended there, since her employer did not have a policy to put injured workers on light duty. New York City, however, had recently passed the Pregnant Workers Fairness Act, requiring employers to provide accommodation for pregnant workers, unless it proves an "undue hardship for the employer." Plus, Floralba had a union that made sure to educate her about her rights and that fought for her. Before her union consulted with the lawyers and found out about the new legislation, she faced desperate straits.

New York City did the right thing and included all workers by extending its coverage to domestic workers as well and not cutting out small employers. Thirteen states have followed New York's lead and require employers to provide some accommodations for pregnant workers.[23] At the federal level, in 2013, Senator Bob Casey (D-PA) and Representative Jerrold Nadler (D-NY) introduced the Pregnant Workers Fairness Act, which would require pregnancy to be accommodated under the Americans with Disabilities Act, the position taken in its guidance by the EEOC.[24] But for now, most women faced with a situation like Floralba's have no recourse.

Women get paid less because they are women. Act like a man in all ways and you will be fine. But once you show that you are actually a woman, there's no protection. For all of us, pregnant or not, there's an unstated wage penalty, with employers factoring in the potential cost of women employees having children and needing or asking for time off. And there's the blatant wage gap that emerges when women actually do get pregnant. Women with children suffer wage losses even with respect to other women—not surprisingly, men do not suffer any penalty for being fathers per se, only for wanting to or trying to spend time with their families.[25] Ironically, the employees most likely to have sick leave or even paid family leave are precisely those who already have the most protections under the law—high earning, and mostly white and male.[26]

Professor Joan Williams, a law professor at the University of California's Hastings College of the Law and founding director of the Center for WorkLife Law at the University of California Hastings College of the Law, has pioneered the idea of family responsibility discrimination as a type of discrimination that should be subject to challenge under the civil rights statutes. According to the Center for WorkLife Law, "Family Responsibilities Discrimination (FRD), also called caregiver discrimination, is employment discrimination against workers based on their family caregiving responsibilities. Pregnant women, mothers and fathers of young children, and employees with aging parents or sick spouses or partners may encounter FRD. They may be rejected for hire, passed over for promotion, demoted, harassed, or terminated—despite good performance—simply because their employers make personnel decisions based on stereotypical notions of how they will or should act given their family responsibilities."[27] The lawsuits based on this theory have increased 400 percent from 1998 to 2008.[28]

If the approach taken by the EEOC withstands the inevitable attacks and more courts accept family responsibility discrimination as a basis for a lawsuit, we will have begun to dismantle the bias against women as mothers, potential mothers, and caregivers. But that's just a beginning in strengthening the laws meant to protect us.

The substance of the law is not the only hurdle victims face to enforcing their rights. Pursuing a legal claim for discrimination is complicated, and the risks are great, including losing one's job and life's savings in the course of a lawsuit. The courts are quite hostile to discrimination claims.[29]

Betty Dukes had worked in retail for twenty years. She started at Walmart as a part-time cashier in 1994, making $5 an hour. Thinking Walmart might help her transform her hard-luck life, she saw the job as a big opportunity. "I was focused on Wal-Mart's aggressive customer service," she said to a reporter during a lunch interview while the case was ongoing. "I wanted to advance. I wanted to make that money."[30] So when she had the chance to move up the ladder, she jumped at it, becoming a customer service manager in 1997. But soon after her promotion, she found obstacles to further advancement at every turn. When she complained to management, she was written up for a disciplinary infraction, allegedly for returning late from a break, which she said her male and white co-workers had done without reprisal, sometimes even failing to clock out without the supervisors objecting. By 1999, she was fed up. She wanted more from her job, hoping to make it into a "career" and not just a small paycheck, so she again brought her concerns to her supervisors—but where she sought help, she found instead demotion for "misconduct" and a pay cut. By asking a colleague to make change for her during her break by opening the cash register for a one-cent transaction—something she says the employees did frequently for each other—she gave management the pretext they were looking for to retaliate against her for her outspokenness, for daring to "lean in." With little money to spare, Dukes grew angrier and angrier, especially when the company cut her hours after having already taken an axe to her paycheck. She was earning so little, the middle-aged divorcée had to move in with her mother. Her supervisors' unjustifiable actions made her think that her obstacles in moving up at the company had more to do with her race and sex than with her abilities. As Dukes said to a reporter, "It was just so outrageous. . . . From that point, I started looking for some venue of change to hear my call."[31] She wasn't alone, and her treatment soon led to a lawsuit that was joined by thousands of women, many women of color like herself, who had been subjected to similar treatment.

In a particularly noxious decision for low-wage women, *Wal-Mart v. Dukes*, the Supreme Court rejected Dukes's suit and made it significantly harder for workers to join class action lawsuits to pursue their rights.[32] When the decision was announced, SCOTUSblog, the website pored over by Supreme Court followers from both the right and the left, had this comment:

> For tens of thousands of women who work now, or used to work, for the giant discount retailer, Wal-Mart Stores, the Supreme Court on Monday put out of their reach a nationwide, all-in-one lawsuit over claims of sex bias in the company's 3,400 stores across the country. Each of those women, it appears, will have to complain on her own to federal officials, or file her own lawsuit. For large companies in general, the ruling in *Wal-Mart Stores v. Dukes, et al.* (10-277) offered a second message: the bigger the company, the more varied and decentralized its job practices, the less likely it will have to face a class-action claim. Only workers who have a truly common legal claim may sue as a group, the Court majority made clear—and, even that claim will require rigorous proof that every single worker suffered from exactly the same sort of bias.[33]

These limits to access to class action suits for employees facing widespread and systematic discrimination make it literally impossible for low-wage workers to seek justice. Even if each woman wanted to bring a case as an individual and had all the evidence in her favor, her individual winnings would not be enough to pay for a lawyer in a long and complicated lawsuit. Even the most generous lawyers rarely take cases for which they don't get paid and that cost them a lot of money to litigate. That's the whole reason for the class action—without it, low-wage workers, consumers, and others who suffer small losses individually but whose losses are large in the aggregate can never bring wrongdoers to justice.

And, increasingly, employees are being forced to sign away their right to sue—even as an individual—for discrimination, lower pay, or other unfair treatment. While many Americans may think that they can always bring a lawsuit if their employer violates the law, for almost a third of nonunion workers (or approximately 36 million people) that is no longer true. Using a new weapon in their fight to undermine workers' rights, more and more companies are forcing prospective and current employees to sign away their right to sue in order to get hired or to avoid being fired and to agree that all disputes will be resolved in private arbitration, rather than in normal courts. Business groups defend arbitration as a better, less costly, and less adversarial option. How handy that the boss gets to choose the arbitrator; considering that corporations are repeat customers in this arena while individual employees rarely are, the arbitrator certainly has an incentive to favor the boss over the worker. Held at a place of the employer's choosing, arbitration is shielded from the public eye, with no record and no opportunity for a losing employee to appeal, even if the arbitrator is wrong on the law or blatantly unfair.[34] It is easy to win the game when your team controls the umpires. As proud as we are to have the Civil Rights Act of 1964 and the other landmark laws in the history books, that's the only place they exist today for a growing share of the American workforce.

Women employees' experiences at American Apparel provide an extreme example of the danger of arbitration clauses. The chief executive, Dov Charney, was a serial sexual harasser who was able to cover up his misconduct for a decade because his staff had all signed agreements not to sue, keeping it secret from the public, investors, and his board and preventing these women from having a real remedy. Multiple women brought suit, challenging the arbitration clauses as biased toward the company, and most lost, including one woman who said that she had been forced to be Charney's "sex slave." Reporter Steven Davidoff Solomon asked, "If American Apparel and Mr. Charney had been subject to public lawsuits, how long could Mr. Charney have lasted? After all, there were five suits in the space of a few months in 2011 alone. And those are the claims we know about." Charney was a CEO who bragged to a reporter that "masturbation in front of women is underrated."[35]

In *Ashcroft v. Iqbal*, another of the many decisions in which courts have shut down civil rights claims, the Supreme Court held that plaintiffs have to have all the facts about their case *before* litigation—that is, before the beginning of the process of discovery, when plaintiffs can seek documents or interview witnesses to get evidence to support their case.[36] In a civil rights case brought by an Arab American for unlawful detention after 9/11, the Court expanded on an earlier ruling to hold that Javad Iqbal had not provided enough facts in his initial legal filing, or complaint, to allow his case to go forward.[37] For civil rights plaintiffs in particular, the discovery process, which allows access to an employer's documents or to witnesses, has been the only way to find out the truth.[38] Reminiscent of the television game show *The Price Is Right*, victims of discrimination now have to know what is behind the curtain of secrecy before they can move forward, and the courts don't allow them to make an educated guess. It isn't surprising that in most cases where employees believe they have been fired or paid less because of their sex or race, the boss is not likely to make a public announcement saying, "I fired her because she's black; I demoted her because I think women should earn less." Discrimination has grown more subtle since the days of Senator "Cotton" Ed Smith. Instead, when a woman strongly suspects her wages are lower than those of her male colleagues, she needs access to information about her supervisors' private meetings, any meeting notes, documents dealing with salary issues, and who might have been party to the decisions or know something about them.[39] Unsurprisingly, employers take great care not to share this information with anyone. The upshot is that if a woman who has been paid less strongly suspects the unfairness is due to sexism, a court can nonetheless dismiss her case if she doesn't yet have the smoking gun as evidence. Sadly, these cases are only a few of those in which the courts, doing the dirty work of the business lobby, have eliminated rights people thought were secured by statute.[40]

Making it even harder to enforce the law, the Equal Employment Opportunity Commission, created to help victims pursue their claims, is significantly underfunded and understaffed. Despite a 38 percent increase in claims brought to the agency by victims of discrimination in the past twenty years, between 2000 and 2008 it lost almost 30 percent of its funding and staff. There was a slight improvement with the election of President Barack Obama but, with the recession, the agency's funding was cut and it faced hiring freezes.[41]

The civil rights laws are still on the books, but the experience of women facing discrimination proves the truth of the adage: a right without a remedy is no right at all.

～

For a significant group of women, even the weak protections of the law are not available. History tells the story behind why the antidiscrimination laws explicitly carve out so many women—those in certain job categories or those who work for smaller employers—allowing their employers to discriminate with impunity. In the course of the adoption of these laudable initiatives, designed to ensure fair wages, hours, and benefits, as well as freedom from discrimination, some groups of women were so powerless that they were left out of the grand bargains forged by others. Making concessions to legislators who wanted to maintain their exploitation of the women who cleaned their houses, cooked their meals, or cared for their children, reformers allowed these workers to be thrown over the side. The legacy of that misogyny and racism continues to hinder the effectiveness of our laws and the ability of people to win justice.

Barbara Ehrenreich perfectly describes the vulnerable state of this workforce:

> They are underpaid, in many cases less than the minimum wage, and often at levels too low to adequately care for their own families. They are almost universally excluded from coverage by labor laws and usually work without a contract or any kind of agreement, written or oral, with their employers. They often perform work that is physically punishing, involving heavy lifting, long hours, and exposure to potentially harmful cleaning products. They may be subject to physical and verbal abuse by their employers, even enduring, in the case of live-in immigrant workers, conditions indistinguishable from slavery.[42]

Legislators erected a variety of barriers to bar certain workers from invoking the antidiscrimination laws. Several laws explicitly carve out certain groups of workers. The Equal Pay Act is a good example. Amending the Fair Labor Standards Act, it adopted the FLSA's exclusion of domestic and farmworkers.[43] Workers whose employers have designated them as independent contractors also cannot call on the law to protect them from discrimination. These "nonemployees" have no recourse to the antidiscrimination protections unless they have been "misclassified" as independent contractors. But to challenge misclassification, low-wage workers have to know about the law and either go to an enforcement agency to file a claim or bring a lawsuit, neither of which is easy for a janitor or health aide.[44] Perversely, another exclusion bars undocumented workers from seeking protection, allowing unscrupulous employers to mistreat vulnerable workers even more than they otherwise could.[45]

In addition to these explicit exemptions, the antidiscrimination statutes don't protect employees of small firms. While more comprehensive than the Family and Medical Leave Act, which carves out half of the workforce due to a combination of excluding firms with fewer than fifty people and minimum length-of-service requirements, Title VII and the Equal Pay Act still leave many workers, particularly women, people of color, and contingent workers, subject to direct discrimination with no recourse. The Equal Pay Act follows the FLSA in limiting its applications to employers who generate more than $500,000 in dollar volume per year. Title VII is limited to companies with fifteen or more employees, requiring only those employers to avoid discriminating in hiring, firing, promotion, pay, benefits, and working conditions. Seemingly narrow, the exception sweeps in far more workers than one would anticipate—it allows companies, in any sector, with millions of dollars in profit, whether its workers are manual laborers, typists, chemists, or surgeons, to escape liability.[46]

For workers in these "smaller" companies, there is no basis for a lawsuit if the employer chooses to pay women less than men, treat Latino workers unfairly, or exclude African Americans altogether from its workforce. Such was the case for Karen Stone, who worked for the Pinnacle Credit Union in Indiana. After eight years working for Pinnacle, she was summarily fired. Stone believed she was fired because of her sex and disability and decided to sue her employer for discrimination and retaliation. But the courthouse doors were closed to her because her employer was too small to be an "employer" under the Americans with Disabilities Act and Title VII of the Civil Rights Act of 1964.[47] So for women like Karen who work in small businesses—even very profitable ones—discrimination is the price of the job.

Discrimination is also a fact of life for the women who work as health aides and nannies, employed by small companies or directly by families. Patricia, a nanny profiled by PBS news, had a common story:

> Patricia had always wanted to have a baby, but her doctors told her she never would. Instead, she worked as a nanny, caring for someone else's child. She worked long hours, under the table—from 8 a.m. to 7 p.m., sometimes more. She was paid what sounded to a recent immigrant like a decent salary of $500 a week. That works out to $9 an hour, which doesn't go very far in New York City. [She] lived in East New York, one of the poorest and most dangerous neighborhoods in Brooklyn, an hour and 15 minutes from the Upper East Side home where she worked. But despite the long commute and the lack of overtime pay, she was happy in the job. . . . Then Patricia found out she was pregnant. . . . She was so excited that she called her employer

from the hospital after the sonogram. The next day she
was fired. No notice, no severance pay.[48]

Pregnancy Discrimination Act? It didn't apply—her employer
wasn't covered.[49] Letting smaller employers off the hook leaves
many women without protection—in fact, 15 percent of the overall workforce and a higher percentage of the female workforce.[50]

Not being protected from discrimination affects pay directly
and indirectly. Women in the excluded workforce suffer from a
variety of abuses—sexual and psychological—that have a long-
term impact on women's ability to earn fair pay. Moreover, hostile working environments force women to change jobs more
frequently, which affects their earnings in the long term and
certainly their productivity in the short term. In allowing some
business owners to discriminate, our laws open the doors to sexu-
alized, racialized, and oppressive working environments. Women
know when they are being harassed, so they are willing to speak
about it to researchers; it is harder to get exact data on pay discrimination against excluded workers because employers keep information about salaries secret, and so, while women may suspect
they are being underpaid, they don't know it as surely as they
know they are being pinched in the ass or fondled. The prevalence of harassment can, however, serve as a proxy for the general
level of discrimination against women in these workplaces—
from harassment to unequal pay and lower benefits. Studies
have documented that sexual harassment leads to loss of wages
for women, even for those protected by law. According to Equal
Rights Advocates, an advocacy group working for low-wage
women, over the course of two years, federal employees lost more
than $4.4 million in wages and more than 973,000 hours of leave
per year, and more recent research shows that sexual harassment
"has negative consequences for workers, including increased job

turnover, higher absenteeism, reduced job satisfaction, lower productivity, and adverse health outcomes."[51] For women excluded
from the law, who have no recourse against bosses who demand
sexual favors, we can only assume the consequences are even
more dire.

Sexual harassment has more to do with power than with
sex, which explains why women who are particularly powerless
because they are single parents who desperately need a wage,
because of their immigration status, or because their lack of education limits their opportunities suffer disproportionately—they
are the perfect victims because filing a complaint or bringing
legal charges puts them at greater risk of job loss, retaliation,
deportation, or ostracism. According to the Equal Employment
Opportunity Commission, women in the restaurant industry are
at the top of the list for the most sexual harassment at work.
Women surveyed report it as "part of the culture" of the restaurant industry.[52] This culture sadly exists in many industries, and
low-wage women overall suffer from this kind of victimization at
shockingly high levels.

For farmworkers, harassment is similarly pervasive—80 percent of female farmworkers in one survey stated that they have
been subjected to sexual harassment with serious consequences
in their working life.[53] After a crew leader began to show up outside her trailer as soon as her husband had left for work, a farmworker went to the human resources office of her employer for
help. Instead of disciplining or firing the crew leader, the company promptly fired her, her husband, and their son and threw
them out of the company-owned trailer, rendering them home-
less as well as jobless.[54] For some, harassment turns to violence,
including sexual assault and rape. In California's agricultural industry, attacks are so frequent that the *Los Angeles Times* begged
officials to pay attention. In an editorial on the prevalence of

sexual violence in the fields, the *Times* told the story of Olivia Tamayo, whose supervisor "raped her three times. The first attack occurred in his car when she accepted a ride to work. The second, under a stand of almond trees. The third, at her home while her husband was at work and her children asleep. The company's solution . . . reassign her to an isolated spot in a field nearer to her attacker's house."[55] Although Tamayo won a significant civil suit against the company, hiring a lawyer and filing a lawsuit is an option for only a very few of these women. A report by the Southern Poverty Law Center states that, as of 2010, no other case had come before a federal jury. That report goes on to provide many other stories of women who could not protect themselves, recounting how women farmworkers had dubbed one company's fields the *field de calzon*, or "field of panties," and another's "the green motel" because so many women had been raped by supervisors on those farms.[56]

Home health aides also often work in environments where they suffer harassment regularly. Andrea, a caregiver in California, came forward to tell her story, one that it is only too common: "One of my employers began to sexually harass me; as if he owned me because I lived and worked in his home. His wife often worked late at night and this is when he would approach me and try to take advantage of me. For a time, I ignored him and continued my work, because I needed my job. As a single mother, and the sole provider for my family I was concerned that I would not be able to take care of my family."[57] Other caregivers related similar stories. Myrla, a home health aide in Chicago, told me about one client who would not wear his pants while she was there and kept trying to touch and kiss her. She tried to ignore it and stay out of his grasp, but her efforts to avoid his touches made him angry and he made her work difficult in retaliation. Another client kept demanding that Myrla help her masturbate.

As Myrla said to me, "Seven incidents of harassment with only thirty patients—what would happen if I was really full-time? What if I was staying there overnight?"[58]

Lisa, also a home health aide in Chicago, faced both racial harassment and sexual come-ons. One of the patients she cared for had a son who called her a "nigger bitch" and verbally abused her, using sexual innuendos and racial epithets. She literally had to run out on that job on the day he came after her with a knife, threatening to rape her. Lisa flew out of the house to escape him, leaving her purse and phone behind. Far from home, she had to beg a passerby for change to call her son from a pay phone so he could come pick her up. Another one of Lisa's clients had a daughter, whose office was in the client's house. Thinking Lisa was an easy target, the daughter began to proposition her and then to try to get close and touch her. She quickly moved to asking Lisa explicitly to have sex with her. When Lisa said no, she was fired.

Yes, sexual harassment is illegal under our antidiscrimination laws. But many of the most vulnerable women are not covered. And it is protection they desperately need.[59] In rare situations, where the environment is particularly toxic, workers have taken things into their own hands. For example, the Coalition of Immokalee Workers pushed for an agreement with Florida tomato growers that provided for worker training on sexual harassment during the workday and included penalties for employers that do not discipline harassers.[60] But should low-wage workers suffering from sexual harassment have to risk their jobs to push for changes by their employers? For many, probably most, workers, the fear of losing their small income serves as an effective gag on complaints, allowing harassers to continue their sexual banter, outright propositions, and unwanted fondling, making life a living hell for their victims.

Implicitly, our lawmakers have determined that discrimination and harassment are acceptable in certain contexts. Cloaking their arguments in economic jargon, some argue that legal remedies for discrimination simply cost too much for small businesses relative to larger companies. But comparing the relative impact of other regulations underscores the different values our society places on protecting working women versus, for example, environmental rules, which are both far more costly and do apply to small firms.[61] But why *shouldn't* "training" for supervisors in how to ensure equal compensation for women as well as how to prevent harassment be a cost of doing business? Should we accept as a fact that discrimination is a natural part of work life? Many have accepted that businesses, even small businesses, should not be able to externalize the costs of the smog or the wastewater their facilities discharge simply to achieve higher returns for shareholders and excessive pay packages for their executives—we agree that profit-driven corporations have a certain responsibility to avoid polluting our water and air, and in principle, our labor laws are designed to ensure that companies cannot make excessive profits through worker exploitation. But small businesses and certain other employers can indeed engage in worker exploitation. Why do we expect them to comply with laws that protect the environment but not those that cover the Latina home care worker or the women answering phones in a law firm or cleaning its bathrooms?

For argument's sake, we might not need to eliminate the exemption for small employers or specific job exclusions if we had a better safety net for affected workers. If we assume that people can and do discriminate and that small employers (real small employers and not shell game employers) should have some protection against liability, why don't we ensure a robust unemployment insurance system, access to health care, and other supports?

Or a universal basic income that would truly allow worker mobility—if each American were to get $1,000 per month, up to a certain income level, we wouldn't have to worry about our loophole-ridden job protections. If victims of harassment could leave a hostile workplace without falling into poverty or worse, perhaps we could defend this system—but under the current circumstances, the system we have means far too many women, especially women of color, are thrown under the bus.

But we cannot let the weakening of these employment laws tarnish the legacy of the civil rights advocates and feminists who fought for their passage. Instead, we need to push for expanded coverage so that all employers face legal consequences for harassing, underpaying, or excluding women from their workplaces. This is not a radical proposition. A number of states and localities apply their fair employment laws to businesses with fewer than fifteen employees, covering nannies and home care workers, and add protections for sexual orientation and gender identity— and some even go so far as to prohibit discrimination against people with children. More than sixty-three local governments in twenty-two states have some law prohibiting discriminating against workers caring for children or disabled family members.[62] Others have protected pregnant women. These successes provide a model, and a rallying cry, for those across the country who want to see stronger laws.

We also need to push Congress and the states to enforce the laws we have by funding the agencies responsible for that task. And we need to fix the procedural rules that make it so hard for victimized workers to get justice. While pleading standards, arbitration requirements, bars on class actions, limits on attorneys' fees, and other barriers to the courthouse don't sound like civil rights issues, they are. Everyone knows that you can have the best baseball team in the world, but if the other team gets to pick the umpires, you are going to lose. The business community knows what the stakes are and has fought to control the rules of the game. While there are some progressive groups that have focused on this battle, many seem oblivious to the fact that their hard-fought victories in passing good laws have been undercut because of lack of enforcement and legal barriers. Civil rights activists and plaintiffs' lawyers need to find their common interest in fixing the laws, funding enforcement, and making access to justice a reality.

THE LADIES' ROOM: SEPARATE IS NOT EQUAL

Professions dominated by women, such as secretarial work and nursing, pay less than those where men are the majority of workers, even when the jobs demand the same level of training and experience. While some occupations have gotten more integrated over time, many have not. This creates at least two problems. First, we are losing out as a nation on the talents and ambitions of women and men who are unable, or perceive it to be socially unacceptable, to work in a job associated with the opposite sex. Second, in addition to direct discrimination and the other barriers to fair pay for women, occupational segregation contributes substantially to the wage differential between men and women. Jobs traditionally filled by women pay less than those filled by men. The bottom line shows the impact of this segregation: women still only make 77 cents on the dollar compared to men.[63]

Women continue to dominate certain occupations. In 2009, nearly one-fifth of all women were employed in just five jobs: secretary, registered nurse, elementary school teacher, cashier, and nursing aide.[64] And almost 44 percent of women fill only twenty job categories, including dental assistant, hairdresser, nursery and

kindergarten teacher, and librarian.[65] For men, there are many
more choices, with only a third of men filling the twenty top
male job categories.[66] During a period of time in the 1970s and
1980s, women made real strides in moving into a broader range
of professions, but since the 1990s, no progress has been made in
breaking down these barriers.[67] And the problem of job segregation with its resulting lower pay falls more heavily on women of
color. Researchers have shown that, generally, minorities, recent
immigrants, especially those whose English is not proficient, and
those with less education are concentrated in fewer job categories than whites with higher education.[68] Although job segregation has a considerable racial aspect, according to the Institute
for Women's Policy Research, race was not as determinative as
gender: "Our data shows that race and ethnic background are
significant factors in explaining occupational patterns when
considering women and men separately. That is, women of different race and ethnic backgrounds have different occupational
patterns (as do men). Yet the data clearly confirm that gender is
the predominant factor in occupational segregation in all major
race and ethnic groups."[69]

The impact is clear—it means that women are less able to
earn a living wage and to support their families. But is the cause
the chicken or the egg—because these jobs are filled by women,
they pay lower salaries, or conversely, because these jobs are
lower paid, women are the dominant workforce? The Institute for
Women's Policy Research, one of the leading think tanks studying women's wages, argues that certain low-wage jobs pay less
than comparable jobs precisely because they are filled by women:
"Even though low-skilled occupations typically pay low wages in
general, wage levels are particularly low for workers in the occupations predominantly done by women. Across occupations, the
median earnings of all full-time workers in female-dominated,

low-skilled occupations are only $408 per week, 73.8 percent of the median weekly earnings paid in male-dominated, low-skilled occupations ($553)." The numbers for child care workers, almost exclusively women, are even worse: their median earnings in 2009 were only $367 per week. A single mother working full-time and year-round would earn just enough to go above the poverty line, which is $18,310 for a family of three.[70] Ironically, when men move into traditional women's jobs, such as nursing or teaching, they tend to get on a "glass escalator"—getting pay increases and promotions more quickly than women.[71] So there's the answer to the chicken and egg problem—it isn't the job itself but the sex of those who fill it that makes it low paying.

Why have we paid so little attention to this nagging problem? Both the unfairness of paying these jobs less and the difficulty women face in entering different professions have immediate and long-term ramifications. In the short term, families get short-changed with less money for rent, groceries, child care, and the other necessities of life. In the long term, occupational segregation and its attendant lower wages for women help explain the high poverty rates for elderly women—and for children.

Certainly, some women may choose to be secretaries or nurses and some men to be construction workers or truck drivers. Our culture reinforces stereotypes about appropriate pursuits for each gender, and both women and men are influenced by these pervasive messages. But for many women, even apart from cultural barriers, they have no real choice because of the variety of obstacles they face when they try to move into a male-dominated field; in part this lack of choice results from ignorance of the opportunities in other fields and in part it comes from hostility and disapproval.[72] Women in construction, for example, still represent less than 3 percent of that workforce, with pitifully few women of color among them.[73] Shané LaSaint-Bell's story goes a long way in explaining why there aren't more women. She loved her job when she started training.

> The minute I lit a torch and started cutting metal, I fell in love with it. I graduated at the top of my class and was thrilled to be offered a job as an apprentice with the Ironworkers. I loved the work, but the hostility and discrimination I faced every day on the job shocked me. On the construction site, men don't see you as a plumber or as an electrician—they only see you as a woman who shouldn't be there. They give you a hard time to press you to quit. Women are groped, grabbed, and relentlessly harassed. A lot of women leave the job before a year is out. It's just too stressful. It'll never change without having more women on the work site and training women to compete in Ironwork. I'm one of three women still working in welding out of the 22 that started in my apprentice class. I love welding and make a good living, but I'm frustrated by constantly having to prove myself just to be considered a player in the game. And even then, I don't get the opportunities to advance that I deserve.[74]

Construction is far from the solitary boys-only club. A twenty-six-year much-decorated veteran of the St. Paul Police Department was fired when she complained to her supervisors about a colleague who persisted in describing his erotic dreams about her, told her how "aroused" she made him, and asked her if she masturbated at work. Her supervisors reacted by accusing her of being "overly emotional" as well as insubordinate, and put her on leave, taking away her gun and badge and barring her from the police department's building. After she sued for sexual harassment and retaliation, the department asked her to resign "voluntarily." She won $60,000 in her lawsuit but is not working as a cop anymore.[75] Another police officer sued her department after her supervisors made her life hell by talking about sex every time she came into the office, making suggestive comments about her and even acting threateningly.[76] A forklift operator at a railroad had a boss who made it clear he thought her job should be held by a man—when she complained, instead of being treated better, she was put on unpaid suspension for more than a month.[77] These aren't isolated stories—many cases challenging oppressive and sexualized workplaces involve women who tried to step into these male-dominated roles. The fact is that these jobs pay significantly better than those filled by women, so keeping women out of them means blocking new opportunities and broader horizons.

Similarly, women in the restaurant industry are often shunted into downscale establishments and into lower-paying positions. While men work in higher-end establishments, women often work in chain restaurants that are informal, "quick-serve and family style," which means smaller tips—and have a harder time positioning themselves for consideration for higher-paying jobs.[78] But even within each restaurant, there are hierarchies of positions. A study done in 2009 of New York's restaurants documented rampant segregation by race, ethnicity, and gender—with the best jobs going predominantly to white men. We rarely, if ever, see women or people of color as maîtres d'hôtel, sommeliers, or bartenders—and there's not much an aspiring sommelier can do about it under laws that exempt smaller employers from antidiscrimination statutes.[79] For women, the only jobs out front seem to be hostess or coat check positions—not a lot of money in that. The leading advocate for women in the restaurant industry, the Restaurant Opportunities Center United (ROC-United), reports that "at the lowest end of the pay scale, women are highly concentrated in four of the ten lowest paid occupations of any

industry: host, counter attendant, combined food prep and serving worker, and server."[80]

You have to give credit to the TV shows *Top Chef* and *Iron
Chef* because they are able to find a supply of chefs who are
women and people of color to fill out their shows. The chefs on
those programs, unfortunately, seem to come from an alternative universe. Back in our universe, "women fill only 19 percent
of chef positions, one of the highest paying restaurant positions
with a median wage of $19.23." Tom Colicchio, one of the chefs
who serve as judges on *Top Chef* (as opposed to a "cheftestant"),
has actually worked to improve the situation of workers in his
restaurant empire. Advocates give him and his company a lot of
credit for understanding that retaining and promoting employees
is good for business and requires making sure women and minorities are not shut out of good opportunities, as is so often the case
in the informal good-old-boy world of many restaurants.[81]

But even if women stay in traditionally female jobs, why should
we accept that these professions pay so much less than those requiring comparable skills and experience that tend to be filled by
men? For one thing, this work is not going away—"women's jobs"
are the jobs of the future for the entire workforce. According to
the Bureau of Labor Statistics, job growth in the coming decade
will be concentrated in the service sector, where jobs are typically low wage and do not require any higher education, let alone
an advanced degree. Of the top fifteen jobs projected to grow,
women make up the vast majority of employees in ten.[82] If wages
remain low in these professions and their share of the workforce
continues to grow, so also will the great inequality in wealth that
afflicts our nation.

Unfortunately, we have few legal tools to combat the lower
wages paid to women in female-dominated jobs. Title VII offers no remedy to job segregation, although it has helped women

and particularly women of color in other ways: after its adoption, through affirmative action and other measures, it did much more to help tackle discrimination against minorities within the confines of the female job sector than it did to help any women to make gains relative to white men.[83] Like Title VII, the Equal Pay Act of 1963 does not help women qua women, but only in reference to men. Already when it was passed, some advocates, particularly labor union women, recognized the weakness of the Equal Pay Act. They wanted stronger language that would have addressed disparate pay between sectors of the economy and not just between men and women doing the exact same job. They argued that if the skill level was comparable, the pay should be as well. Instead, the new law only required "equal pay for equal work," which did little for women who were stuck in female-dominated professions.[84] Similarly, the Paycheck Fairness Act, if it ever becomes law, will not provide women with a vehicle to advocate for equalizing wages between professions of similar skill levels and experience.[85] It would strengthen remedies available to victims of pay discrimination and provide more significant damage awards, make it easier to bring class action lawsuits, and prohibit retaliation against employees who share information about their pay, but it would not provide a way to attack the different pay scales between occupations filled by women and those filled by men.

Senator Tom Harkin (D-IA) has been a champion in the cause of creating a legislative response to occupational segregation. He stated when he reintroduced his bill that "the *Fair Pay Act* would address the more systematic forms of discrimination and the historic pattern of undervaluing and underpaying so-called 'women's' work. Millions of women have jobs—for example, social workers, teachers, child care workers and nurses—that are equivalent in skills, effort, responsibility and working conditions to jobs that are usually held by men. However, the jobs that are predominantly held by women pay significantly less."[86] His bill would finally provide a legal remedy to women who make less money than men when doing jobs "comparable in skill, effort, responsibility and working conditions, and would give workers the information they need to determine when jobs are undervalued." But it has never gotten a vote, let alone passed, and, like other protective statutes, it exempts smaller employers, where many of the affected women work.[87] And, sadly, Senator Harkin is retiring.

Minnesota is the only state to have attempted to address this problem in any way. Even its efforts focus only on the pay gap in government jobs and do not touch the private sector. The Minnesota State Employee Pay Equity Act makes it "the policy of this state to attempt to establish equitable compensation relationships between female-dominated, male-dominated, and balanced classes of employees in the executive branch," mandating that "the primary consideration in negotiating, establishing, recommending, and approving total compensation is comparability of the value of the work in relationship to other positions in the executive branch."[88] For both state and local governments, the Minnesota statute defines "comparability of the value of the work" as "the value of the work measured by the composite of the skill, effort, responsibility, and working conditions normally required in the performance of the work."[89]

The law has several weaknesses—it applies only to government employees and is somewhat vague on how to measure "comparable value," which is set by the employer.[90] A better law would cover all employees and would have a neutral party analyze the jobs and make judgments about skill levels. But Minnesota has worked to limit employer discretion by relying on a task force to review the job evaluation system in place.[91] At least as a starting place, the Minnesota experience gives cause for hope. According to independent evaluations, "the average pay increase was approximately $2,200," and "overall, women's pay increased by approximately nine percent, with no significant impact on employment for women within the state system."[92]

Outside of the United States, Ontario, Canada, was the first jurisdiction to enact pay equity in both the public and the private sector.[93] It did so in order "to redress gender discrimination in the compensation of employees employed in female job classes in Ontario."[94] The law requires employers to evaluate different job classes to assess whether male- and female-dominated jobs with similar skill, effort, responsibility, and working conditions are paid comparably, and, if not, to adjust wages.[95] It is worth noting that international law requires Canada, as a signatory of the International Labour Organization (ILO)'s Discrimination (Employment and Occupation) Convention, to ensure that each of its provinces promotes equal pay.[96] This convention is one of the most widely ratified, according to the ILO—but not by the United States.[97]

While broader in application than the Fair Pay Act or the Minnesota law, the Ontario Pay Equity Act still has some limitations. First, the setting of wages "is a self-managed process," which gives room for employer chauvinism and subjectivity, as does allowing the boss to evaluate the worth of a particular job to the employer personally.[98] Nonetheless, at least anecdotally, Ontario has seen some successes. For example, a school district reviewed the skill level of secretaries as well as audiovisual technicians and moved the women's yearly pay up by $7,650; a company that makes shoes adjusted the salaries of the female-dominated console operators upward by $4,660 after comparing their earnings to the equivalently skilled male cutters; and a local government paid clerks $7,424.72 more after considering what drivers were paid.[99]

While national legislative advances may not be imminent, these examples give some guidance to advocates and show that success is possible. In the interim, there are other ways to combat occupational segregation. And this is where Sheryl Sandberg gets it right: women should "lean in"—for themselves and for fellow women. But women shouldn't have to go it alone without the helping hand of good public policy. First, we can address some of the cultural barriers that impede women's moving into more lucrative professions by developing programs to encourage girls and women to broaden their horizons in terms of the types of jobs they contemplate pursuing—as well as give them support through training and opportunities, including affirmative action. And real enforcement of existing equal pay and antidiscrimination laws would better protect those women who try to or do venture into more male-dominated jobs.[100]

Wider Opportunities for Women is an important voice in both advocating for broader job choices for women and providing mentoring, training, and encouragement. It focuses on a wide range of jobs, including construction, manual labor, and science. Other groups make a particular focus of getting more women into science, technology, engineering, and math, including the American Association of University Women—and women like Sandberg have their own powerful impact as role models for girls who like math or science but are afraid of being called "unfeminine." Unions like the American Federation of State, County and Municipal Employees work to open up jobs to all of their members—fighting for both men and women to have the opportunity to be bus drivers and prison guards, police officers and firefighters, teachers and nurses. And it is clear from the Canadian examples that we can actually change the paradigm that condemns women to lower-paid and lower-valued jobs.

Claudia worked as a server in a chain restaurant. Leaving her hometown of Monterrey, Mexico, she said good-bye to her family and came to the United States in search of a better life. With eight older siblings in an impoverished family, Claudia did not see much of a future for herself staying at home. Once she got to the United States, she tried going to high school while working at the restaurant, but she struggled to make ends meet. As is often the case for servers, her tips did not make up the difference between the base wage of $2.13 and the minimum wage of $7.25, as is required by law. Her supervisors told her to lie about her tips on her time sheets so the company would not have to supplement her wages to bring her pay up to $7.25 per hour. Her bosses also often stiffed her for the overtime hours she worked.

> They told me to clock out before doing side work. I was always scheduled to work 5pm to 12am, and exactly at midnight . . . I had to clock out. Sometimes I'd stay two more hours. Late at night they'd only keep one or two people, and we had to do all the side work—make silverware packets, clean coffee pots, orange juice pots, soda machine, refill the butter, syrup, ketchup, . . . sugar, salt, and pepper. I had to make sure the supply room was clean, organized and labeled. I had to make sure the stock room was refreshed, and cut lemons myself.[101]

Claudia got paid nothing in exchange for her extra work and loss of sleep. And along with the other women servers, she was often given the graveyard shifts with few customers and almost nonexistent tips—and the bosses still forced them to lie and report that they had gotten tips, enough to push their hourly earnings above the minimum-wage level. On top of all that, the company stuck the servers with the bill if a customer snuck out without paying.[102]

Women are the backbone of the low-wage economy because of discrimination and because they are concentrated in female-dominated occupations, making them the majority of workers who earn the minimum wage, as well as those who make less and slightly more. The minimum wage is historically low, currently at $7.25, with many minimum-wage workers forced to rely on food stamps or other assistance to supplement their meager wages.[103] Raising it would benefit women more than men; even though women are slightly less than half of the American workforce, they make up 55 percent of those whose wages would be raised by lifting the minimum wage.[104]

First, we need to correct a few myths that have been spread about the minimum wage and minimum-wage workers in our country. Contrary to right-wing mythology, minimum-wage jobs are held by adults who support families and not, as business owners who oppose an increase would have us believe, predominantly by teens working a few hours a week to make money for weekend date nights at the soda shop. In fact, the average age of workers who would benefit from a higher minimum wage is thirty-five, and only 12.5 percent are teens. A higher percentage of minimum-wage workers are over fifty-five than are teenagers.[105] Almost 88 percent of these workers are twenty or older, and a third of them are over forty. Far from being high school kids working after school to supplement an allowance, most of these workers are full-time (54 percent) and more than two-thirds of them come from families with less than $60,000 in total income.[106]

Opponents' false claims against raising the minimum wage

bear a strong resemblance to earlier arguments against providing women fair wages because they were only working for "pin money" or not covering hospital workers under protective wage laws because they do their work "out of love." There is no more effective way to deny people the earnings they are entitled to than by denigrating their interest in fair treatment and devaluing their work. An Economic Policy Institute report debunks these specious claims, noting that "low- and minimum-wage workers are often dismissed as 'secondary earners,' implying that the income earned by these workers is primarily discretionary income, unessential to their family's well-being. This is patently false: The workers who would be affected by increasing the minimum wage to $10.10 earn, on average, 50 percent of their family's total income." And women with children are a large component of this workforce—more than 25 percent of workers whose wages would go up because of an increase in the federal minimum wage are parents. Almost 20 percent of the 75 million children in this country have at least one parent who would benefit from an increase in the wage to $10.10. Right now, a parent earning the minimum wage falls well below the federal poverty line.[107]

Overall, raising the minimum wage would make a real difference in the lives of these women and their families and would make at least a small dent in our growing income inequality. As the minimum wage has declined in real value, income inequality in the United States has grown. In prior decades, workers earning the minimum wage suffered a smaller gap with respect to workers earning the average U.S. wage. Minimum-wage workers during the mid-1960s to the early 1980s earned about 50 percent of the average wages of other workers. Now that figure has shrunk to a little over a third. But with an increase to $10.10, minimum-wage workers could once again bring home half of the average wage—that may not seem like a huge change for many people, but for those on the brink, it would be a lifeline.[108] Moreover, contrary to the moans of the chamber of commerce, raising the minimum wage would have a negligible impact on the economy overall and consumer prices in particular. A recent study shows that if retail workers went from making $7.25 to $12.25 per hour, the cost would equal only 1 percent of the $2.17 trillion in sales of major stores. Another study, done by the University of California, found that a minimum wage of $9.80 would make hamburgers about 2 percent more expensive and raise the cost of groceries by less than 1 percent.[109]

Minimum-wage workers are seriously underpaid, but tipped employees may have it the worst. They are a subcategory of minimum-wage workers in which women make up an even higher percentage of the workforce. Tipped employees, under the Fair Labor Standards Act, are defined as "those who customarily and regularly receive more than $30 per month in tips. Tips are the property of the employee. The employer is prohibited from using an employee's tips for any reason other than as a credit against its minimum wage obligation to the employee ('tip credit') or in furtherance of a valid tip pool. Only tips received by the employee may be counted in determining whether the employee is a tipped employee and in applying the tip credit."[110] Just like the other low-wage jobs dominated by women, tipped jobs are growing, with projections of an increase over a ten-year period of almost 28 percent for personal care jobs, such as manicurists and pedicurists, and an increase of 10 percent for restaurant jobs.[111] Tipped employees include hairdressers and barbers, nail salon workers and cosmetologists, car wash and parking lot attendants, dealers in casinos, and taxi drivers. But most of them are restaurant workers—two-thirds of the 5-million-person tipped workforce—and three-quarters of these restaurant workers are women.[112] The media often portray a typical waiter as an elegantly dressed man in a dimly lit French or Italian restaurant, recommending wine or serving an amuse-bouche to charmed patrons who subsequently leave him a large tip in recompense for his services. The reality is quite different. Waiters are far more likely to be women working at restaurants like Applebee's or Macaroni Grill or the local diner, making less than the minimum wage and most likely not making up the difference through the tips they may or may not receive—and probably having their asses pinched periodically by their customers or co-workers.

In 1996, Congress raised the minimum wage, but as has happened frequently, members of Congress cut a deal that excluded a group of workers that not so coincidentally is largely made up of women. The legislation left the wages of millions of so-called tipped employees at the same level as before, even while it raised the overall minimum wage.[113] The powerful restaurant industry argued that these workers would more than make up for their lost wages by the generous tips they would receive from their grateful customers. The lobbyists opened their checkbooks and wined and dined lawmakers, easily getting lawmakers to swallow the unpersuasive argument that tipped employees are paid very well, or at least well enough. They shored up their lobbying efforts with more than $90,000 in direct campaign contributions to members of the relevant committee in the House of Representatives, the House Committee on Education and the Workforce, for the 1994 and 1996 campaign cycles, when restaurant industry lobbyists succeeded in unlinking the tipped minimum wage from the regular minimum wage.[114] The money has not stopped flowing. An investigation by *The Progressive* documents that "the $683 billion industry's trade association itself has poured $12.6 million directly into federal politicians' campaign coffers since 1989. NRA [National Restaurant Association] member organizations have chipped-in around $51 million more."[115]

The sad fact was that lobbying on the workers' side had to rely on moral suasion. Money won. My first year with Senator Daschle was 1996; I worked closely with Senator Edward Kennedy's Labor Committee staff on the effort to raise the minimum wage for tipped employees. We just did not have enough allies to do it. Unfortunately, the industry's game plan still works: Maryland raised the state minimum wage in 2014 but left tipped employees where they were.[116] The domestic workers I met at a CASA of Maryland meeting in the spring of 2014 had been in Annapolis lobbying for the wage increase and were so disappointed when even blue-state Maryland succumbed to the dollars of the restaurant industry and shafted tipped employees—but lobbyists know that if they pay off enough legislators, they can win many battles. It is not surprising that the National Restaurant Association is known to servers as "the other NRA."

Disgracefully, the tipped wage remains at $2.13 today, exactly where it stood in 1996, when restaurant industry lobbyists successfully unlinked it from the minimum wage, to which it had been pegged at 60 percent. To understand how low this wage is, one has only to know that, in 1991 dollars, it would be only $1.24.[117] Servers suffer from three times the poverty rate of other workers and are twice as likely—a sad irony—to depend on food assistance programs to feed their families. This is even more true for people of color, with almost 24 percent of African American and 22.1 percent of Latino servers living under the poverty level, compared to approximately 18 percent of white waitstaff.[118] Women's earnings are particularly appalling. According to research done by the Restaurant Opportunities Center United, "female servers working full-time, year-round, typically are paid 68 cents for every dollar paid to their male counterparts. The annual median earnings for full time, year round servers are $17,000 for women, and $25,000 for men, a discrepancy of $8,000." That's especially tough for the 20 percent of them who have children.[119] All women in the restaurant industry suffer a wage penalty compared to male workers, but the impact on wages of being a female of color is significantly greater. Controlling for education and work experience, women who work in front-of-the-house positions (waiting tables, serving as a maître d'hôtel or a sommelier, for example) in the New York restaurant industry lose $4,508 annually compared to men; women of color lose an additional $1,287 per year, resulting in a total of $5,795 less in wages than male workers in the same jobs with the same background.[120]

Nineteen percent of restaurant employees do not earn the minimum wage even when their tips are added to the $2.13 per hour they earn as base pay.[121] In theory, tips are supposed to make up the difference between $2.13 and $7.25, but employees often fail to make that much in tips, and their employer may not follow the law's requirement that they supplement workers' pay so they reach the minimum wage.[122] The restaurant industry is notorious for ignoring its legal obligations with respect to workers—minimum wage and overtime violations are rampant, as is employers' outright theft of hard-earned tips.[123] According to a recent White House report, "while the failure to ensure that employees are earning the minimum wage is the most prevalent wage and hour violation, other violations occur. For example, other violations include failing to pay overtime wages as required for weekly hours worked over 40; failing to pay the full minimum wage when tipped employees are asked to perform non-tipped work such as cooking, cleaning, and stocking in excess of 20 percent of their time; or failing to pay employees any wage at all (leaving them to work only for the tips they make)."[124] Like Claudia, the server whose story is told at the beginning of this section, many workers encounter unscrupulous employers who whittle down their small earnings by forcing them to put in some time with no pay at all—like the McDonald's workers who have sued the company for "erasing hours from their timecards, not paying overtime and ordering them to work off the clock."[125]

Recently, the Department of Labor successfully pushed a chain of sports bars, Chickie's & Pete's, to pay $6.8 million in back wages and damages for taking tips from the servers. The owner had required the waitstaff to pay what they called "Pete's tax," a tip pool from which the company skimmed 60 percent off the top. The chain was so tightfisted with its employees that, not only did the company fail to provide waiters with the full minimum wage by making up the difference if tips plus base pay did not equal $7.25, but it also often failed to pay even the measly $2.13 per hour or pay workers time and a half when they had worked overtime.[126] We should cheer to see these servers prevail against such a bad actor. But for servers in smaller restaurants, it is a lot harder to be brave than it is for those who stand with 1,159 other workers and who have the Department of Labor on their side. And in most cases, employers can take the little workers earn with impunity because the repercussions are so minimal: the firm often only has to pay back wages, exactly what it would have paid if it had followed the law. So for unscrupulous bosses it is often worth the gamble: little risk, big gain. Stealing tips, refusing to pay overtime, creating fraudulent deductions from workers' paychecks, misclassifying workers as independent contractors, forcing them to work off the clock, denying them pay for necessary prep time, charging them for uniforms or other required work tools—at the end of the day, all employers might have to do if they get caught is pay the money they owe.[127]

This major weakness of the wage and hour law means that employers can truly violate it without consequences. The costs are so predictable for employers that it makes sense just to factor in wage theft as part of a business plan. And only employees who explicitly opt in to the lawsuit can recover back wages. For many workers, suing the boss comes with the fear of losing a job and a toehold on financial stability; because of that, only 5 to 20 percent of workers are willing to take the step of explicitly joining a lawsuit.[128] It is an especially hard calculation for the many women and single mothers.

There's much that needs to be done to help women in tipped jobs—protect them against pay discrimination and harassment, enforce laws against wage theft and forcing them to work off the clock—but one immediate and effective means to give them a better standard of living would be to raise the minimum wage and eliminate the discrepancy for tipped workers. Thirty-two states (including D.C.) set the tipped wage at a higher level than the federal level, and seven states have done away with the difference altogether.[129] One only has to look at the different poverty rates for servers in states without a subminimum wage versus the rates in states that have left tipped employees at $2.13: 13.6 percent versus 19.4 percent.[130]

This increase would directly affect the earnings of an estimated 837,200 tipped workers, of whom 630,000 are female, and their families, but would also exert a healthy upward pressure on the wages of other low-paid workers in the restaurant industry.[131] And, despite what the business community, and the restaurant industry in particular, argues, the increase would have a minimal impact on prices. Nonetheless, the companies are pulling out all the stops to keep the wage at its grossly inadequate level, even working to target those who advocate for this vulnerable workforce. They are running advertisements attacking these groups and ginning up investigations by friendly government officials, all to stymie efforts to get workers a wage over $2.13 per hour. As Saru Jayaraman, the founder of the Restaurant Opportunities Center, said, "It's flattering. . . . The fact that they're attacking us is a sign that they feel threatened. That's what happens when you challenge the industry to do the right thing."[132]

The problem is that this industry has very little history of doing the right thing. Following the lead of the National Restaurant Association (NRA), business interests have fought hard against every increase, both for tipped workers and in the minimum wage. As *Dissent* magazine reminds us, "In 1996, Herman Cain, onetime 2012 GOP presidential hopeful and alleged serial sexual harasser, became [the] chair [of the NRA] and then CEO. The previous year, Cain, as CEO of Godfather's Pizza, had testified to a joint economic committee in Washington that a proposed minimum wage increase, from $4.25 to $5.15 per hour, would destroy jobs and price first-time job seekers out of the market."[133] Under Cain's leadership, the NRA persuaded Congress to decouple the wages of tipped workers from the minimum wage in 1994, leaving them stuck at $2.13. Today, the NRA and its members are spending more than ever on lobbyists and campaign contributions, determined to thwart efforts to give minimum-wage workers a long-overdue raise. In addition to using their leverage to get government officials to open investigations of worker advocates, designed to intimidate them and enfeeble reform efforts, the industry groups are funding think tanks and paid talking heads to challenge the economics of raising the wages and to attack the reputation of the servers and their advocates.[134] We can't expect this industry—at least as represented by the NRA—to develop a moral conscience or to care about its workers. We will have to force it do so.

Overall, raising the minimum wage should be one of the easier political ways to address inequality in the United States. A recent poll conducted by the *Washington Post* and ABC News demonstrates overwhelming support among Americans—once again. Close to 60 percent support an increase and two-thirds believe that our government's policies favor the wealthy. According to the poll, Americans generally support a minimum wage of $9.41, as opposed to the current $7.25. Even Republicans backed a wage at least $1 higher than what it is now. From 2009 to 2012, the top 1 percent of earners saw their income grow by 31 percent. For everyone else, incomes grew a measly 0.4 percent.[135] It is not lost on most Americans that our nation is mired in gross inequality. Although it would not do nearly enough to erase the huge gap, an increase in the minimum wage would make a difference for those at the bottom of the wage scale, minimum-wage workers, but also for those above them, through a ripple effect ultimately lifting the wages of almost 35 million workers, or a third of the workforce.[136]

We can do better by pushing for more than the minimum wage; what is necessary is a living wage—the wage that anyone would really need to survive in the city where she lives, almost by definition higher than the minimum wage.[137] Some local governments have moved in this direction, requiring government contractors to pay a higher wage. But local and state governments can do more than simply police their own contractors. Few governments ensure that their economic development funding goes to companies with fair labor practices. This is a lost opportunity. When providing economic development funding to the private sector, why shouldn't it be a requirement that these businesses create full-time jobs with a living wage and not have a history of labor law violations? Living wage policies are already in place in Los Angeles, San Francisco, Hartford, and Minneapolis, and forty-two states have adopted wage requirements for businesses to receive economic development funds. And the evidence shows that such living wage requirements have not caused job loss and instead have helped companies by reducing turnover.[138]

LOOK FOR THE UNION LABEL

Union membership for women carries a real dollar value. Unions have helped eliminate differential pay between jobs held mostly by women and those held by men, and between management and lower-level employees.[139] Not only do female members of a union earn wages that are 11.2 percent—about $2 per hour—higher than those of women in similar jobs not in a union, but they also are more likely to have paid leave and are almost always full-time.[140] Public employee unions have a substantial female membership, and as a result, it is a sector where women get higher pay and benefits with respect to men than other types of employment. Overall, women are 45 percent of union members and a large majority of the membership of public sector unions.

But the shrinking of the labor movement and the attacks on public sector unions in particular have hit women very hard. According to Ruth Milkman, a professor of sociology at the CUNY Graduate Center and an expert on labor organization and the workplace, "These attacks will roll back many of the gains women made since the 1960s. In 2012, the average hourly earnings of unionized women stood at $24.18, compared to $18.74 for nonunion women workers."[141] Currently, in the private sector, unions represent only 7 percent of workers; with the addition of the public sector, only 11 percent of American workers belong to a union.

Sadly, union membership is not even an option for many women. In 1935, when the National Labor Relations Act was adopted, it explicitly excluded certain types of workers whose presence in the workforce today has been growing rapidly, and who are mostly women and minority workers. "Temporary" workers, even those who have spent months or years at one company, cannot unionize.[142] Approximately one-third of health aides who are classified as performing "domestic service"—that is, approximately half a million women—are shut out. Similarly, the statute's bar on independent contractors forming a union cuts out more than 3 million people designated by their employers as independent contractors. Some of these independent contractors are nannies; others are hairdressers; some are taxi drivers. And, not surprisingly, the law also precludes the substantial number of undocumented immigrant workers from joining a union, which leaves out around 7 million workers, or nearly 5 percent of private sector workers. Adding up all these exempted employees, it is likely that more than 20 million workers have no right to join a union or engage in collective action to improve their wages and working conditions. And a large share of this 20 million is women of color.[143]

Even for employees who are eligible, organizing a union poses a formidable challenge, prompting labor unions to realize how important it is to catalyze new approaches to worker empowerment. An AFL-CIO publication recognizes that "previous models of labor organizing and labor policy are based on centralized jobsites, single large employers, permanent workforces, skilled workers and an economy based on industrial production. In today's service-based economy, jobsites are dispersed, bosses are constantly shifting and unskilled and semi-skilled temporary work proliferates. These conditions, combined with a dispersal of once well-paid industrial jobs and politically inflamed tensions between low-wage workers, calls for a rethinking of labor organizing and organization in the 21st century."[144]

Worker centers, like the Restaurant Opportunities Center, the Retail Action Network, and the National Domestic Worker Alliance, have stepped into this void. The centers now stretch across the United States, from a mere five in 1992 to more than

230 today, with networks that connect the centers to one another.[145] Victor Narro, the project director at the UCLA Center for Labor Research and Education, explains that "worker centers emerged to respond to the increasing exploitation of low-wage immigrant workers and persistent racism and xenophobia in labor markets and society in general. These worker centers are community-based. Worker centers do not focus exclusively on labor and employment—or on immigration issues. They are about something much bigger and much more visionary in that they see themselves as a movement."[146] Workers come together to create a tighter solidaristic bond, with the centers serving as a hub, providing information and organizing about legal issues, including immigration and worker rights, but going beyond that to offer language classes and other learning programs, financial planning, health care, recreation, and group discussion sessions.[147]

Most important perhaps, they seek to develop the leadership potential of their members, empowering these women to fight for themselves and their families. At CASA of Maryland, the women I met shared stories and lessons learned about the whole range of issues they faced. Rocking children on their knees, they talked about an upcoming conference for domestic workers, lobbying in Annapolis, the fight for immigration reform, an upcoming "rescue" for a diplomat's servant/slave; shared their individual stories; and planned a weekend soccer match and barbecue for them and their families. Like CASA, other worker centers use creative strategies, including aggressive tactics to attract media—like their "rescues" of domestic workers in diplomatic households who have been denied pay and access to friends and family, who can't protest because they lack immigration status apart from their employer—since their constituents are often excluded from the protections of civil rights and employment law and they can't rely on the usual legal tools.

The AFL-CIO sees worker centers as the new frontier in protecting workers' rights, especially in light of the decline of manufacturing and its denser workforces. Even for workers who have a protected right to join a union, organizing is very hard in a more service-oriented economy with smaller and more spread-out work sites. The painstaking efforts to reach and educate workers, let alone win an election to represent them, is very difficult and resource intensive under current law. Joining together, "unions and workers centers are collaborating on campaigns to change regional labor laws and explore new enforcement and agreement models. This includes creating new policies and laws that set standards for large numbers of workers, including those who are covered under government contracts and hired using public to private incentive programs."[148]

The worker centers have achieved some real victories in the states, raising wages and improving benefits for tipped employees, bargaining for better working conditions and safer workplaces, and winning the right to organize. They have successfully sued big corporations for back wages after unscrupulous employers stole tips from workers or forced them to work off the clock.[149] In Vermont, the Vermont Workers' Center, called Put People First, and several unions joined together to push for policy changes including universal health care for all Vermonters as well as allowing home care providers to organize. Those workers subsequently joined Vermont Home Care United, part of the American Federation of State, County and Municipal Employees, and have just bargained their first contract.[150]

The domestic worker bill of rights campaigns provide another illustration of successful efforts led by worker centers with the help and support of unions. To date, three states, New York, California, and Hawaii, have enacted legislation to improve the status of domestic workers. New York passed its legislation in 2010.[151] The New York law covers home workers, including nannies, housekeepers, and those who care for the elderly, an estimated two hundred thousand workers just in the New York City area. In California, workers successfully passed a Domestic Workers' Bill of Rights, on September 26, 2013.[152] In Hawaii, legislators applied the state's prohibition on discrimination to domestic workers.[153] Massachusetts is now advancing similar legislation, pushed by the Massachusetts Coalition for Domestic Workers. It still remains a project to get these laws enforced, as many of these workers are not familiar with their newly acquired protections and the enforcement funding hasn't met the need. In New York, even after the law had been close to a year on the books, few of the affected workers were aware of the changes.[154] But there's hope as both nonprofit and government agencies have stepped in to educate workers and help them pursue their rights, already winning back pay and other penalties for dozens of them.[155]

This piecemeal approach has drawbacks, with some workers in certain states winning victories and others left behind. Domestic workers outside of New York, California, and, perhaps soon, Massachusetts, have only the federal regulation addressing overtime to hope for. They are still excluded from Title VII, OSHA, and the National Labor Relations Act, as well as other job protections.[156] In Vermont, after the victories of the Put People First campaign, home care workers now have the right to bargain, but those workers in other states do not. Moreover, taking on one slice of injustice at a time does not necessarily create solidarity between and among low-wage workers. And anything that workers achieve in only one or a few states is always a target of rollback efforts by the Right and has to have muscle behind its implementation. As one organizer said to me, in questioning the domestic worker bill of rights strategy despite its successes, "What about enforcement? Is there money? If not, is this victory?"[157]

While more work remains, these victories do demonstrate the capacity of low-wage women to fight for dignity and to win better treatment. Focused on certain professions or a local community, the centers offer a model that has helped many workers—but the most creative and far-reaching have also built bridges to workers in other professions and other places. They are challenging barriers to organizing that affect many workers, in many occupations beyond home care and child care. By questioning the legal structures that allow employers to avoid paying decent wages or providing benefits for certain workers, that exempt them from other legal protection, these workers may be laying the groundwork that allows all of us a fair shake in the workplace. As a report of the Excluded Workers Congress suggests, "The hope and vibrancy attributed to contemporary immigrant workers' struggle are actually broader dynamics that are emerging across racial, sectoral and regional lines; these positive developments demonstrate the potential for excluded workers to help rejuvenate and transform the broader labor movement."[158]

THE FINAL STRAW: RETIREMENT (IN)SECURITY: THE CONSEQUENCES OF WAGE DISCRIMINATION

Lower wages do not mean only insecurity in the everyday lives of women workers but also poverty in their older years. The lasting legacy of unfair pay is reduced pensions and Social Security payments forever after. According to Senator Harkin, "The average woman loses more than $400,000 over her lifetime due to unequal pay practices, and evidence shows that discrimination accounts for much of the disparity."[159]

Lilly Ledbetter is again a sad example of that reality. Known for the Supreme Court decision bearing her name that gave employers a license to discriminate so long as they conceal it from their workers—later overturned by Congress in the Lilly Ledbetter Fair Pay Act of 2009[160]—she also epitomizes the impact such unfairness has on women's retirement. Ledbetter said later, "I was making 40 percent less than those men. After realizing that, I finally got enough energy to do my 12 hour shift, then thought about how my overtime, my retirement, 401K and social security were all based on what I was earning."[161] Ledbetter decided to file a complaint with the Equal Employment Opportunities Commission, after which she was promptly pushed out of Goodyear and forced into early retirement.[162]

She won a jury verdict of $3.3 million in compensatory damages, as well as punitive damages because of how egregious and long-standing the pay disparity had been. But while Ledbetter may have won a symbolic victory, she did not get her damages reinstated and thus lost a lifetime of fair wages—and had a much smaller retirement fund as a result. Lilly Ledbetter is a hero for fighting for justice, but she is currently struggling to get by.[163]

In addition to the myriad ways in which women are disadvantaged by lifelong lower earnings, our retirement scheme—and Social Security is for many workers the only retirement benefit they will receive—skews against women, particularly mothers. Social Security benefits are calculated based on how many quarters per year a worker is employed over his or her lifetime. Like the other New Deal programs, Social Security was founded on an assumption that families would maintain a "traditional structure," with the father working and the mother staying at home. But with more and more women working outside of the home, but often not as consistently as men, since they may take some time off for childbearing and early child care, the system makes less and less sense. An employee qualifies for benefits after working forty quarters or ten years. Women who have been married can collect benefits based on the husband's income, if they are widowed, and men, too, can now choose whether to take their own benefit, based on personal earnings, or the spousal benefit, whichever proves higher. In the past, this structure was very beneficial to women. But for many families, this formula no longer works. When both parents work and take time off to care for children or elderly parents, and certainly in the case of single-parent households, the family pays a double penalty by losing wages during time off but also by losing Social Security benefits.[164]

Even for more traditional families, the way benefits are awarded can harm women. If a woman stays home to raise the children but the marriage falls apart before ten years are over, she gets nothing. And if the couple divorces after ten years, the spouse with lower earnings, usually the woman—particularly if there are young children—is entitled to only the spousal benefit, which is just 50 percent of her ex-husband's benefit. Ann O'Leary and Karen Kornbluh describe in *The Shriver Report* how stay-at-home moms are disadvantaged: "The spousal benefit is based purely on marriage, not on an individual's caregiving responsibilities. This means caregivers who take time out of the work-place or limit their hours (and therefore earnings) to care for family members get no credit toward retirement for their caregiving directly but only as a derivative of their spouse's earnings. This is not only demeaning, it means they lose out if they divorce, are widowed before age 60, or are otherwise single parents."[165]

In addition to fixing Social Security, we can do more to address the pension gap by providing help for workers to save for retirement along the way. For one thing, we should push for the government to fund a universal 401(k), which, unlike the current system, which gives a fat tax benefit to high earners, would help all Americans save. Gene B. Sperling, the former head of the Obama White House's National Economic Council (and my colleague in the Clinton White House), makes a persuasive case for a government dollar-for-dollar match for lower-income workers' savings of up to $4,000, which could help build a nest egg[166]— but only if they can afford to put aside $4,000, which may overwhelm the resources of a single mom waiting tables. Still, it is a useful idea and one we should pursue.

Most important, women will have more secure retirements if they earn a fair wage during their working life—and that's what we need to fight for.

While there are a number of different reasons for women's lower earnings, there are synergistic forces that push women's pay down. Discrimination and occupational segregation have helped keep women in the lowest-paying jobs in our economy, and our laws have not given women enough muscle to contest their unfair wages effectively. Barred from unions or simply lacking access to them, most women have not been able to benefit from the real impact labor organizations have had in remedying unequal pay scales. Many women work as hairdressers and servers, trying to scrape together enough tips to earn a living, but often don't earn even the minimum wage. And even if they do earn the minimum wage, their earnings rarely lift them above the poverty line. As a nation and as moral people, we need to care about this problem. These women make up a growing community of overstressed and underpaid workers, many of them struggling to care for children or elderly parents and often having a hard time even feeding themselves. The jobs these women hold are those most economists expect to grow rapidly in the coming years and decades. Unless we address the needs of the lowest paid, we will face an unconscionable and unsustainable inequality in America, an inequality that is already challenging what it means to be a democracy.

3

PUNCHING THE CLOCK:
PART-TIME, JUST-IN-TIME, AND OVERTIME

On Mother's Day 2013, the New York City Police Department told 911 operators, most of whom are women, that they would have to work overtime that day. The women who were already covering that day's three eight-hour shifts were told that they would have to stay an additional four hours and perhaps longer, even though it was Sunday. The choice of spending time with family was off the table—anyone who refused would be fired. Rubbing salt in the wounds, the NYPD required anyone who called in sick to provide documentary evidence of their illness. Said one operator, "It's double-jeopardy for us, because handling crime calls all day, with no break to go home to your family, plays with the psyche. You worry about making a mistake and getting written up, but moreover, you worry about making a mistake that will hurt somebody."[1] And these workers even had a union.

When Congress passed the Fair Labor Standards Act (FLSA) in 1938, there was high unemployment, but for those with jobs, there were also brutally long days and little time off. The FLSA, for the first time, in addition to setting a minimum wage, established the length of the workweek employees could be expected to work without being paid overtime. By requiring extra pay—time and a half—for any hours worked in excess of the newly enshrined forty-four-hour workweek,[2] supporters of the law thought it would provide an incentive for employers to hire more workers to spread the work around and save on overtime costs, thus reducing unemployment. They also sought to provide a fairer wage and regular, sustainable hours, especially for workers who did not have the protection of a union or who worked in low-skilled jobs without much bargaining power. The Supreme Court, in an early case interpreting the act, described its purpose as protecting the "unprotected, unorganized and lowest paid of the nation's working population."[3]

But the law's stated goal was undermined from the outset. As legislators hammered out the bill, they made political trade-offs and concessions to secure its passage that dropped many workers out—indeed, only 20 percent of workers were helped by the FLSA at the beginning.[4] The southern members of Congress demanded the explicit exclusion of the workers who cooked, cleaned, and cared for children in their homes and the field hands who worked their lands—virtually all African American—so their plantation economy could remain intact. President Roosevelt and his allies in Congress had not wanted to carve out so many workers, but they needed southern votes to pass the law so they traded preserving Jim Crow conditions for some in favor of better pay and overtime for others. And business interests were able to whittle down the covered workforce even further, cutting out those laboring in laundries, tailoring, and dry cleaning in 1945.[5] Ironically, partly because of the FLSA's limitations and exclusions, those workers who fit the profile of the most vulnerable are those least likely to be protected.[6]

In addition to excluding domestic workers, farmworkers, and others, the law was limited to larger employers, initially because of the worry that the Supreme Court might strike down the law.[7] Many business opponents of the bill had specifically challenged its constitutionality as too broad a reading of the Commerce Clause, which had been a successful argument against earlier bills.[8] Seeking to alleviate opponents' concerns, Senator Hugo Black of Alabama assured them that factories and large unionized facilities fell under the act, but not retail stores and services: "The prevailing sentiment of the committee, if not the unanimous sentiment of the committee . . . [is] that businesses of a purely local type which serve a local community, and which do not send their products into the streams of interstate commerce, can be better regulated by the laws of the communities and of the [s]tates in which the business units operate."[9] It goes without saying that legislators understood that the act would play a very small role in the less-industrialized South—especially in conjunction with the explicit exemptions for agricultural and domestic workers. Later, courts and Congress came to see that almost all workers are actually "engaged in commerce," and the coverage of the FLSA came to encompass a larger and larger group of workers. In 1989, however, after lobbying by powerful industry groups, like the National Federation of Independent Business, President George H.W. Bush maneuvered Democrats in Congress into adding an exemption for smaller companies by agreeing to an increase in the minimum wage. So once again, certain businesses were given a license to demand excessive work hours without paying overtime. Millions of workers lost their rights.

In drafting the FLSA, legislators made another choice that led to the exclusion of vast numbers of workers when they limited overtime provisions to "hourly employees," giving companies wiggle room to write their workers out of the law by calling them "salaried." George W. Bush followed his father's lead by adopting a regulation that radically expanded the number of workers who could be called salaried, taking away their right to overtime with the stroke of a pen. When the rule was adopted, analysts found that an additional 8 million workers lost overtime protections; that number is approximately 6 percent of the labor force.

In the same pattern as other statutes, the FLSA leaves out some workers through the explicit exclusion of their job category, others by the size of their employers, and yet others by virtue of being designated as "salaried" and not "hourly" employees.[10] These categories cover more and more people, and the hours Americans work are going up and up. Not having to pay time and a half is a great incentive to work people to exhaustion. Even for those who earn overtime pay, the forty-hour workweek does not mean employers can't ask—or rather, demand—that employees work longer hours; they only have to pay them time and a half. Unexpected changes in schedules or additional hours can throw havoc into the carefully organized but often precarious plans of low-wage workers with children or sick parents or who have a second job. A woman who says no to extra hours, like the 911 operators, may be saying good-bye to her job at the same time.

On the flip side, many workers work less than they would like. The United States has seen a great increase in its part-time workforce, with women filling the majority of these jobs. Part-time jobs not only pay less overall because of reduced hours but also pay less per hour—employers impose a wage penalty on their part-time workers that compounds the difficulty faced by women and families scraping to get by. Some employers drop the number of hours employees work, to avoid having to provide any benefits. Other employers, particularly in the retail and restaurant industries, have added insult to injury by abandoning regular schedules altogether and forcing workers to call in daily to know whether they should report that day.

As our economy has shifted from manufacturing to service jobs, with more and more mothers in the workforce, and with our expectations of 24/7 commerce, women suffer particularly from the failure of the FLSA to give workers control over their workdays.[11] The twenty-first-century workplace is one of too many hours or too few, one where employers can change workers' schedules with no warning, where some workers know if they have work on a certain day only by calling in to their employers, where the FLSA's lofty promises are irrelevant. Those most likely to control their working hours as well as their time off are those who have the most bargaining power. Flexibility and predictability are the province of those at the top of the food chain.

WELL OVER FORTY: TOO MANY HOURS AND TOO LITTLE PAY

Myrla Baldonado told me that she had not set out to become an activist. But in the course of working as a certified nursing assistant and caregiver for the elderly in Chicago, she has been sexually harassed, underpaid, and forced to work long hours with no overtime and has struggled to pay her rent, let alone send money home to her children in the Philippines. Myrla was lucky to find Latino Union, a worker center started by women day laborers that has become part of the national network of day laborers and domestic workers. She went further, though, than simply becoming a member—she became a volunteer organizer and leader, learning the stories of other workers and working to push for stronger workplace protections. When Secretary of Labor Tom Perez came to Chicago to gather evidence for a new rule that would finally give home care workers overtime pay, she gave poignant testimony about her working conditions:

> I worked from 6 am–9 pm or 15 hours excluding interrupted sleep without meal breaks and day offs. More than the household work, meal prep, bed making and clothes

washing which are described as companionship under the
law, I fed the patient, prepared and oftentimes administered medicines, bathed, turned and cleaned up the patient
3-4 times during the day, dressed and groomed the patient
or changed diapers, transferred or lifted the patient from
bed to wheelchair, assisted in rising or getting up, assisted
in walking, monitored vitals, exercised the patient, and
with patients who had dementia and Alzheimer's I became
their psychologist.

The task is endless which even includes oftentimes taking care of an elderly husband or the grandchild. I was
working for an average of 90 hours a week. My pay is $110
per day which comes up 4.58 dollars per hour.

Even while working with the agency I wasn't given overtime pay. The highest pay that I got for a month's work was
$1,780 a month. I was eating mostly eggs and bananas to be
able to send money to my children, which wasn't enough
for their food, education and medical needs. I was having
difficulty paying my rent and did not have any insurance
and couldn't even go on a day off to go to the doctor. My
situation is typical of what many a caregiver goes thru.[12]

The FLSA's objective of keeping working hours humane
has been severely undermined. Americans work more hours
than ever before—and more than workers in other industrial-
ized countries.[13] Over the course of twenty years, from 1979 to
2000, the share of workers putting in more than fifty hours per
week went from 21 to 27 percent for men and from 5 to 11 percent for women. While many tend to think that eighty-hour
weeks and working nights and weekends are the province of the
billable-hours professions—lawyers and investment bankers—
extremely long days are also true in many blue- and pink-collar

jobs, and many of the professions that face abuses of overtime are dominated by women.[14] According to the American Nurses Association, "mandatory overtime is one of the many workplace issues that may be contributing to nurses leaving the workforce."[15]

Mandatory overtime is acutely hard on women. Especially in a country without affordable child care, limited availability of paid sick or family leave, let alone flexible schedules, the increase in hours demanded by employers has hurt all women, not just those in low-wage positions but also those who want to compete for higher-paid jobs or break out of female-dominated positions.[16] It is hard enough for most parents to juggle work and family, but those expected to work extra-long hours struggle to find the time or energy to help their kids with math, shop for food, clean the house, let alone have an hour to relax, take a nap, or talk to their spouse. The stresses and strains can be overwhelming, with a mix of guilt for neglecting the family and fear of not doing the job well enough. Lack of sleep makes workers more prone to accidents and mistakes, which can have a real safety impact for consumers and patients, and more likely to develop stress-related illnesses. And clearly the children and the family pay a cost.[17]

Workers like Myrla Baldonado whose jobs are omitted from the FLSA's overtime protections are most at risk of brutally long workdays. These women work night and day in large part *because* employers do not have to pay them time and a half for working more than forty hours per week. Domestic workers provide one of the most poignant examples of how employers exploit the lack of overtime to wring excessive profits out of their workforce. Testimony from an anonymous but typical home care worker explains how this model helps pad the wallets of the home care executives:

I average 120 to 160 hours every two weeks. My husband loads trucks 40 hours a week. It takes me almost twice as long to earn what he does. I can work in two weeks what some people work in an entire month. That's because we home care aides don't get paid time and a half for overtime in Florida. A couple days a week I work 8:00 in the morning until 8:00 at night. Sometimes I work from 8:00 at night until 3:00 in the afternoon. I spend a lot of my day just going from one client to another. These days I'm not driving too far between clients, but there were times when I was traveling 30 to 50 miles a day to get from one client to the next. We used to get paid for that travel and mileage. Now we don't anymore. Gas costs a lot more now than it used to. When I started working for this company about three years ago I was making $9.50 an hour. Now I earn $10.00 an hour. I wouldn't have gotten even those two 25 cent raises if I didn't make myself available 24/7 to make sure my clients get the coverage they need. Sometimes I stay overnight with someone who just needs light care. They call that "companion care." When I do that, I just get $8.00 an hour. Your clients feel like part of your family when you spend time with them and love them like I do. But my husband and kids need me, too.[18]

Cut out of the FLSA right from the beginning, with no right to overtime or even a minimum wage, domestic workers finally pushed Congress to give them protections in 1974, when legislators made clear that domestic workers were indeed engaged in commerce and thus covered by the law.[19] But while Congress might have thought so, the Republican-controlled executive branch didn't agree. So without any apparent justification, and in total contradiction to the newly passed law, the Department of

Labor (DOL) issued regulations that immediately excluded most of the workers, even though, as the DOL now admits, "there is no indication in the legislation or the Congressional history that those employees covered before this amendment, domestic workers employed by third parties, were to be excluded."[20] But what is clear is that the home care agencies—those are the "third parties"—had powerful lobbyists.

There were obvious financial interests at stake—companies designed their business plans on the assumption that home care workers could be worked endless hours without overtime and attracted investments to capitalize on this advantage.[21] In a report on the economics of the industry, the Paraprofessional Healthcare Institute describes how low wages and long hours have helped the industry boom, with national chains rapidly adding franchises to take advantage of the vast market opportunity and high profit margins. As the report explains, "Underlying these margins are significant spreads between the billing rates for services, on the one hand, and the wages paid to aides, on the other."[22]

These women kept fighting, nearly succeeding in fixing the mistake at the end of the Clinton administration, but just before the new rule became final, the incoming Bush administration was able to kill it.[23] Home care workers moved to the courts, and while they did not win, the Supreme Court ruling in *Long Island Care at Home, Ltd., et al. v. Coke* made it clear that the DOL had discretion to change the rule.[24]

After years of fighting for relief, advocates finally have a sympathetic ear. President Obama has proposed a change to the FLSA that would provide home health aides the protections they should have gotten under the law passed in 1974.[25] This simple change would put an estimated 2 million workers under the FLSA's safeguards, giving them overtime and a minimum wage.[26]

But still left out are those women who are hired directly by the family and who live with them; they won't get overtime. (We can call that "the live-in nanny exception"—so everyone on the Upper East Side and Greenwich can relax.) Unfortunately, for the newly covered workers, the regulation itself does not actually go into effect until January 1, 2015. According to *Franchise Business Review*, in 2011, industry leader Home Instead Senior Care has already invested at least $362,000 against the proposed rule, in the meantime enjoying "an 18.8 yield ratio of investment to revenue," one of the best in the magazine's survey.[27] Home Instead and the other agencies will no doubt keep throwing cash at lawmakers to prevent the regulation from coming into force.

Attention paid to the impending victory for home care workers may obscure the remaining injustice that leaves farm laborers and a few other categories of low-wage workers explicitly exempted, despite obvious reasons to protect them. A simple reading of the list of remaining exemptions unmasks the power of hardball lobbying by certain industries and the deep imprint of campaign contributions on the rules. For example, one might find it hard to square the exclusion of farmworkers with the intention behind the FLSA to provide protections to the most vulnerable. While inexplicable in terms of the stated purpose behind the FLSA, it is not so hard to understand in light of the Jim Crow history, followed by the flow of campaign cash for members of Congress. Three lawyers discuss the reasons for this exclusion in a somewhat naïve article: "Specifically, the legislative history of the agricultural exemption indicates that it was based upon the fear that application of overtime requirements would result in higher produce prices, would impact most harshly upon smaller growers and would prove unmanageable where growers utilized piece-rate harvesters. Lobbyists were [also] successful in persuading Congress to exempt other industries as well by arguing that the maximum hours standard would drive up prices and harm fisheries, logging operations, bulk petroleum distributors and local newspapers and broadcasters. It is unclear why Congress believed that the FLSA was a threat to these industries and not others."[28] Beyond a simple review of the *Congressional Record*, which tells the story of the racist intentions quite clearly, I think the word "lobbyist" provides the very explanation these authors are searching for—agribusiness had lots of them and the farmworkers did not, and the worker advocates did not have bags of cash to throw around.

Even those employers not able to neatly excise their workers from overtime protections through an explicit exclusion have been given a means to exclude low-paid staff by calling them "salaried." The FLSA creates an incentive for employers to give low-wage employees inflated titles because certain white-collar positions are not entitled to overtime. Under the law, known as the "salary test," employers need not pay either the minimum wage or overtime to workers they designate as "bona fide executive, administrative, professional and outside sales employees," so long as their daily tasks meet the DOL definition and they make more than $455 per week.[29] For employers, there's a clear financial incentive to fudge on these designations. Workers have had to challenge their denial of overtime when their employers tried to get out of the requirement by adding "manager" or "leader" to their title when their actual work consisted of serving fast food, shelving merchandise, or ringing up customers' purchases.[30]

In a recent case, an employee, called a "store manager" by Dollar General, sued arguing that she had been improperly denied overtime. Issuing an initial ruling for the woman plaintiff, the court described the actual duties performed by the employee: "Hale spent forty percent of her time alone in the store, during which she supervised no one and she performed tasks typically done by a clerk. A juror could conclude that her mental management of the store, such as spotting empty shelves while performing menial labor, did not constitute management or supervision of others. Further, a reasonable juror could determine that the company's strict policies and stringent allocation of staff labor hours resulted in Hale forgoing true management duties in order to perform menial tasks so the store could simply remain open."[31]

In this way, too, the FLSA is archaic—the job duties test is laughable and salary level has not been updated in years. Contrary to the statute's original purpose, many workers put in the "salaried" category do little if any supervisory work. While in theory, "their duties must include managing a part of the enterprise and supervising other employees or exercising independent judgment on significant matters or require advanced knowledge,"[32] the reality is quite different. This loophole allows employers to tell women that as a receptionist or typist they are administrative or professional, while in fact they have little or no supervisory responsibilities. But what they do get, in addition to a nicer title, is the right to work overtime without overtime pay. The Bush administration used regulatory black magic to push more workers into this category in 2004. That DOL rule cost an additional 8 million employees their overtime pay.[33] Even without chicanery, the rules have become so lax that many employees are called "salaried" who should be earning overtime under the FLSA's original purpose. According to an economist at the Economic Policy Institute, "under current rules, it literally means that you can spend 95 percent of the time sweeping floors and stocking shelves, and if you're responsible for supervising people 5 percent of the time, you can then be considered executive and be exempt."[34]

And in 2014, how many employees performing real "executive, administrative or professional" work make below $455 per week?[35] Even with stagnant wages that's not plausible. Interviewed for a story on a proposed reform, Seth Harris, who had recently stepped down as deputy secretary of labor, expressed amazement that anyone would oppose the long-overdue fix. Calling the current salary level of $455 "laughably low," Harris noted that "it's only a few dollars more per week than the proposed new minimum wage would require for all workers."[36] Indeed, some of these employees earn less than the minimum wage because of the number of hours without overtime they have to work—meaning that the number of workers earning at or below minimum wage is undercounted because salaried workers are not considered in calculating the minimum-wage workforce.[37] Keeping the threshold low for salaried work makes it enticing to employers to work these employers well beyond forty hours because there is no overtime to pay at all.[38]

President Obama proposed a new regulation to raise the dollar threshold for the salaried worker exemption as well as to make it harder for employers to manipulate employees' job titles to avoid paying overtime.[39] Women make up the majority of the workers who could start earning overtime, many of whom currently work well over forty hours per week without additional pay. Almost 30 percent of the affected workers are people of color.[40]

Lifting the salary level alone will help many women earn a better wage. Tightening the definition will enable even more women access to overtime pay. And increasing enforcement will help deter employers from continuing to call workers "supervisory" or "salaried" or "white-collar" in order to avoid paying what the law requires. And for many women—domestic workers as well as office workers—coming under the overtime provisions will mean that they will actually have more time for their families and other pursuits—but if they are indeed forced to work long hours, at least they will be paid for it.

TOO FEW HOURS TO MAKE A LIVING: THE RISE OF THE PART-TIME WORKER

The recent economic downturn has accelerated the trend of employers making more of their workforce part-time. After laying off full-time workers during the recession, many employers hired part-time workers to replace them as the economy began to improve. According to the Bureau of Labor Statistics, there are now more than 8 million involuntary part-time workers—people who would really like a full-time job but cannot find one. The Bureau of Labor Statistics euphemistically calls these workers "part-time for economic reasons."[41]

Dolly Martinez was working at an art supply store in Manhattan. Utrecht was a collegial place, and many employees had been there for years. Some of them were artists or artisans who liked being around the tools of the trade. But things began to sour when the parent company was bought out, bringing many changes, including a shift to part-time work for all the employees. "Our hours were capped [at] twenty-five hours per week. A lot of employees got angry," she told me. Everyone who did not have a managerial position had a big bite taken out of their hours. All of a sudden, their jobs could not provide them a living. For many of these workers, the change in hours was devastating because their families depended on the income brought in by a full-time job.[42]

Instead of giving in or simply looking for other jobs, these employees got mad, decided to fight back, and organized themselves, joining the Retail, Wholesale and Department Store Union. The new owners bitterly contested the efforts. But even in the face of an aggressive anti-union campaign by the company, including "captive audience" meetings, where workers were forced to sit through management threats about the consequences of supporting a union, the union won a decisive vote. According to the lead union organizer, Stephanie Basille, "Workers were subjected to an aggressive anti-union campaign that included multiple meetings with top management and long pamphlets filled with distortions and lies. . . . The employees at Utrecht are incredibly hard working and passionate about what they do, and tried on multiple occasions to ask for basic things like better pay and having their hours restored."[43] The Utrecht employees are now trying to negotiate a contract with Utrecht that, among other things, demands a living wage, including adequate hours, and advance notice of schedules.[44] Dolly, who was a lead organizer of the union drive, was fired by the company in retaliation, but the union has filed an unfair labor practice complaint that may entitle her to get her job back. For workers like Dolly who have the right to join a union, a right provided to too few, it is illegal for the employer to fire them because they support the union drive. As of this writing, Dolly's case was still in process. In the meantime, she's thrown herself into organizing other retail workers, helping them to get full-time hours, and is now on staff full-time at the Retail Action Project.

Part-time work is not always an unwanted choice. For some workers, especially women, the option to work part-time may be an attractive alternative that allows them to spend time with their children or care for elderly relatives and still bring some money home (some argue, however, that a number of women who tell researchers that they are part-time by choice say so because they do not want to designate caring for children or parents as an undesirable way to spend their time, resulting in an undercount of the involuntary part-time workforce).[45] Some employees work their way through school to defray expenses. But for many, an increasingly large number, part-time work is the best they can get despite wanting and needing more. And even for workers who prefer or need to work part-time, few of them actually would choose to opt out of benefits.[46]

Women make up almost two-thirds of the part-time workforce, with a median weekly income of $236.[47] The rate of involuntary part-time work has doubled for women since 2007.[48] For example, retail workers, a majority of whom are women, are more and more likely to be hired as part-time rather than full-time, with black and Latino women workers most at risk.[49] The consequences for families are significant. The Carsey Institute, a think tank at the University of New Hampshire that does research on vulnerable children, youths, and families, has used economic data to show the strong correlation between poverty and involuntary part-time work. It reported, "In 2012, more than one-fourth of women who worked involuntarily part time lived in poverty, and more than one-half were low-income, that is living in families with total income below 200 percent of the federal poverty line." Not only do these jobs not provide enough hours for workers to earn a living; they often pay less per hour than full-time jobs, provide few or no benefits, and are notably less secure than other positions.[50]

While some companies trumpet their generosity in paying slightly over the minimum wage,[51] what they keep secret is that while raising the hourly wage, they have lowered the number of hours they assign to their workers. Sitting with a group of other organizers in the offices of the Retail Action Network, Nala Toussaint described to me the way retail employers continually undermine workers' ability to earn a decent wage, manipulating their hours and changing their schedules. Nala, a transgender woman, had more to contend with than most employees. "I worked at the Gap. In 2010, when I started, they were initially giving me a lot of hours, forty to forty-five," said Nala. "I originally started part-time because I was in college and couldn't commit to full-time. When I graduated, they started to cut my hours. And when I got paid more, I got even fewer hours. They would say they couldn't give me any more hours because they didn't have the money, but I would see them hire more employees. While I was transitioning, they didn't know what to do with me. It is as if they would say, 'What do we do with you? Should we keep you in the back or put you in the front?' I probably didn't get hours because of transitioning."[52]

Ten dollars an hour is better than $7, but if a worker gets only twenty hours per week, he or she can't survive. Joseph Williams, having lost his job as a reporter, took a job at a sporting goods store. In order to keep him from earning benefits or overtime, his employer kept his hours under thirty, while regularly working him longer than his scheduled shift. Even though he made more than the minimum wage, he did not earn enough to live on. "Sporting Goods Inc., I came to realize, was fine with paying me a few dollars more than the minimum wage . . . because it had other ways to compensate itself, including disqualifying me from overtime or paid sick days. Requiring me to play Cinderella on the closing shift also saved management the money it would have had to pay a cleaning company to maintain the store. Yet even $10 an hour . . . can barely keep a single adult afloat in a city like Washington," he wrote.[53] Paying a bit more than the minimum wage may be a nice, if small, gesture, but when it is coupled with a policy of keeping workers part-time, it is clearly more public relations than compassion.

In addition to simply wanting to avoid overtime and to pay less in wages, employers have cut workers' hours to make sure they can't claim benefits. Both voluntary benefits, such as pensions and paid leave, and government-mandated ones, such as family leave and affordable health care, are available only to employees who work more than a specified number of hours, excluding part-time workers from coverage. Passed in 2010, the Affordable Care Act ("Obamacare"), President Obama's signature legislative accomplishment, was designed to expand the number of Americans who have health insurance, providing more than 30 million previously uninsured people with coverage. Despite helping many formerly uninsured people get coverage, the Affordable Care Act applies only to larger employers and requires companies to insure only full-time workers. Under the act, covered employees—those with fifty or more full-time workers (which means those who work an average of thirty or more hours per week)—must provide affordable health insurance or pay a penalty of $2,000 per worker.[54]

Many commentators have recognized the perverse incentive created by the Affordable Care Act in encouraging employers to drop workers' hours to avoid covering their health care costs. A report by the Retail Action Project explains these concerns: "The 'employer responsibility' provision that is scheduled to take effect in 2014 would . . . only require employers to provide requisite health insurance or pay a penalty for full-time employees. There is no penalty assessed based on the number of full-time equivalents, no matter how many are employed at a business. . . . The employer-based health care law—at least in the retail sector—may have the effect of fueling the shift towards a part-time workforce that would qualify for a range of government supports, including Medicaid."[55] Rather than providing the benefit itself or paying a penalty, a business can simply cut the hours of its staff and force them to get their health insurance on the exchange along with the self-employed and the unemployed. The worst consequence for these vulnerable workers may not be enrolling in the exchange but the fact that they will lose hours and wages when their work schedule is cut down so their company can avoid the cost of insurance. Companies from Regal Entertainment to Sodexo have lowered hours for their workers to avoid paying for their insurance and thereby lowered their wages at the same time.[56]

A data analysis by the University of California, Berkeley's Labor Center finds that the workers "most vulnerable to work reduction" are those "working 30 to 36 hours, with incomes below 400% of the Federal Poverty Level and not covered by their own employer [for health insurance]," and that the lion's share of those workers are concentrated in restaurants, retail, accommodations, nursing homes, and building services.[57] We know that women, often women of color and single mothers, are overrepresented in these jobs—and now likely to suffer a wage loss because of reduction in hours and a denial of employer-provided health care under the Affordable Care Act. There are also reports of local governments cutting hours to avoid providing health care for their part-time employees. Substitute teachers, bus drivers, and others are seeing their hours cut, and if they hold two part-time jobs in a school system, such as softball coach and bus driver, they are told to pick one.[58] Public sector jobs had been one area where women have done pretty well, making this doubly painful.

Fewer hours, of course, mean lower wages, and that loss of income can be disastrous. And employers have succeeded in offloading a cost of doing business onto workers and taxpayers. By adding more part-time and reducing full-time workers, these businesses can avoid almost all costs of providing benefits, even the minimal penalty under Obamacare. The health care law is only one example, but it provides useful data about incentives—about how corporations looking for profits will respond to new legislation. They can continue to claim they generously provide benefits to full-time employees, who are the exception rather than the rule in their workplaces. Meanwhile, their part-time employees have to turn to public assistance for health care and food programs, leaving the costs to be borne by the taxpayer, the worker, and the workers' children, but certainly not by the executives or the shareholders.

THE HUMAN YO-YO: JUST-IN-TIME SCHEDULING AND LOSS OF CONTROL

Tamara, a mother working two jobs, struggles with trying to survive as a retail worker:

> I'm a parent with two children living in Brooklyn, and I work another part-time in addition to my retail job to make ends meet. I work six to seven days a week and it still doesn't cut it. During the holidays, I am forced to work late so that the corporation makes huge holiday profits. . . . I was even pressured by my boss to work when my daughter was in the hospital, despite the fact that I gave as much advance notice as the situation allowed. I feel like my work is forcing me to choose between keeping my job or caring for my children. How am I supposed to take care of my children when I earn so little, despite working two jobs?[59]

Tamara's story is becoming more and more typical, with the old-style forty-hour workweek quickly disappearing. Because of lack of bargaining power in a weak economy, employees find themselves at the mercy of companies that have adopted a just-in-time system of management, meaning they keep a pool of workers on call subject to the demands of the restaurant or retail establishment. These workers, treated by their employers like car parts in a Toyota factory, get no fixed hours and must be available when the boss needs them. If summoned, the on-call workers have to drop everything and rush to work, affecting child care arrangements, or conversely their shift gets canceled at the last minute, undermining their desperate efforts to stay above water financially.[60] For many of these workers, the coupling of too few paying work hours with too much volatility creates chaos in their lives and adds to the constant stress of being a low-wage worker. Workers' schedules have become more unpredictable and less manageable—tough for anyone, but for a low-wage mother, devastating.

The retail workers I interviewed described in vivid and painful detail how hard it was to complete their degree, take care of children or elderly parents, and earn money they desperately needed—not to mention the wear and tear on their bodies of constantly changing sleep patterns and the impact on their ability to have a private life—when they didn't know when they might have to work, when they might have to stay late or start early, or when they might lose a shift altogether. Despite giving their employers advance notice of when they were available for work and when they had a conflict, such as a class or family responsibility, these women continued to get shifts that disrupted their other commitments. The only options they had were to skip class, be absent from family obligations, or lose their job.

Rebekah Christie spoke softly, her face and demeanor making her seem even younger than she was. Interested in starting her own jewelry-making company on the side, she used any free time to do her art and try to get to shows where she could display her work. So many retail workers need extra income to survive because of their low pay and scattershot hours, but Rebekah thought she was lucky because she had a talent that would help her earn money in a way she enjoyed: "I worked at a clothing store. I started while I was living in a dorm room working in retail and another job and being a part-time student getting my degree. I was starting a business making jewelry. It was very hard to coordinate the shows because I was given a lot of mid-shifts. That's twelve to eight or one to nine, and it would affect the whole day. There was no time to do anything else in the day. The shifts went up every two weeks; we would get them just a few days in advance. But the worst would be the changing shifts because I couldn't work around the school schedule. They wouldn't try to make it work around your life. It was frustrating because they wouldn't take into account life."[61]

In the retail industry, where this practice has become increasingly prevalent with the rise of big-box stores, managers have implemented call-in shifts that allow them to adjust workers' hours to the number of customers they expect. That means for workers that they have to call in at the beginning of the day to find out if they have work or will go another day without pay. For the company, it means that it can pocket any savings and transfer the risk of a slow day to the staff.[62] Since few of these workers can count on a full week's wages, they need a second job to survive, but combining a second job with one with unpredictable hours is nearly impossible. So the call-in system gives employers another perverse advantage—it makes it hard for the staff to protest with their feet and find another job. With the Manhattan store where she works selling clothes giving her only part-time hours, Akaisa O'Kieffe has been looking for stable work with enough hours to pay her bills. The twenty-one-year-old single mother has only one set day of work per week, Wednesday, but otherwise never knows when she might work, and she gets her work schedule only on Fridays, giving her little time to make arrangements. Never knowing how many hours she will work makes it hard to plan her life and ensure she can meet her payments, not to mention finding someone to watch her child. "It's a real pain. . . . I honestly feel they're taking advantage of us," she told CNBC.com.

As much as she would like a more predictable job, the unpredictable hours she has now make it hard to make a change. She added, "The day you plan to look for a job is always the day they call you in to work, and so you can't do it. . . . It's ridiculous."[63]

With generally predictable opening and closing hours and fairly uniform staffing needs, if employers wanted to provide some stability they could certainly do so in most cases. Some do— Macy's and even Walmart are credited with taking some steps to give employees some control.[64] But even with the resulting harm to worker morale and productivity, not to mention greater turnover, the business culture is moving ever more in the direction of autocratic management and unpredictable schedules. European companies follow a more enlightened model, where stores inform workers well in advance of their hours, even up to a year ahead of time; that is, until they open stores in the United States. Here, these same companies quickly conform to the American practice and stop giving schedules to staff ahead of time.[65] American exceptionalism at work again.

RESTORING THE FLSA'S PROMISE: PROTECTING THE "UNPROTECTED, UNORGANIZED AND LOWEST PAID OF THE NATION'S WORKING POPULATION"

Working too much or too little or anytime the boss says does not describe the life anyone wants or merits. To make FLSA meaningful, we need to enforce a humane workday, giving workers more control over their hours and putting more money in their pockets. First, we need to add in the excluded workers and make sure they can collect overtime: farmworkers, home care workers, and nannies, among others. Without a doubt, they would work fewer hours, but with the added bonus of earning a bit more if they do work overtime. In addition, the salary test and the threshold salary level have to be updated. How long has it been since a true professional salaried worker earned only $455 per week? These so-called salaried workers should and must get overtime pay. To give workers more control over extra hours, we could set a maximum number of hours that they could be expected to work per week, absent a collective bargaining agreement or other contractual arrangement between the worker and the employer. They would have the right to refuse extra hours except for essential personnel and exceptional circumstances enforced by penalties under employment discrimination statutes.[66] While this concept seems novel, workers represented by a labor union do have this right. And we have the example of the states that have passed legislation giving nurses, a group of workers who regularly work excessive hours, the right to turn down overtime.[67] As far as possible, workers who are part-time should be part-time because they want to be. By requiring employers to offer additional hours to their part-time workers before adding more part-time staff, we would encourage the move to more full-time workers; some jurisdictions have adopted such rules.[68] Workers also should have the right to know their schedules in advance and expect that their employers try to respect their external obligations.[69] Employers should have to pay for a minimum number of hours if workers are sent home before working a full shift and should have to provide workers called in on short notice a pay bump, as is proposed in legislation by Representative George Miller (D-CA).[70] Part-time workers should have guaranteed hours and not be expected to work fifty hours one week only to be dropped to fifteen the next.[71] These simple measures would help the FLSA better live up to its lofty goals.

And perhaps we should consider allowing people to get time rather than cash for their extra work hours. In the past, business lobbyists have attempted to dismantle the protections of overtime pay by substituting time off for extra pay. Their cynical version, however, not only would have cut wages for workers but also would have given the boss total control over when the workers could use the time—which is exactly contrary to the point! Losing overtime pay for low-wage workers is bad enough; not being able to attend the parent-teacher conference, take the kids to the doctor, or celebrate a family event would completely undo any of the benefit of time off if it could not be used at times when the worker wants and needs some time away from the workplace.[72] In the context of rethinking how we regulate wages and hours and in light of a growing number of women with children in the workforce, we need to come up with a new framework. If a parent could earn paid time and a half in hours instead of dollars, that might provide just as much of a disincentive for employers to demand extra work and, if the father or mother could decide when to use the hours, the change in policy might provide some families with a lot more stability. And to discourage employers from laying people off and making the remaining workers put in more hours, we should restructure unemployment taxes by actually raising taxes on those companies who lay off some people and then up the work time for others.[73] But regardless of whether we tighten any definitions or add any new protections, we still need to beef up enforcement. It makes no sense to waste time fighting for statutory and regulatory reforms just to see the courthouse doors slammed in the faces of workers because corporate America still writes the rule book.

But we can do more than give workers the right to say no to extra hours; we should be thinking about how to ensure greater flexibility overall—flexibility that helps the worker mesh work and life outside—not schedule manipulation by employers to wring every cent of profits by cutting hours and changing workdays. With the increasing number of mothers working and the imperative that men share some of the parenting responsibilities, it is time we rethought the rigid schedules of the American workplace. Thirty years ago, research done by the Work in America Institute identified the increasing creakiness of the statute's framework: "Because the assumption underlying the FLSA is that workers are employed full time and have a stay-at-home spouse to fulfill caregiving obligations, the law did not deal with or encourage workplace flexibility."[74] And not only would more flexibility help workers, but it could help the economy. The Work in America Institute recommends flexible schedules as a way to "raise employee morale and boost productivity. And work sharing, which avoids layoffs by distributing reduced work time among all of a plant's employees, can serve as a cushion against cyclical recessions."[75]

Employers already have the ability to provide greater flexibility to workers, even within the forty-hour workweek, by allowing them to work longer hours but fewer days per week or alternate their schedules on different days. But this kind of scheduling is totally under the control of the employer, and few provide it. So for most employees, working from home, coming in early and leaving early or coming in late and leaving late, or working a four-day, ten-hour-per-day schedule will happen only if the boss decides it is okay. Without any requirement to offer flexible schedules, few employers do. If they do allow flexible schedules, like other benefits, they are available mostly at the upper end of the salary scale.[76] The irony of the well-off having the most flexible schedules has an unfortunate downside. Politicians and opinion leaders, who regularly make it to their kids' baseball games or performances, and certainly can always make their own doctors' appointments (and have nannies to take their kids to their appointments), have no idea how much other families have to juggle.

But there are some advances. Both San Francisco and Vermont have adopted legislation allowing workers to request flexibility without suffering job consequences. While it is not a huge step forward, elsewhere workers can get fired for even raising the question. Great Britain, Australia, and New Zealand have also provided this protection and require employers who refuse to allow the worker a more flexible schedule to explain why.[77] Under Prime Minister Tony Blair, the British government adopted a law that allows employees to request a flexible schedule if they have a child under six and have worked more than twenty-six straight weeks for the employer. Employees can request a range of schedule variations, including a shorter workweek with longer hours per day, flextime, work from home, a job split with someone else, alternative hours, and different shifts, accompanied by an explanation of how such a schedule could be implemented. Employers can deny requests because of cost or inconvenience, but overall the business community in Great Britain has found the law something it can work with. This didn't happen without a lot of effort to create the right climate for business to support the law. The Blair government pitched the change as a partnership with business and one that would spur productivity rather than harm profits. The leaders focused on the benefits to business, and even provided a funding stream for companies to hire consultants to make it easier for them to develop and promulgate policies. And, writer Karen Kornbluh notes, while employers can deny requests, they must provide a written denial, which may have helped keep denials lower than they might have been without the documentation. According to Kornbluh, part of this outcome is due to shame: "It's one thing to believe that business goals are more important than employee schedules; it's quite another to state for the record that you'd rather Jane didn't pick up her children from school because you prefer holding staff meetings at six in the evening. By throwing daylight on some of the unreasonable burdens that have been placed on employees without debate and without their agreement, the initiative creates a dialogue between employers and employees."[78]

Representative Carolyn Maloney (D-NY) and Senator Bob Casey (D-PA) have introduced the Working Families Flexibility Act, which would give American workers the right to request flexibility.[79] Better yet would be legislation that would allow workers, in addition to requesting schedule variations, to opt out of overtime unless the employer can show need.[80] Nonetheless, it is cause for hope that some lawmakers are taking the issue seriously. We need to support these efforts and challenge the rest of our elected officials and business leaders to do better.

One of the most important actions we could take would be to remove the financial incentive for employers to cut workers' hours or hire only part-time staff. By decoupling benefits from full-time status, we would take away the impetus for many companies to push their employees below forty (or even thirty) hours of work time. Worker advocates are pushing for federal legislation that would require health care coverage under Obamacare to cover part-time workers, or employers would have to pay a penalty, calculated by prorating the $2,000 fine they now pay for not covering their full-timers. The bill would also expand eligibility under the Family and Medical Leave Act by removing the requirement that only employees who work more than a minimum number of hours are covered and would allow part-time workers to take advantage of employer pension plans.[81] While the moment may not yet be upon us when this legislation will become law, its introduction shows that members of Congress are hearing from workers about fixes that need to be made to change the incentive structure for schedule manipulation. The FMLA took years to get passed, and only with the election of President Obama have we made progress on a national health insurance scheme—we can get this done, too, if we fight for it.

In addition, advocates are pushing for partial unemployment benefits that would provide a safety net for part-time workers not now covered by unemployment—which, like requiring a pro-rated health care benefit under Obamacare, would also remove some of the financial incentive for employers to avoid full-time workers. Instead of making benefits contingent on full-time status, we could simply prorate them based on hours worked. Employers would have less financial incentive to cut workers' hours to avoid any liability for unemployment insurance, health care, family leave, and other benefits.[82] As a model, the Dutch have developed a system of "flexicurity" that guarantees workers a certain level of health insurance, pensions, and other benefits and thereby serves as a deterrent to categorizing a job as contingent or to creating shorter-hour, benefit-free jobs.[83] Ireland is another country that has sought to deter the expansion of an involuntary part-time workforce, requiring that employers treat all workers equally with respect to benefits, making part-time work less precarious, and at the same time ensuring that it is the worker's choice and not something foisted upon her.[84] America should do as much.

We can't blame the FLSA for all of the ills of the twenty-first-century work schedule. But the practice, begun by that law, of using the number of hours worked by an employee, as well as the distinction between "salaried" and "hourly" employees, as the benchmark for whether one gets benefits has led to some serious unintended consequences. The financial inducements for employers are substantial—to circumvent minimum-wage and overtime requirements by classifying employees as salaried and avoid providing many benefits by hiring part-time rather than full-time workers. By building all of our protections for wages and hours, as well as health and safety, family leave, and retirement benefits on top of the employment structure, rather than as national, universal programs, we have created a whole variety of perverse incentives for employers to manipulate the schedules and status of their employees to get out from under coverage or to outsource employees altogether.

Picking through the various statutes, assorted exemptions, multiple loopholes, and regulatory omissions, it is clear that the best and only way to ensure low-wage women and those with little bargaining power an end to excessively long workdays, denial of overtime, chaotic scheduling, and lack of benefits is to provide universal programs, like Medicare, available to all. Only when all Americans are equally entitled will we see the day when employers are not constantly searching for the regulatory exit door.

4

THE WILD WEST:
THE LAWLESS WORLD OF THE
CONTINGENT WORKFORCE

I shop online, like a lot of people do. And, like most people, once I'm off the computer, having ordered a birthday present for my mother or a few books for my husband, I don't think again about the order, except to check that it arrives. I haven't ever thought much about how the flowers or the MP3 player or the running shoes actually got from here to there, about the fact that there are workers who sort, pack, and load the goods for shipment. Hired by temporary employment agencies filling contracts for warehouse companies, which in turn are working for online retailers like Amazon, Walmart, and Target, this is the contingent workforce of the cloud, a new virtual working class—and a sign of things to come. Writing for *The Nation*, Gabriel Thompson became one of these workers, hired through a temp agency to help with the pre-Thanksgiving rush. Adding and subtracting workers for peak periods holds great attraction for companies that can bring staff on and then spit them out once they aren't needed anymore. Bosses track day-to-day productivity, late arrivals, and days missed for sickness and quickly replace a "low-performing" employee with one of the many hungry people waiting to jump in.

Thompson describes the first day:

After waiting twenty minutes, we are ushered into a room upstairs. A woman from the agency hands each of us a time sheet. For the sign-in, she tells us to write 8:30. "I know you were told to be here at 8:15," she says, anticipating a protest that never comes, "but that was just to make sure you got here early." And, like that, fifteen minutes are lopped from our paycheck. It's a small but important lesson in what it means to be a "flexible" worker. We are not in control here. Shifts may last four hours, eight hours or twelve; start times will bounce around as well. I'm originally hired for a shift that begins at 7 am, but that later moves up an hour, to 8, and then, in a rush to move goods out the door, to four o'clock in the morning. In the online world of holiday shopping, where demand can surge and retreat with the click of (many) buttons, workers must respond in real time, shoving other commitments aside. For people without cars, the ever-changing schedule makes it hard to coordinate transportation. One middle-aged woman, caught off guard on a day we're dismissed at noon, will spend three hours walking the eight miles home. That she returns for the next shift—rubbing her feet and complaining under her breath—is a testament to her "flexibility," to how far she's learned to bend in the new economy.[1]

There are a lot of ways to avoid paying the minimum wage or overtime, to work staff beyond forty hours a week or shorten their schedules without warning, to escape liability for discrimination or violating health and safety laws. But perhaps the most ingenious approach taken by certain companies is saying that those who work for them aren't actually their workers, shrugging off any liability at all. By calling certain staff members "independent contractors" and hiring others through temporary agencies, the boss is suddenly free from many of the financial burdens but not the benefits of having employees.

In a law review article in the mid-1990s, Jonathan P. Hiatt, then general counsel of the Service Employees International Union (SEIU) and now the chief of staff to the president of the AFL-CIO, raised the specter of a workforce in transformation, with degraded or nonexistent legal protections, where employers opted out of legal obligations by reclassifying their employees as contractors, franchisees, or temps. He wrote, "The SEIU discovered one Seattle cleaning contractor who established himself as the lowest bidder on commercial office building cleaning contracts. That contractor 'sold' franchises for the right to clean floors of downtown office buildings for $4,000 to $7,000 a floor—mostly to Central American and Asian immigrants. As a franchisor, the contractor disclaimed responsibility for Social Security and unemployment compensation payments, minimum wages and overtime payments, and tax withholdings of any kind."[2] Just as MacDonald's or Taco Bell works through franchises (and for much the same reason), the cleaning company claimed that each floor was its own business and a separate legal entity. As crazy as it sounds, that contractor's behavior was not all that unusual, and since that time employers have become even more ingenious in reclassifying their workers as something other than employees to avoid legal liabilities and raise profits.

When the New Deal laws were drafted, few could have imagined the creativity of the American employer. At its inception, the FLSA, like later statutes, was written only to apply to "employees," because no one anticipated how that term would be manipulated. But the FLSA helped set in motion the legal contortions used by employers today by giving smaller companies the freedom to pay less than the minimum wage and avoid overtime pay.[3] Similarly, Title VII and the other antidiscrimination statutes, as well as the Family and Medical Leave Act and the Affordable Care Act, are limited to firms with more than a certain number of employees. The financial incentive is obvious. The combined impact of protecting only "employees" and applying the legal requirements only to larger firms drives companies to shed employees by designating workers as independent contractors, or by hiring temps. In addition, employers have devised creative structures, with holding companies, shell operations, and franchises, to continue to avoid any liability for minimum wages, overtime, or discrimination. These companies often have common ownership and common management, including officers and directors—and even pool their workforces and use interrelated operations—yet argue, often successfully, that they don't reach the $500,000 threshold or requisite number of employees because each entity is an independent employer.[4] Some go so far as to "go in and out of business" to escape legal requirements.[5]

What was originally defended as reasonable policy to limit the burdens on small companies has morphed into a major loophole in our workplace protection laws. Over the years, these novel approaches have grown routine and a contingent workforce has become the new normal. In 1993, secretary of labor Robert B. Reich and secretary of commerce Ronald H. Brown commissioned a study to examine the evolving workplace at the end of the twentieth century, reviewing labor-management cooperation in the workplace, collective bargaining, and safety and health issues, but taking particular note of the dangers of the fragmentation of legal protections for certain workers. According to the commission, "The growing number of 'contingent' and other nonstandard workers poses the problem of how to balance employers' needs for flexibility with workers' needs for adequate income protections, job security, and the application of public laws that these arrangements often preclude, including labor protection and labor-relations statutes." Chaired by John Dunlop, who had served as secretary of labor during the Ford administration, and comprised of union and business leaders as well as economists and other experts, the commission made several recommendations to shield workers against efforts to deny them legal protections, including suggestions to tighten the definition of "employee" to prevent misclassification of workers. Specifically, the report found that the legal definition of "employee" was out of date, contradictory, and obsolete: "There are two major problems with the definition of employee in current labor and employment law: (1) each statute makes the distinction in its own way, presenting employers with an unnecessarily complicated regulatory maze; (2) in substance, the law is based on a nineteenth century concept whose purposes are wholly unrelated to contemporary employment policy."[6]

But Congress took no action in response to the Dunlop Commission's report and the problem has only grown. The societal consequences are significant, allowing the circumvention of hard-fought labor protections and antidiscrimination laws. As soon as they were confronted with a broad set of rules requiring equal treatment for employees in terms of wages and benefits, employers had strong financial reasons to hire fewer "employees" but rather to fill positions with temps, contractors, or leased staff and wriggle out of the law's constraints. In addition, giving employers such latitude to use temps and independent contractors has segmented the workforce, even within a single employer, between those real employees, more often white and professional, who get benefits, and those non-employees, more likely to be female and minority, who get nothing. In his 1995 law review article, Hiatt perceptively described this weakness in our legal system as one that allows companies to "distance themselves from the exploitation of the low-wage workers while benefitting from their exploitation."[7]

THE RISE OF THE PERMANENT TEMP

Temporary workers are a growing cohort of the American workforce. In 2005, according to the Department of Labor's statistics, almost 4.5 million employees worked as temps. That's nearly 4 percent of the workforce.[8] And women and minorities are dominant in this sector, with women filling two-thirds of temp jobs, while minorities are the majority in building services, a major employer of temps.[9] And the number only grows.

The law's perverse incentive for companies to stay small to avoid minimum-wage and overtime liability—not to mention the application of civil rights laws and other worker protection statutes—is just as powerful for the temp agency, which is also typically a small firm. It is a mutually beneficial arrangement— the agency makes money by leasing workers, and both employers are free from almost all legal obligations. Through sustained and effective lobbying, the temp industry has developed and exploited the loopholes that have allowed it to thrive. In the 1960s, the industry pressed hard to break down the definition of employee, waging what one legal scholar described as "intense lobbying campaigns in the state legislatures to persuade them to enact statutes proclaiming temporary agencies were the employers of record for purposes of state labor law obligations."[10] Not only was this good for business—the agencies could assure potential clients that hiring temps would free them from employer obligations, which made the arrangements more attractive to the customers—but it also succeeded in undoing labor protections for many workers.

Temporary workers can come to the firm in a variety of ways.

Some come to an employer from an agency that specializes in providing workers for a short period of time, to fill in for an employee on vacation or to meet high demand. Other workers may work for a leasing company that may provide a larger group of employees, typically an entire department, to another company. For example, some companies will hire their human resources or accounting department through a leasing firm.[11] And some other temporary workers work on an as-needed basis and are essentially on call when the firm needs them. Some temporary arrangements are benign—filling in for an employee on leave, for example, or as a job for people who want to work only occasionally. But in many cases, the so-called temps serve for a long time in one workplace and do work that is the same as or very similar to the work the employees on staff do. In other cases, companies bring on additional people during a peak period and just as quickly let them go, without any strings, liabilities, or continued relationship. Corporate America can do the math: temps cannot join a union, cannot demand the minimum wage or overtime, and have no rights to complain about discrimination, let alone get vacation pay or sick leave.

As an example, some of the foreign companies that have set up factories in the American South have not only escaped a unionized workforce but have gone so far as to hire a large portion of their workforce through temp agencies. Not satisfied to use a temp agency solely to cover for an employee on vacation or at a time of an upsurge in demand, some of these companies actually have a much larger portion of their workforce who come from an agency than they hire directly—hardly temps, often they work for many years and still are not considered "employees." At Nissan's auto plant in Smyrna, Tennessee, according to a former supervisor, well over two-thirds of the workers come from agencies and earn only about 50 percent of what Nissan's own

employees earn.[12] And of course, their benefits are also much
less than what the permanent workforce receives, making them
even cheaper for the company. More and more companies are
using this strategy in a variety of sectors. In the South, reports
the *Washington Post*, Nissan is just one of many—"companies
such as Amazon, Asurion and Dell [that] have outsourced their
warehouses and call centers to hundreds of staffing agencies that
have cropped up in the region." But the South isn't an outlier
region—companies across the country have hired more and
more temps or renamed their current workers as such. Overall,
the use of temps has grown rapidly across the workforce not just
in the service sector but in blue-collar jobs as well. In 2008,
the Bureau of Labor Statistics calculated that firms had hired
654,030 temporary workers in manufacturing out of a workforce
of 13.5 million.[13]

Not only do temps cost less in wages and benefits, but employers also save money by not investing in the workers' training or vocational education. Moreover, temps are often scared
to report unsafe conditions because they can so easily lose their
jobs for doing so—making the workplace less safe for all workers.
Guadalupe Palma, an organizer for Warehouse Workers United,
says that "because of the temp nature of the work, it's very easy
for a worker who speaks out to be retaliated against. . . . They
might not be called back to work the following day, or have their
hours decreased."[14] Instead, they keep working—with terrible
consequences. In Taunton, Massachusetts, a company that made
hummus hired temps to operate machines in its plant even after
being told by a consultant that the facility was unsafe. Facing a
measly $9,500 fine from the U.S. Department of Labor's Occupa-
tional Safety and Health Administration, the company ignored
the warnings and hired untrained temps to run the machinery.
Unfortunately, one of the temps was killed, something that could

easily have been avoided if the company had addressed the safety issues.[15] Even though the firm controls the employee's work, the temp agency is still the employer of record.[16] Same worker, same responsibilities, but very different protections for wages, hours, and benefits, not to mention health and safety.

The temp agency helps employers play a shell game that makes workers' rights disappear, sometimes by stepping in when a company wants to deny its employment relationship with a group of workers to avoid legal liabilities. At a Toyota facility in Los Angeles, for example, a group of janitors was hired by and got wages from a company called Advance Building Maintenance, a contractor for Toyota. But when the janitors started to push for better wages and benefits and to join a union, all of a sudden they had a new employer and their paychecks came from Stafcor, a Texas-based employee-leasing company. Advance Building Maintenance disclaimed any relationship with the workers apart from brokering the contract, and Toyota pretended not even to know of the existence of Stafcor. Unclear about which company employed them, the janitors had no focus for their workplace demands and no idea of their rights. And Toyota, which directed the operations of the plant where they worked, continued to insist they were not its employees.[17]

Being a temporary worker has consequences beyond lost wages, benefits, and protections from discrimination. Not only does the employer not treat these workers as "employees," but neither does the state government—a temp worker can be fired or laid off by a firm, but unlike her terminated colleagues she probably cannot collect unemployment insurance. State laws often set requirements that are difficult or impossible for this type of employee to meet, including having worked a specific length of time and earned wages above a defined minimum level from a covered employer—typically needing two quarters of work and

wages of $1,734 to get a monthly benefit. This is obviously par-
ticularly difficult for temp workers. Moreover, both the temp firm
and the company where the temp is working often contest that
they are the "employer" of the worker seeking the benefit because
the employer has to pay the tax that covers unemployment.[18]

Some legislators are taking note, proposing that the charade of
calling employees "temps" shouldn't allow companies to shrug off
legal responsibility. One proposal would consider employers who
bring on workers from temp agencies "joint employers" with the
temp agency, making them liable for both violations of health
and safety and other workplace laws. Illinois and Massachusetts
have adopted legislation, and it's on the move in California.[19]
Recently, the general counsel for the National Labor Relations
Board issued a decision finding McDonald's liable as a joint employer for the wage and overtime violations of its franchisees;
this action is considered "outrageous" by the businesses that have
long been able to exploit this legal fiction, but hopefully it signals
that we may see some progress soon.[20]

THIS ROSE HAS THORNS

As William Shakespeare said, "What's in a name? That which
we call a rose by any other name would smell as sweet."[21]
Unfortunately, what is true for the rose is not true for the law. A
woman may work regularly doing the same work every day for the
same company, but somehow, she's not an employee. Meet the
independent contractor.

Not too long ago, I started chatting with the woman doing
my makeup before an appearance on a liberal cable show and
discovered how blind I have been to the circumstances of people
who provide many services in our service-dominated economy;
we regularly talk to people who clean houses, cut our hair or do

our nails, or provide some other service, but we don't often think about the laws that do or don't govern their work. As we talked, I asked her about whether she also worked for other shows. "Other shows?" She laughed. "Try other networks. None of the networks allows makeup artists to work more than twenty hours per week." A bell went off in my head as I remembered that in my other chats with makeup artists they had all mentioned working for various networks as well as politicians and talking heads. I am not a frequent guest on TV shows but have always enjoyed talking to the women (always women!) who do my makeup before going on the air. The networks, like so many employers, want to make sure that none of these women can claim that they are employees. As independent contractors, they cannot invoke any labor law protections and receive no benefits. This could be true for your hairstylist, manicurist, and maybe the janitor in your office building. Right under our noses, every day, these women toil without any of the basic job safety or security protections we take for granted. Independent contracting is the Wild West of the workplace. No law applies. None.[22]

According to the Bureau of Labor Statistics, in 2005, more than 8 percent of the workforce, or more than 10 million workers, were counted as independent contractors. This part of the labor force has shown amazing growth—indeed, it is the fastest-growing part of the job market, having increased 577 percent between 1982 and 1998.[23] While not all independent contractors are low-wage workers (some of them are consultants by choice, who receive decent compensation, like certified financial planners), many of them are. At least 3 million people, or a third of the more than 10 million considered independent contractors, are employed in low-wage jobs. Some industries are infamous for trying to characterize their regular workforce as independent contractors, particularly the janitorial, home care, and secretarial services, which are dominated by women and immigrant workers, thereby eliminating the workers' right to a union, a minimum wage, or overtime and wiping out any responsibility for unemployment and workers' compensation, or safety and health violations.[24] In 2000, the Department of Labor commissioned a study that estimated that nearly a third of all employers misclassified some employees; a study in 2005 found that more than 10 percent of workers in the private sector had been wrongly designated as contractors.[25]

Once again, the tech community is at the forefront of change, and certainly in this case the change is not positive. Take the advent of "crowdworking." Pioneered by Amazon in 2005, it is a market for labor where the buyer is in the driver's seat. Perhaps a half a million people, more than two-thirds of them women, bid to do very small tasks for companies of all sizes, generating huge profits for very small returns. Estimates are that the average wage is $2 per hour—that's even less than tipped employees make. Most of the work involves transcription, tagging, and other Internet-related tasks the online user never realizes have been done to make the sites work. Even more than other types of independent contracting, crowdwork is totally unregulated, with large numbers of people competing for tedious assignments, at extremely low and nonnegotiable prices, creating easy opportunities for companies to use the work and not even pay for it. One proud executive boasted, "Before the Internet, it would be really difficult to find someone, sit them down for ten minutes and get them to work for you, and then fire them after those ten minutes. But with technology, you can actually find them, pay them the tiny amount of money, and then get rid of them when you don't need them anymore."[26] The miracle of technology—making the workforce disappear with the click of a mouse.

Not only do these workers get excluded from all labor laws,

critics point out that the companies may even be using child labor. One crowdworker expressed amazement when Amazon disclaimed all legal responsibility for the work it helps barter, declaring, "That's like saying someone is running a slave market on my property, and they're paying me, but I have no responsibility." But many of the people, primarily women, who do this work are desperate, and the low wages and lack of protections are no disincentive, because they have nothing else. Nonetheless, a group of workers willing to risk their standing as crowdworkers is suing, arguing they are not contractors but actually employees and should have been paid the minimum wage, well above the $1 to $2 per hour many of them earned, some of that amount paid in online game credits or virtual money.[27] The case is ongoing, but the questions it raises about how companies classify "employees" are long overdue for consideration.

In SEIU's struggle to organize a group of home care workers, the union's general counsel, Jonathan Hiatt, described how even government officials were not above playing bait and switch with workers' employment status:

> 50,000 California Homecare workers in Los Angeles County sought to unionize with SEIU. . . . Initially, they assumed their employer was the State, which gave them their paychecks each week. The State said, "not us, perhaps the County." So the homecare workers looked to the County which assigned them to clients and set their hours. The County said, "not us, perhaps the clients themselves." Three years of litigation later, with no entity willing to admit to being their employer, these minimum-wage Los Angeles homecare workers were told by the court that they were all "independent contractors" having no one to bargain with.[28]

But SEIU was not content to leave the situation as it was, embarking on a political effort to change the legal status of these workers. Fearing the impact of the court's decision because it is illegal under federal antitrust law for independent contractors to form a union—so-called contractors joining together in an organization is deemed "anti-competitive behavior"—SEIU decided it needed to try to get these workers considered employees. In coalition with a variety of groups (including senior citizen groups, consumer advocacy groups, and disability activists), the union pressured the state to pass legislation in 1992 that made the counties the employer for purposes of negotiating wages and benefits. In 1999, 74,000 home care workers in Los Angeles County voted to have SEIU represent them. This election made history as adding the largest group of workers to a union's membership since World War II.[29]

Since that time, unions have moved successfully to organize home care workers in other states. Using the same model pioneered in California, where the state or county served as the employer for purposes of collective bargaining, these efforts have led to higher wages and better benefits for workers and a higher quality of care for patients. Unfortunately, because the right cannot tolerate low-wage women getting better treatment, the National Right to Work Committee successfully challenged this arrangement in *Harris v. Quinn*, with the conservatives on the Supreme Court agreeing that these home care workers are not in fact real public employees, but only "partial" or "quasi-employees." Not being true employees, but rather some type of contractor, they could not be required to pay the fair-share fees to the union that pay for collective bargaining services.[30] It is no surprise that when workers can get the benefits of the wages bargained by the union but don't have to chip in for the fees, they may choose to become free riders. Nonetheless, many of these women now understand that joining a union gives them higher wages and stronger voices and will decide to pay the small fee that helps sustain the union. Indeed, immediately after the decision in *Harris v. Quinn*, SEIU moved forward to schedule an election to represent home care workers in Minnesota, in what would be the largest union election ever in that state.[31] Even if these home care workers get some representation, they will be "employees" only for the purposes of wages, but not for antidiscrimination law or other protective statutes.

The move to hire independent contractors to avoid paying for benefits is not unique to construction or house-cleaning jobs. In fact, universities have been turning more and more to so-called adjuncts to teach courses, the equivalent of hiring independent contractors. In the 1990s, approximately one-third of academic jobs were tenure-track. Now that has declined to only 25 percent. And, as with other employers, universities do everything they can to keep these adjunct workers from being able to call themselves "employees" and thus be entitled to benefits. A recent study shows that a large portion of universities and colleges closely track their adjuncts' teaching hours to avoid providing health insurance.[32] And take, for example, the story of Allstate insurance agents, as reported by the *New York Times*:

> When his children were young, Nathan Littlejohn was a regional salesman in search of a position that would allow him to spend more time with his family. So when he heard about Allstate's neighborhood agent program in 1990, he was intrigued. Over the next several years, he said, he worked round the clock to build his customer base and poured about $40,000 of his own money into his agency, located in Overland Park, Kan. He figured it was a long-term investment. Using similar logic, Craig Crease was able

to justify investing $120,000 in his Kansas City Allstate agency over the course of 14 years. The same went for Ron Harper in Thomson, Ga., who spent about $80,000.

But after building up their agencies for nearly a decade or more, the agents said they were called into meetings in late 1999 by Allstate managers. The agents could keep on selling Allstate policies, they were told, but they would no longer be entitled to health insurance, a retirement account or profit-sharing, and their pension benefits would no longer accrue. Instead, they would become independent contractors.[33]

Some 6,200 agents, 90 percent over age forty, were told they were no longer on the Allstate books as employees and were forced to sign waivers giving up their right to sue.[34]

While hiring an independent contractor is not illegal per se, many employers come close to or go over the line, stretching the facts to make an employee not an employee. Certain industries—construction, day labor, home health care, child care, and agriculture, among others—have a particularly bad record of increasing profits by improperly calling workers independent contractors.[35] Sometimes, as was the case for the Allstate agents, even as they are being stripped of their status as regular employees and made contractors, workers are forced to sign a document waiving any right to sue.[36] So even if they continue to do the same job they did as full-time employees, suddenly they have far fewer job protections and no benefits, and the courthouse door is closed to them. The insurance agents had the wherewithal to bring a lawsuit, but many are pushed into being contractors without the requisite means to fight it—and even the Allstate agents have endured thirteen years of litigation trying to convince a court that their age discrimination suit should go forward despite their signing away their right to sue. Mr. Littlejohn is now bankrupt.

Companies' efforts to avoid legal obligations for their workforce are not new. Even during World War II, when women were a critical part of the war effort and were guaranteed equal wages for equal work, employers would keep women's wages lower by using what historian Philip Foner describes as "such ruses as paying women hourly rates on jobs for which men received higher piece-work rates or giving different titles to similar jobs and thus changing job classifications from skilled to unskilled."[37] Changing job titles within a company now seems like a baby step on the road to creating a whole workforce that works *at* the company but doesn't work *for* the company.

Despite their efforts, however, these companies haven't been entirely successful. Courts have helped to create some limits on these contortions by scrutinizing such arrangements to make sure that the worker is properly categorized and that the employer is not manipulating job titles to avoid liability.[38] But while the courts have put some brakes on these efforts, how easy is it really for a worker, who has been told she's not an employee but an independent contractor, to know her rights? The courts use a *twelve-point test*—that's a fact. And even then, "no one factor is controlling, nor is the list exhaustive. . . . The weight of each factor depends on the light it sheds on the putative employee's dependence on the alleged employer, which in turn depends on the facts of the case," stated a federal district court in a case where a pregnant employee challenged her designation as a contractor.[39] What nonsense for a janitor or health aide to have to satisfy a judge that she's really a worker, particularly when every one of the twelve points of the test is so subjective. Chief Justice Roberts may have famously claimed that judges, like umpires, only "call balls and strikes," but this legal regime seems more like chutes and ladders than a baseball game.

Recent efforts by the Department of Labor to attack misclassification have been met with full-throated opposition by the business community. But there's money to be made for the United States from lost taxes and payments to Social Security, so the IRS and the DOL are working together to do a better job, combining forces to go after the truly bad actors. Similarly, Senator Bob Casey (D-PA) is pushing a bill, entitled the Payroll Fraud Prevention Act, that would increase enforcement efforts. And some states are moving forward to bring legal action against companies that have stretched the limits of the definition of "independent contractor."[40]

At the end of the day, however, what we really need is a statutory regime that doesn't slice and dice employment protections based on a twelve-part test. Remedying the problem of the non-employee employee will require a comprehensive approach. Like squeezing a balloon, if we fix only one issue, such as the loophole for temps or independent contractors, part-time workers or employees of small, exempt establishments, the problems will just bulge out somewhere else.

There was a period of time, in the mid-1990s, when experts recognized that it was troubling to have a growing contingent workforce. The Department of Labor established the Dunlop Commission, which transmitted its analysis and recommendations to the agency after a fact-finding process. Finding the laws defining "employee" hopelessly out of date and easy to abuse, the board suggested to the Department of Labor that it should push for a streamlined definition that would work across statutes and be harder to evade.[41] Around the same time, several members of Congress, including Senator Howard Metzenbaum and Representative Patricia Schroeder, introduced related legislation.[42]

The Senate bill took a broad approach, addressing temporary staffing, part-time work, and the use of independent contractors, as well as the growing reliance on contract and leased employees. Although the House bill was narrower, focusing on temps and part-time work exclusively, Schroeder worked hard to advance the issue. Unfortunately, she was not successful; nor was Senator Metzenbaum, and we are left with a cancer that has metastasized.

While their efforts were not successful, they did provide some solutions that remain relevant today. The most basic recommendation of the Dunlop Commission was to look at the realities of the workplace in determining who is an employee and who is an employer.[43] The commission's suggestions were extremely modest, and it declined to endorse suggestions expanding "the coverage of various statutes to seasonal workers; affording farm workers the protections of the National Labor Relations Act; mandating equal pay for equal work as well as equal benefits on a pro-rata basis for part-time employees; giving employees of contractors a right of first refusal when they are displaced because their employer loses a contract for ongoing services; and putting a time limit on temporary positions, so that they would convert to regular employee positions with the client firm after a specified time period"[44]—all of which are policies we should adopt. While disappointing in its timidity, the Dunlop Commission gave us a starting place with its recommendations, which after twenty years are more germane than ever. For all employees, we need to go back to the basic concept of what an employee does. Titles can be manipulated—it is duties that matter. But we should push for the other changes the commission declined to champion. All types of workers, seasonal and domestic included, should have legal rights. The business where the temp actually spends his or her day working should be considered a joint employer with the temporary agency so that they cannot conspire to keep their size under the law's limit. And temporary workers should indeed be temporary—there should be an upper limit on the amount of time that can go by before an employee becomes an "employee."

Because, after all, "rose is a rose is a rose is a rose."[45]

5

BYE-BYE, BABY:
GIVING BIRTH AND BACK TO WORK

Americans dote on babies. Commercials feature talking infants, toddlers doing flips and pirouettes, precious pink princesses and rough-and-tumble junior cowboys. Cute sells products. Unfortunately, it doesn't seem to inspire good public policy—which makes the lives of low-income women even more stressful and precarious. With only two weeks' leave from one of her two jobs and eight weeks' mostly unpaid from the other, Christina S. fell into money troubles right away after having her baby. Working as a psychologist, she had tried to save up money in advance by taking on extra hours, but when she went on leave and lost her income, she could not help going into debt on her credit card, struggling with rent payments, and eventually going to a food bank for groceries. Another woman, Juliana E., got some pay during her leave of two months, but loss of a full paycheck put her in a bind on basic expenses. Bringing up a new baby alone, she found her expenses beyond her means on the reduced income. Even after going to family and friends to borrow money, she still could not keep up with payments due on her car and ended up needing food stamps and welfare for several months.[1]

One of the easiest ways to fall from the middle class into poverty, or from poverty into destitution, is to have children.[2]

Families climb down the economic ladder for many reasons, but in almost 9 percent of cases where they go under the poverty line, the precipitating factor was the birth of a child. The impact is immediate—almost 13 percent of these families descend into poverty within a month of the child being born, and nearly 25 percent of these families succumb to poverty in thirty days when they are dependent on the earnings of a single mother. Many of them end up needing public assistance, and some are forced into bankruptcy. According to a report by Human Rights Watch, "One study of over 1,700 bankruptcy cases found 7 percent of the debtors identified the birth of a baby as a reason for filing for bankruptcy."[3] This is stress at its worst, worrying that a new baby will actually tip the family over the cliff into destitution.

UNPAID FAMILY LEAVE: THE GREAT PROTECTION FEW CAN AFFORD

Decades after adopting critical safeguards for workers, such as the Fair Labor Standards Act and Title VII, Congress finally got around to addressing the needs of a modern workforce in balancing home and work. With more and more women working and more mothers not at home to take care of children, something had to be done to ensure that women were not penalized for taking time off to have a child. So in 1993, the United States finally adopted legislation providing unpaid leave for new parents. The Family and Medical Leave Act (FMLA) was a big step forward, providing some workers with the right to take twelve weeks of leave for the birth or adoption of a child or other family health care needs. But even more so than other statutes, the FMLA's benefits were limited to a small number of employees. First, the employer needs to provide the leave only if it has at least fifty employees, and, second, the employee must have worked at least 1,250 hours in the previous year. Because of these two limitations, more than 40 percent of private sector workers fail to qualify for FMLA leave. Many ineligible workers work for smaller employers, but others, especially young parents, do not qualify because they have not worked long enough for one employer.[4] As few as 20 percent of new mothers qualify for the benefit.[5] Of young African American workers who are between eighteen and twenty-five with a child under two at home, only 48 percent have enough hours to qualify.[6] Overall, the workers with least access to FMLA leave are those most in need—younger, low-wage women of color.[7]

And since the FMLA provides only unpaid leave, even those mothers who qualify often opt out because they can't afford to lose wages.[8] According to a survey by the Department of Labor in 2012, 46 percent of workers who needed leave were not able to take it because they could not sustain the loss of wages.[9] A trio of labor economists, after reviewing the data since the adoption of the FMLA, concluded that unpaid leave has had a limited impact in helping workers: "Losing a day's pay is a real hardship for many families. If a low-wage worker making $10 an hour has a family of two children and misses more than three days of work without paid leave, the family would fall below the poverty line due to lost wages. Moreover, workers with less education—who are also more likely to be in low-paying jobs—suffer disproportionately when they are forced to choose between lost wages or their caregiving responsibilities."[10]

Those weaknesses explain why what may have been a step forward for some did not register as an achievement at all for most of the workforce. The legislation did nothing to answer the following questions: What happens when a low-income woman goes into labor? Will she be able to keep her job when she leaves work to have the baby? Can she stay home for a period of time and can the father also spend time with his child? Will they get paid when they are at home or will they have to use savings to finance the critical bonding period? And then, when the parents return to work, how do they care for their child? What happens when the baby gets sick? For most families, these questions are not merely rhetorical, but remain truly existential.

Paid family leave seems an obvious answer—and one that has been apparent to most other countries in the world. Yet economists who have run the numbers show that it is exactly that segment of the American workforce that would most benefit from paid leave that has the least ability to get it, and vice versa, with well-paid workers being much more likely to have paid leave benefits.[11] And that's not all—the highest-paid workers also have paid vacation and sick leave, so they have a much greater ability to combine different leaves for a longer paid time off. Making their lives even easier relative to lower-earning employees, they are more likely to be entitled to flexibility in their workday to deal with unexpected emergencies, from child care problems to a sick child—and they don't lose wages as a result of time away.[12]

According to the Bureau of Labor Statistics, only 11 percent of the workforce has paid leave—that means the other 89 percent are left to their own financial resources (if, indeed, they have the right to take leave at all). According to one survey, almost three-quarters of workers with an income below $20,000 per year did not have paid leave, as opposed to only one-quarter of employees whose income fell between $50,000 and $75,000.[13] The double irony is that men, because they occupy more of the higher-paid jobs, are more likely to be eligible for both paid and unpaid leave,[14] but because of the social stigma still attached to being a stay-at-home dad, few of these men take the leave.

Families depend more and more on women's income, meaning that unpaid leave is the same as no leave for too many. Low-income women workers often put their own health or that of their children at risk by returning to work before fully recovering from childbirth; this is compounded by lack of workplace flexibility to breastfeed.[15] Human Rights Watch exhaustively documented "consistent accounts of the harmful consequences of inadequate paid family and sick leave after childbirth or adoption, employer reticence to offer breastfeeding support for flexible schedules, and career fallout from becoming parents. Parents with short and unpaid leaves described delaying immunizations and health care visits for babies; physical and mental health problems for parents; short periods or early cessation of breastfeeding and dismal conditions for pumping; financial hardship; debt; demotion; and denials of raises or promotions." Babies are less likely to be vaccinated or see a doctor, and mothers are stymied in breastfeeding. Moreover, in addition to a higher mortality rate for the children and higher rate of depression for mothers who go back to work after a short leave, lack of paid leave can throw families into poverty, especially those headed by a single mother.[16] A worker named Samantha B. told the researchers how she went back to work only eight weeks after giving birth despite having a very painful infection from her cesarean section. Other women described early returns to work after harrowing pregnancies, including complications from hemorrhaging, postpartum depression, and an inability to get needed care for either the mother or the child. For the children, when a mother has to return to work quickly after having a baby, the health consequences can be significant.

Unfortunately, these sad stories are not merely anecdotal but representative of the very substantial limitations of the FMLA. Just like they've done with Obamacare and the FLSA, employers can game the statute by moving more workers into part-time work, thus ensuring that they do not have the requisite number of hours per year to be covered, or designating them as independent contractors, both of which serve to keep the firm as a whole under the requisite number of full-time employees and thereby totally exempt.[17] With far fewer women able to take advantage of unpaid leave, the FMLA has disappointed the expectations of its early proponents. And, by contrast with many other developed countries, in the United States very few men have availed themselves of the leave provided by the FMLA.[18]

FMLA supporters also hoped it would spur more employers to offer paid leave. That, too, was a false hope. FMLA has not changed the share of workers with paid leave at all.[19] By contrast, when the federal government has provided a tax incentive for employers to provide health coverage or retirement accounts, private sector employers have offered such benefits. In 2009, 74 percent of civilian employers provided some health care benefits and 71 percent offered a retirement plan.[20] Paid family leave, on the other hand, is available to very few employees. And part-time employees are totally out of luck.

As a result, families often face something of a Hobson's choice, deciding between critical wages and the health and well-being of mother and child. If a woman who is not covered by the FMLA stays away from the office either by choice or by necessity after giving birth, she may not have a job to come back to. With family leave still far from the norm, even women in workplaces covered by the FMLA have felt that their request for leave has led to negative consequences. Researchers talked to women around the country and found countless examples of retaliation against employees who want to have time off.

> Many women said that merely revealing they were pregnant
> and requesting leave triggered tensions with employers,

and sometimes demotions or pay cuts. Kimberley N.'s employer was hostile to her maternity leave request, and gave her a terrible performance review after returning to work, utterly different from the glowing reviews of prior years. Abigail Y.'s employer said it was imperative that no one get the impression she was taking maternity leave, and insisted that she teach all her college class hours before giving birth. Many women, including Kimberley and Abigail, consequently quit their jobs and wound up in far less senior, lucrative, or rewarding positions. US law does protect against discrimination on the basis of sex, including pregnancy, but proving such discrimination is not easy, and women said they feared that pursuing discrimination claims would endanger their jobs or careers.[21]

It is true that federal antidiscrimination law technically covers women during and after pregnancy, but, as described in chapter 2, its protections are limited. Even for women who work for employers with the requisite number of employees to be covered by Title VII (fifteen, as opposed to fifty for FMLA), the activities associated with impending parenthood and childbirth, let alone the responsibilities of parenting after a child is born, are not covered at all. First of all, the Pregnancy Discrimination Act says nothing at all about leave for childbirth and provides no guarantee of job protection if an employer fires or demotes a new parent because the demands of caretaking are affecting the worker's performance or hours at work. Only if an employer provides disability leave for its employees does the Pregnancy Discrimination Act kick in.[22] The irony is that, while the law protects women from discrimination on the job because of a pregnancy, it does not protect them from discrimination based on needing to take time off to give birth or care for a child. Without these protections, expectant mothers can be shown the door just when they most need an income.

Some workers cobble together leave for childbirth from sick leave and vacation days, but only some Americans have either of those benefits. Excluding those serving in the military, more than one-third of the workforce—and three-quarters of low-income workers—lacks paid sick leave, and 25 percent do not have vacation pay. For some workers, temporary disability insurance, which covers pregnancy- and childbirth-related disability, may help defray the costs, but fewer than 40 percent of nonmilitary workers are covered by such policies. And women who work part-time have even less access to temporary disability insurance, paid sick leave, or vacation time.[23]

Paid leave makes sense. It helps keep families out of poverty. It enables women to take the time to recover from childbirth instead of rushing back to work because of financial stress. It allows parents to bond with a new child and respond to any medical issues the newborn may have. It reduces the stress of caring for an older relative by giving time to spend on their needs as well. It keeps sick people out of the office. But importantly, it also helps advance the goal of making women truly equal in society by reducing the wage penalty of having a baby. Making sure that all women, and not just a few, have paid leave will help address the economic inequality that is growing ever larger in America.

While these worries are particularly severe for low-income parents, all parents suffer from the incompatibility of the current structure of work and our obligations to our families. In 2004, pollsters Anna Greenberg and Bill McInturff surveyed likely voters, finding that 75 percent believed bringing in adequate income and finding time for children are very hard for parents, and 84 percent did not think that parents' long workdays were good for children.[24] The numbers only get stronger. A 2013 survey found that 80 percent of women and 70 percent of men supported paid family leave, with both Republicans and Democrats strongly in favor of such a program.[25]

For now, the state level is where the action is. Currently, we have a hodgepodge of policies, but for the most part, the few states that have paid family leave have used temporary disability insurance, or TDI, to pay for at least a few weeks of leave.[26] California, New Jersey, and Rhode Island use TDI, financed by payroll deductions, but because the leave is structured as a disability policy, it is not, by definition, available to men or adoptive mothers. In California, which passed its law in 2002, the efforts brought together a broad coalition of advocates—labor, civil rights groups, and women's organizations, among others—that created a model for winning paid leave. Before the FMLA was adopted nationally, in 1991, California passed legislation to require unpaid leave. The earlier campaign forged the bonds that allowed advocates to push for more. In 1999, then state senator (and future member of Congress and secretary of labor) Hilda Solis pushed a bill through the state legislature to study the impact of adding "family needs"—that is, more extended care for a newborn as opposed simply to labor and giving birth—as a disability under TDI. When the numbers came back and showed that the cost was minimal, they were able to move forward with getting the program passed. The factors that made it happen were a strong and diverse coalition, a committed legislator, and a governor who would sign the bill.[27] New Jersey followed California in 2008, and Rhode Island in 2013.

In addition to expanding TDI to provide a few weeks of paid leave after giving birth, Rhode Island and California also adopted a paid family leave law to allow men and adoptive parents to qualify. Rhode Island's new program provides job protections for workers while on leave and is funded by workers themselves, who pay 1.2 percent of the first $61,400 they earn into the state's temporary disability fund. The new law provides up to four weeks of paid leave for a new child or sick family member in addition to leave a worker might take for his or her own disability. The fund will cover up to 60 percent of the worker's salary, capped at approximately $750 per week. In addition, Rhode Island prohibits retaliation by employers against workers who take the paid leave.[28] Peculiarly, California does not, meaning the state law ensures leave but employers can terminate someone for using it. It seems nonsensical that the law ensures that a parent can receive some financial assistance while taking time off for a newborn but does not protect that parent from being fired and having no job to go back to.[29] As a result, a significant portion of mothers who use TDI in California forgo the additional family leave—as do the fathers.

In all of the states, another reason parents may not use the family leave is that they simply don't know that it is available because states haven't done much to market it. In California, a study found that "in 2003, 22 percent of respondents were aware of the program. By 2007, awareness increased only slightly: 28 percent of respondents knew about the paid leave program. Those most in need of paid family leave benefits are also the least likely to be aware of the program: low-income, minority, and young respondents were among the groups least likely to know about paid family leave. Overall, there was greater awareness of FMLA and the state's TDI program than paid family leave."[30]

But what these states have done right is make sure a greater share of the workforce is covered by applying the law to employers of all sizes. To avoid penalizing workers who have paid into the system, these states have created universal programs, available to all employees who have worked some set period of time, that do not exclude small employers and that do not penalize workers for changing jobs. It is a portable benefit paid for by the workers themselves.[31] Legislators in Connecticut, Vermont, and North Carolina are studying how to adopt a state family leave program, and those in New York and Massachusetts have begun to move legislation.[32] In Washington State, a paid parental leave program was passed in 2007 but is not yet in effect, as of this writing.[33] Hopefully with lessons learned from the initial efforts, other states will fine-tune their legislation to cover all workers, men included, and to prohibit retaliation.

For poorer families, paid leave helps significantly in avoiding the plunge into dire poverty associated with childbearing. According to the National Center for Children in Poverty, in California, the onset of paid leave gave low-income workers greater "economic security, especially for workers in 'low quality' jobs, or those that pay $20 or less per hour and/or do not provide employer-paid health insurance. Nearly 84 percent of workers employed in low-quality jobs who took advantage of the state's paid family leave law received at least half of their usual pay during leave, compared to only 31 percent of those who took family leave but did not avail themselves of the new law—often because they were unaware of its existence." And paid leave keeps mothers in the labor force, which is critical in the long term for them and their families. New Jersey shows similar results. The National Center for Children in Poverty found that under New Jersey's paid family leave program, "women who report taking paid leave are more likely to be employed nine to 12 months after a child's birth compared to those taking no leave at all. Women who report leaves of 30 days or longer are also much more likely to report wage increases in the year following the birth compared to those taking no leave. The study suggests that paid leave strengthens mothers' labor force commitment by giving them an option other than quitting when they need to care for a new baby."[34]

Paid leave is also good for business. Originally, advocates in the states faced a firestorm of opposition from employers who had argued that it would make the states uncompetitive and hurt the economy. But many of them have come to appreciate the positive effects of paid leave on the bottom line, and now polls of affected businesses show strong support for state family leave programs.[35] Indeed, companies agree that the effects have been minimal on business operations. In New Jersey, the government official responsible for administering the state's paid family leave insurance program described the "deafeningly silent" reaction he gets when he asks members of the business community to detail their concerns about the burden imposed on them by the program. More than that, he said, the employers actually feel very positive about the program: "It comes up a lot that people say they would give time off anyway. . . . They say, 'as a good employer I would do this [grant leave] to help employees. It's nice to see they can get a few dollars as well.'"[36] And in California, a recent study shows that not only has the family leave law not been burdensome for business, but it has really made a difference in the lives of women in a way that serves the corporate bottom line—by reducing turnover. Over the ten-year period from 1999 to 2010, with the advent of paid leave, use of maternity leave doubled from three to six weeks, especially among the most vulnerable workers.[37] One documented impact of paid leave is that it brings women back to the same employer after childbirth in much higher numbers than women without it—meaning that employers have much lower turnover costs (employers lose an estimated 21 percent of yearly salary in recruiting and training replacement staff).[38] That's money in the bank.

And paid leave is good for the economy. The Centre for the

Study of Living Standards, based in Canada, has examined the impact of different social policies on the national economies, finding that paid leave better serves the nation's fisc than unpaid leave. According to its report, "one study on productivity growth in 19 Organization for Economic Co-Operation and Development countries from 1979 to 2003 found that paid parental leave had a significantly greater positive effect on productivity than unpaid leave. The study also estimated that instituting 15 weeks of paid maternity leave in countries (such as the US) without paid leave could increase multifactor productivity by 1.1 percent in the long run."[39]

Even without factoring in the productivity impact or the cost savings for taxpayers in keeping people off of assistance programs, the fact is that a leave policy will not break the nation's piggy bank. Studies from other countries show how minimal the costs really are. Countries that have well-financed leave programs spend a modest amount relative to their gross domestic product (GDP) and population size. Estimates put the average cost of public outlays for maternity leave in Europe and the OECD at only 0.3 percent of GDP, with no impact on unemployment. In fact, those countries that provide leave have the most competitive economies.[40]

These countries, and not just those who share America's prosperity, have made it a priority to ensure that parents—not just mothers—can take time off from work for a birth (or adoption) and for a period of time afterward. An in-depth study of parental leave policies in twenty-one developed countries put the United States in twentieth place overall.[41] The United States is such an outlier that recent studies examining leave policies around the world document that, as of 2011, 178 out of 190 countries have paid leave. Nine countries have policies that are ambiguous, but only three countries have no such program at all: Papua New Guinea, Swaziland, and the United States.[42]

At least some members of Congress have absorbed the lessons—a good policy must provide paid leave and cover a much greater share of the workforce. In 2011, Senator Kirsten Gillibrand and Representative Rosa DeLauro introduced the Family and Medical Insurance Leave, or FAMILY, Act, which makes substantial improvements to the FMLA.[43] First, it provides *paid* leave. Reports the *Washington Post*, "The proposed leave program would provide benefits equal to 66 percent of an individual's typical monthly wages—such as New Jersey's program does—up to a capped amount. These benefits would likely incentivize men and women to share care responsibilities." Significantly, the legislation would also decouple the benefit from the employment relationship but instead make it portable. Allowing each worker twelve weeks of leave for childbirth, adoption, or their own illness, or to provide care for a sick family member, it would cover any workers eligible for Social Security and would work the same way. The benefits are attached to the worker and don't disappear when he or she changes jobs. It would make sure that low-wage, part-time, and younger workers would have access to paid leave, unlike the FMLA, which disproportionally excludes such workers. And it would add domestic partners to the family members one could use leave to care for.[44]

But that should be only the start. In addition to providing sufficient financial support and covering more employees, the leave should also last longer than twelve weeks. Some countries have adopted leave policies that allow parents time out of the office for a longer period, an average of ten months in certain developed countries, and a range of benefits such as paid leave, flexible scheduling, accommodations for breastfeeding, and protections against retaliation for exercising the right to spend time with a new child.

Men need access and encouragement to take leave as well. For example, some countries require men to take some leave to avoid creating a disincentive to hiring women, using a mixture of carrots and sticks to get men to participate. Finland used a very ingenious method to persuade men to take leave, running an ad campaign with billboards that asked how many men on their deathbeds "wish they had spent more time with their bosses?"[45] In Sweden, men who do not take the leave lose it—they cannot transfer it to their wives or partners. With 240 days of paid leave, fathers can spend a significant portion of a child's early months at home. For men who choose not to take the full time off, they must take at least two months in the first eight years after a child's birth or lose the benefit entirely. According to a *Wall Street Journal* article, "Government statistics show the vast majority of fathers take off at least the minimum two months. And about 72% of working-age women living in Sweden are employed at least part-time, according to the Organization for Economic Cooperation and Development. This is more than in most other countries. Iceland and Norway—Nordic nations that also grant generous leave benefits, have more women in the workforce."[46]

But even just making leave paid brings in more fathers. After California passed paid family leave in 2004, fathers began to take leave in significantly higher numbers. There's nothing like adding a little money to get the men to recognize the value, and to lessen the stigma. Before the state offered paid leave, fewer than 20 percent of the leaves were taken by fathers; that has now grown to one-third. Fifty-three thousand fathers took leave in 2012, according to a recent study, more than twice as many as eight years ago.[47]

How leave is financed can either help or hurt women. Unless

the costs are borne broadly, through insurance programs or other schemes, rather than being financed by individual employers, women face discrimination, because employers want to avoid the cost of leave. The most common approach in countries with paid leave is to establish a universal program, funded by payroll taxes or general revenues, rather than one dependent on employer contributions. By removing the leave payment from the employment relationship, these programs help avoid the discrimination that women can face in cases where the employer thinks they may have a child and the firm will have to foot the bill.[48]

These policies play an important role in addressing gender inequity, in particular by limiting the impact of time out of the workforce on women's long-term earnings. Paid leave allows women to take less time out of the labor market, and less time out of the labor market means that their wages stay more in balance with men's. Another significant factor for women and children is that when women stay in the workforce, they are better prepared to weather the financial impact of divorce. And when fathers are pushed to take time off, they forge much closer bonds with their children and there is less societal stigma associated with paternity leave.[49] One of the reasons women's participation in the labor force has gone down in the United States and up in other developed countries is because those countries have surged ahead of us in making work and family compatible.[50]

Countries with generous family leave policies see the greatest success both in keeping women in the workforce and allowing for robust family life (these countries also have the highest birth rates among the developed countries). Germany provides an instructive example of a counterproductive policy. Interested in raising its very low birth rate, the Germans provided strong incentives for women to stay home to raise their children, rather than giving them the ability to stay in the workforce once they have had a child. In addition to the strong cultural disapproval of working mothers and a school system where classes often end by 1 p.m., Germany lags in public child care and instead pays parents (mostly mothers) to stay home.[51] Putting another finger on the scale against women working, the tax system benefits families with a stay-at-home spouse.[52] As a result, the relatively low birth rate in Germany has not improved relative to those of other countries, despite the robust economy in Germany. "If you look closely at the numbers, what you see is the higher the gender equality, the higher the birthrate," said Reiner Klingholz of the Berlin Institute for Population and Development.[53] The policies adopted in the Scandinavian countries as well as France help explain why their birthrates are among the highest in the developed world. While Germany has a fertility rate of 1.37, France's is 1.90, Norway's 1.81, and Sweden's 1.75.[54] Paid family leave is a big part of this equation, as is adequate health care and early child care. With paid time off for childbearing as well as a decent child care system, families have a less difficult calculus to make in terms of when and whether a mother should return to work—or whether she should have children at all.

THE SICK WARD: LACK OF SICK LEAVE, OR "PLEASE COUGH IN THE OTHER DIRECTION"

Joining with other domestic workers to push for legal protections, Paola Garcia came to the Massachusetts statehouse to testify about how she was denied basic human dignity on the job, even the simple ability to get medical care when she was sick. She described how "she worked for five years as a live-in nanny. She worked from 6 a.m. to 11 p.m., with her only time off from 10 a.m. to 6 p.m. on Saturdays. When she had a root canal that got infected, she was unable to take time off. 'Working that many hours for so many years without a full day of rest in the week, or the right to go see a doctor when you need it is wrong,'" she said.[55]

A lot of us may take it for granted that we can stay home when we are sick—or even when a child is sick. The highest earners are most likely to have paid sick days and, among the top 10 percent, almost 90 percent can count on being able to stay home when ill and not see their pay docked. In contrast, this is true for only 19 percent of those in the bottom 10 percent and a third of those in the bottom quartile of earners. Just an unpaid day or two off for illness can wreak havoc on a budget where every penny counts. Workers without paid sick leave earn a median wage of $10 per hour compared to those who do have such leave, whose median hourly wage is $19.[56] Illness, like the birth of a child, can push families on the margins into bankruptcy.[57] If workers cannot afford to—or are not permitted to—stay home, they will come to work, and that has its own costs: loss of productivity as well as infected coworkers, who also will not be able to take time off to recover. Some estimates say these costs exceed the cost of providing paid sick days.[58]

For those people who complain when sick preschoolers go to school and make their children ill, this inconvenience is another shared societal cost of parents without sick leave. If a parent stays home to tend to a sick child or to him- or herself, the consequences may be equally dire, as workers may lose their jobs or be penalized another way. According to a study published by the Economic Policy Institute, "Sixteen percent of American workers report that they or a family member have lost a job or been otherwise punished, or that they would be fired, for taking time off work to care for a sick family member or their own illness."[59] When Dena Lockwood's daughter came down with extremely contagious conjunctivitis, or pinkeye, she called her employer to say she would be taking a sick day. That call resulted in her immediate dismissal even though the company let single people take time when they needed it. A high-performing sales representative for a Chicago company, Lockwood said she was "100 percent sure she was being discriminated [against] because she had children." She's a lucky one because Chicago has a local ordinance that provides stronger protections against discrimination than federal or state laws, and even under those laws many women work for employers that are not legally required to give them family leave. But even though Lockwood did win a lawsuit against the company, it took her three years of litigation to win a little over $200,000 in damages. In the meantime, she had to find another job and cover her living expenses.[60] And all because she wanted a day of sick leave to care for her sick daughter.

Despite the clear need for sick leave (who wants a cook sneezing on their hamburger or a colleague spreading germs from the next cubicle at work or a teacher coughing in their children's schoolroom?) and the popular support for legislation mandating some days off, business lobbyists have succeeded in getting ten states to ban cities, counties, and other subdivisions from even adopting such policies.[61] Funded by the Koch brothers and Karl Rove's Crossroads GPS, business groups have fought sick leave across the country. The shadowy American Legislative Exchange Council (ALEC), which is responsible for much of the noxious legislation at the state and local level, from stand-your-ground laws to requirements for photo IDs for voting, drafted the very first anti–sick leave bill in Wisconsin. Joining with the National Federation of Independent Business and the National Restaurant Association, ALEC has helped galvanize corporate America, getting even companies that provide paid sick days to their own employees to put money into fighting local efforts.[62]

In addition to a robust and equitable family leave system, we need to ensure that workers can take sick leave without being fired—even workers with paid sick days can be punished if they don't give advance notice and get permission. That may be nonsensical, but it is true nonetheless. San Francisco, Washington, D.C., Connecticut, Seattle, New York City, Portland, Oregon, Jersey City, and Newark have adopted policies to protect sick workers.[63] At the federal level, the Healthy Families Act, first introduced in 2011 by Senator Tom Harkin (D-IA) and Representative Rosa DeLauro (D-CT), would mandate that workers earn one hour of sick leave for every thirty hours worked, up to seven days per year. Unfortunately, it exempts employers with fewer than fifteen employees.[64] Even without passing legislation, the federal government could take the lead by rewarding contractors who provide some leave to their employees—and by penalizing those who don't. Since so many low-wage workers are employed by these contractors, the impact would be demonstrable.[65] It's no surprise that these companies usually give their higher earners paid leave.

At the end of the day, paid leave is just good policy. It addresses economic inequality and gender inequity. It protects the health of women and children. And it is good for business and the economy.[66]

6

DID MARY POPPINS HAVE KIDS?
CHILD CARE AND THE WORKING MOTHER

Alexandria Wallace wants to work. And she was working until her child care arrangements fell apart. Because she couldn't afford the high cost of professional child care, she relied on ad hoc arrangements, looking to friends and family to help out. When she wasn't able to find anyone to take care of her three-year-old daughter, she had to skip some shifts at the salon where she worked as a hairstylist and eventually got sacked. Without any income, the twenty-two-year-old single mother became eligible to enroll her child in the state's subsidized child care. Unfortunately, because Arizona, where Wallace lives, cut funding for the program, there are far more children than there are slots. Her daughter was added to the list of eleven thousand kids hoping to get in. Wallace's frustrations are shared by parents around the county as many states fail to fund enough slots in their child care systems for families in dire need.[1]

One of the biggest challenges for families in America, up and down the income scale, is how to care for children once they are born. Women's participation in the workforce has grown significantly over time, especially that of women with children: almost 77 percent of women with children between six and seventeen are working; 64.2 percent of women whose children are under six are in the workforce, with unmarried mothers having a higher participation rate than married women overall.[2] And while we have taken some insufficient steps to combat discrimination in the workplace and to open new opportunities to women, we really haven't done much at all to address what to do with their children during the workday.

Many news stories have focused on the middle-class conundrum of whether a mother should stay home because she is paid less than the father, and the cost of child care is more than, or a large share of, her earnings, as well as on the worry of how "opting out" might affect her income over the long term. More obsessively, elite media and parenting websites geared to Park Slope and Chevy Chase dissect the trade-offs between nannies and exclusive child care programs that feed into fancy private schools. A late night at the office or an unexpected dinner out, with child care provided by the nanny, is a part of life for some privileged parents, but few people consider what happens when nannies have children of their own. It seems an obvious question, since the overwhelming majority of such caregivers are women. But how often do we hear about the nannies—or the janitors or fast-food workers—and what happens to their children when they have to work late?

Unfortunately, there are many stories, rarely reported on, of the traumas and sacrifices faced by low-income families and the serious consequences for their children of being placed in suboptimal child care or left alone altogether.[3] The irony of our current situation is that it harkens back to what we think of as a very different era, in the early twentieth century with tenements and factories. As a child growing up in Chicago, I learned about the great social activist Jane Addams, who opened Hull House to help alleviate some of the worst aspects of tenement living for poor immigrants in the city. Were she alive today, she would find that the work she did is still needed. For example, she discovered during the course of her work, to her great horror, that the children of many workers had no one to care for them during the long workday but instead were left completely alone. In her book *Twenty Years at Hull House*, she described the heartbreaking injuries suffered by such children: "The first three crippled children we encountered in the neighborhood had all been injured while their mothers were at work. . . . One had fallen out of a third-story window, another had been burned, and the third had a curved spine due to the fact that for three years he had been tied all day long to the leg of the kitchen table, only released at noon by his older brother who hastily ran in from a neighboring factory to share his lunch with him."[4] This is what happens when kids are in "self-care," the cringeworthy phrase coined by the Department of Labor to describe kids left home alone.

THE QUEUE, THE COST, AND THE QUALITY: CHILD CARE AND ITS MALCONTENTS

Our system of child care—or lack thereof—fails all families with its high costs, limited availability, and often low quality.[5] But while the failings of the system may affect most parents, they most seriously harm those families that are least able to absorb the extra financial and scheduling burden—because the mother's earnings are minimum wage or below and she is not eligible for overtime; because she faces legalized discrimination and retaliation on the job because of her race, sex, language abilities, or parenting responsibilities; because she has no access to leave to care for a sick child or to take her children for necessary medical visits; because she works nights or overtime or her employer won't give her a regular schedule.

Financial hardships from the recent economic downturn have

forced many families to use informal arrangements rather than paid child care.[6] Nearly half of working families who are *able* to find child care rely on a family member, including parents and other relatives. Because they simply cannot afford private child care, families with two parents trade off parenting, finding jobs that take them out of the home at different times; others have family members, including their older children, who take over some care responsibilities; others just leave their kids alone and hope nothing goes wrong; and some decide it is better to slide further into poverty than to leave their children without adequate supervision.[7]

Those parents who cannot rely on family care may opt for day care centers—at high cost and of questionable quality.[8] Getting into a child care program is the first challenge. Many families struggle to find a slot for their children, facing a market where demand and supply are clearly not in sync. Middle-class families go through rounds of interviews and competitive exams as their two- and three-year-old children compete for the few openings in affordable programs. For low-income families trying to get into publicly subsidized programs, there are far fewer openings than children. Despite the fact that the Child Care and Development Block Grant came out of welfare reform—otherwise known as the Personal Responsibility and Work Opportunity Reconciliation Act, which was designed to allow, or rather force, mothers to work—the program is not an entitlement, and that means there is no guarantee that eligible children will be taken care of.[9] Despite the real need and the pronounced efficacy of the programs, spending for these services is actually going down. This is true across the board—for Early Head Start, Head Start, and prekindergarten. Large majorities of eligible children are left out.[10] While funding for early childhood education went up by $1.2 billion from 2006 to 2012, that growth is dwarfed by the growth in need, allowing only 18 percent of eligible children to enroll.[11] Sadly, states are actually pulling back on the child care assistance that is available. In 2011, for the second consecutive year, thirty-seven states made it harder for families to qualify for subsidized child care, with only eleven states covering more families. Overall, the situation has gotten worse for parents since 2001, based on comparable data.[12]

But shortage of slots isn't the only challenge for poor families to overcome before finding a place for their children. States also set income limits, require copayments, and exclude parents who are in the process of searching for employment but do not yet have a job, or even those who do not work enough hours.[13] Ironically, between income limits and slots only for those already employed, our system penalizes families with two employed parents and prevents single parents from searching for employment.[14] Analyzing the set of programs designed ostensibly to reduce poverty, business journalist Eduardo Porter concluded that "for a two-parent family with children and a breadwinner earning $25,000, it makes little financial sense for the other spouse to get a job. After subtracting taxes, lost government benefits and the added cost of child care, the family would take in only some 30 cents of each additional dollar."[15] Our current hodgepodge of child care subsidies and low-income supports is structured so that incremental increases in earnings can actually drop a family over the "cliff" and cost them eligibility.[16] For some parents, these realities mean that when offered a chance at a promotion or a better job, they will decline because the additional responsibilities are not compatible with their child care arrangements or because the additional pay will bump them out of subsidized child care and they would pay out more in child care expenses than they will gain in income.[17]

This chapter opened with the story of Alexandria Wallace,

the hairstylist who lost her job when she missed work because she had no one to care for her little girl, Alaya. She came from a relatively middle-class background, growing up in a Spanish-style house with a pool and views of the distant mountains. But in 2009, she began to slide down into poverty. That year, working at Verizon and making $9.50 an hour, she was able to afford night school, where she was studying to become a cosmetologist. She hoped eventually to earn enough money cutting hair to be able to go to nursing school. Her child care arrangements were still working at that time because she was able to get Alaya into a subsidized child care program, which seemed decent. But much to her consternation, when she tried to renew Alaya's enrollment, she found that she was no longer eligible. Because of a raise of less than 50 cents per hour, her income was now too high to qualify. With no child care, she left the call center job for a lower-paying job that would allow her to be around for her daughter more often while she finished school. Her drop in income let her reapply for child care, but there was now a waiting list, forcing her to turn to friends and family to fill in caring for Alaya. For a while it worked, enabling her to start cutting hair at the salon and making some money. But the improvised arrangements didn't work well enough—she missed work, and that's when she lost her job. Without the financial means to get Alaya into a child care center and without child care, she had no way to find a job and had to go on welfare.[18]

Further complicating access to child care is that low-wage workers tend to work in the types of jobs that make good parenting especially hard: they work night shifts or weekends, they have no ability to leave work for emergencies, let alone school events or parent-teacher meetings, and they don't get any benefits from their employers, like sick leave or paid vacation.[19] Very few child care facilities, especially those that serve low-income families, are open during the hours worked by the 40 percent of American workers who work a nonstandard schedule—nights and weekends. The number of women and children affected is huge. For example, among restaurant workers, whose hours are very unpredictable, 2 million of the 5 million workers have children, and half of those are single mothers with kids under eighteen.[20] Home care workers, who are nearly all women, face a similar struggle to care for their own children when they have to care for patients in the evening or on weekends. Perversely, the increase in the number of part-time workers has made it harder for low-income parents to find care for their children, with so many of those workers working a second job or subject to just-in-time or on-call scheduling with very erratic hours. Parents who cannot control their work hours have a hard time attending school events or doctor's appointments; if they work a night shift or weekend shift, they might not be able to be at home with their children when the children have unsupervised time—leading to more "self-care" and all the risks that that entails.

Even when a child can get a placement in a child care program or prekindergarten, few facilities provide adequate care. They rarely have enough adults to care for the number of children in the center or have staff with sufficient training—sometimes the "teachers" lack even a high school degree. A large survey of state child care providers showed that disturbingly few of the providers were able to meet quality benchmarks.[21] A Child Care Aware of America fact sheet stated, "Our conclusion after six years of studying child care regulations and oversight is that we still cannot say with confidence that America's children are protected by state licensing and oversight systems. Nor can we say that child care policies are in place to help young children learn and be ready for school."[22] The lack of oversight means that many children are in inadequate, not to mention dangerous, facilities, raising nightmarish memories of what Jane Addams saw in Chicago early in the twentieth century.[23]

A story published by the Center for Investigative Reporting chillingly described the dangers of an unregulated market:

> The infant boy had been left alone in a closet. He was strapped into a car seat, facing a wall on the second floor of a Milpitas, Calif., day care. A state inspector discovered the isolated boy when she visited in April and shut down the day care that Stephanie Newbrough had run out of her home for more than 18 years. Newbrough had been a respected member of the local community. Many parents who left children in her care lived nearby or learned about her day care through word of mouth. But behind that neighborly image, the day care had a long history of breaking state rules, including a lack of supervision of children in its care. Parents like Denise Davis knew nothing of the problems. "It's your worst nightmare," she said. The violations were so severe that Newbrough ultimately lost her license and was banned for life from operating a day care in California.[24]

None of this information was accessible for parents looking for quality care because the state does not provide electronic records, forcing parents to go to the regional licensing offices to search in the archives to find out about caregivers. Only twenty-seven states provide online records of inspections for facilities, and only twenty-four do so for care provided in the home.[25] Few harried parents, especially those who have low-paid and inflexible jobs, have the time or means to do that kind of research. Despite all of the complaints and violations that had been filed against Newbrough, including seven previous citations by state officials for the worst violations, her center was not closed until the inspector found the boy locked in the closet.

In addition to access and quality, cost is the issue driving the conversation about child care. Across the board, families with children between ages three and five pay more for child care than for any other expense except housing.[26] And for low-income families, what they pay for child care may actually be their single greatest expense, eclipsing both food and housing.[27] The cost as a percentage of income for low-wage workers is staggering: families living in poverty spend 30 percent of their income on child care. According to the U.S. Census Bureau, "the poorest families pay the largest proportion of their income [for child care], with those below the poverty line paying four times as much of their income as richer families."[28] For higher-income families, the costs can still be hard to afford. A shocked and somewhat naïve reporter exclaimed that "many families pay the equivalent of college tuition, and that's not for a high-priced nanny who can teach your child to speak Mandarin. It's for day care. In 31 states and the District of Columbia, the annual average cost for putting an infant in a day care center full time was higher than a year's tuition and fees at a four-year public college in that state." (But we shouldn't be misled—as this same reporter recognizes later in her article, very few nannies are "high-priced," with wages ranging between $8.26 and $15.19 per hour and averaging only $11.73.)[29]

What our government does to support workers with children is very minimal: parents shoulder most of the financial burden, paying 60 percent of the cost of child care, on average, with government funding covering the remainder through the Child Care and Development Block Grant, the Temporary Assistance for Needy Families program, the Social Services Block Grant (or Title XX), Head Start, and state funds.[30] Wealthier parents may be able to take advantage of flexible spending accounts provided by their employers, which allow an employee to set aside $5,000 in pretax dollars to pay for child care.[31] Similarly, the Child and Dependent Care Credit uses the tax code to provide child care help by providing a tax credit if parents need child care to allow them to work, but only up to $3,000 per year for one child and $6,000 per year for two. Because of the sky-high cost of child care, as much as or more than a public college, this relief does not pencil out to much assistance at all.[32]

The data could not be clearer about the powerful positive impact of early child care and education and the dismaying results when children are left out of these programs, especially for the most at risk—poor children with unstable families.[33] Children face challenges just being poor, suffering from many more stresses and problems than we often acknowledge.[34] Recent studies show that lack of good child care has long-term implications, and the children of teen mothers, parents without a high school diploma, and those who do not speak English suffer the worst consequences.[35] As early as eighteen months, children from wealthier families are well ahead of low-income children in language skills, with the gaps only growing until children enter school, meaning that the low-income children face a significant disadvantage right from the start.[36] But even if policy makers consider only the economic consequences of having a large cohort of children who receive little, inadequate, or no early education, we need to take this problem seriously. While some wealthy people may not understand their interest in having available, affordable child care since they employ nannies in their homes, economists say otherwise.[37] Budget analysts maintain that when more than half of the children in public school in one-third of the states are from poor families, expanding access to early childhood education is money well spent and will save taxpayers in the long run.[38]

STAY-AT-HOME MOMS AND THE WELFARE QUEEN

In a country that helped pioneer universal and free public education, and with the singular importance of early childhood care
and education, why have we done so little? Past is prologue may
be an old saw, but it reflects a reality about America, with our
sentimental view of white mothers who stay home and judgmen-
tal view of black mothers who do so. Political leaders concerned
about the demise of the "traditional family" among whites successfully defeated our only effort to provide universal child care
during the Nixon administration, while hypocritically and cyni-
cally demanding that poor women, predominantly women of
color, keep working while they have young children or lose important financial support for their families.

Our first and only real experiment with public child care began
and ended during World War II. To compensate for the loss of
male workers, who were fighting overseas, American businesses
recruited women to fill jobs in factories critical to the war effort.
As many of these women had children, they needed somewhere to
put them while at work—besides locked in the house or left alone.
These children were called "door key" children because so many
of them were left alone—the name comes from the habit of tying
a door key on a string to hang around a child's neck so he or she
could open the door on coming home from school. So in its only
legislation providing a broad-based program for children, Congress
passed the Lanham Act in 1940, which set up government-
run child care centers that served more than one hundred thousand children. But the centers did not have a long life, as their
fees were often too high for struggling families to afford and their
hours too short to cover many shifts. Most significant, even some
purported advocates for women did not support the program. In
1942, Secretary of Labor Frances Perkins wrote to the head of the
Children's Bureau, asking, "What are you doing to prevent the

spread of the day care nursery, which I regard as the most unfortunate reaction to the hysterical propaganda about recruiting
women workers?"[39] Her views only reflected the commonly held
belief that, while women might be needed for the war effort, *mothers* should be at home with their children. Even Florence Kerr,
the woman running the child care program, had doubts: "We
have . . . what amounts to a national policy that the best service a
mother can do is rear her children in her home. . . . But we are in
a war. . . . Whether we like it or not, mothers of young children *are*
at work. . . . So we do need care centers." The centers were seen,
even by their congressional advocates, as a temporary and targeted program, designed primarily to serve the needs of employers
and only for those mothers who absolutely needed to work.[40]

Without adequate funding to run the program, and with bu-
reaucratic infighting, inconveniently located child care centers,
and high fees, the Lanham Act had limited impact. And, in
a sadly familiar tale, when the war ended, policy makers' first
thought was that women should leave the workforce to free up
all possible jobs for men—so there was no need for child care.
Congress closed the centers and the brief experiment was over.[41]
Only 10 percent of eligible children were served by the Lanham
Act, perhaps because of such deep-seated opposition by those
who were supposed to be helping working women. We can only
assume the rest of the children were in "self-care," locked in the
house or playing outside unsupervised.

Congress made another attempt at a systematic approach,
after the adoption of the Head Start program targeted at low-
income families, to provide child care for a larger group of families with the Child and Family Services Act. But the mere idea
of providing women with subsidized child care was enough to
send the right wing into convulsions. Even though President
Richard Nixon may have been open to signing the legislation,

he was talked out of doing so by Pat Buchanan, then a staff person in the White House, who persuaded him instead to veto the bill. President Nixon, apparently ambivalent about the legislation before Buchanan worked him over, decried its attempt to set up "communal" child care.[42] It is interesting, and dismaying, to see how the burgeoning religious right came together to fight paid child care, winning the battle decisively, with bitter consequences for families in America.[43] Similar to tactics used against the Equal Rights Amendment, opponents trotted out a host of frightening scenarios, from children refusing to do their chores to organizing unions to bargain for rights in the family. ("Doing the dishes is overtime!")

In the early 1970s, talking about public child care was like waving a cape in front of a bull for the right wing in America. One group, called Women Who Want to Be Women (the Four Ws) followed up its successful attacks on the Equal Rights Amendment by organizing against the child care legislation, engaging its local chapters in the effort. These anti-ERA activists had already used the specter of state-mandated child care in propaganda against the ERA, including a piece written by the woman who started the national Four Ws. She decried the ERA as "the most drastic measure in Senate history"—with one certain negative consequence being that it would require children to be put "in a federal day care center." (Oh no! Communism is upon us!) Four W chapters threw themselves into fighting the legislation, along the way getting some local PTA councils to commit to helping to torpedo the bill. They, along with other right-wing groups around the country, lobbied hard, organizing letter-writing efforts that flooded congressional offices with mail asking them to vote no on the Child and Family Services Act. Even though public opinion was still in favor of the bill, most members of Congress voted against it.

Reminiscent of the social backlash against working women during the Depression, the idea of women in the workforce and children in child care tapped into deep anxieties about the end of a certain vision of America. Phyllis Schlafly, a longtime general in the antifeminist army and a leader of Stop ERA, rallied her troops by describing the horrors that would ensue if the United States had a child care system: "We realized [that] if we didn't get out and defend our values, this little feminist pressure group was going to end up changing our schools, our laws, our textbooks, our constitution, our military—everything—and end up taking our husbands' jobs away."[44] Schlafly and her comrades-in-arms fought to protect a vision they had of a perfect family, one with fathers working and mothers staying home. But one that was also white and middle-class.

Despite the overwhelming number of women in the workforce today, and the high number of children in their households, this stereotype of the perfect American family where the woman stays home still has some resonance in our country. In the 1990s, there was much handwringing by and about professional women as they were singled out for failing to quit their jobs to spend time with their children. These women were told that despite their education and whatever preferences they had about working or not working, they should "opt out."[45] And in some cases, they did because of the financial and other difficulties involved in finding child care. According to Stephanie Coontz, researcher and author of numerous scholarly works on contemporary families and women in the workforce, American women left jobs not by choice but because of limited child care and family leave—as well as because women earned lower pay than their husbands. Coontz wrote, "Women's labor-force participation in the United States . . . leveled off in the second half of the 1990s, in contrast to its continued increase in most other countries. . . . [T]here was

a significant jump in the percentage of married women, especially married women with infants, who left the labor force. By
2004, a smaller percentage of married women with children under 3 were in the labor force than in 1993." But as for the women
who left the workforce, most did so not because they were "opting out" but due to structural barriers that led to a higher level
of "work-family conflict" in the United States than in Europe.[46]

At the same time as married women left the workforce, unmarried women with children worked more hours than before.[47]
According to Jason Furman, chairman of President Obama's
Council of Economic Advisors, the Earned Income Tax Credit
under President Nixon and the tax credits for child care that
came with welfare reform in the mid-1990s were part of "a dra-
matic shift in poverty-reduction policy to focusing on promoting work through anti-poverty programs."[48] When it comes to
low-income families, especially minority families, the vision of
perfect motherhood clashes with the demands made by policy
makers that poor women work, no matter whether they have
children or whether they can afford child care (not to mention
transportation to their job, job training, and other necessary expenses like appropriate work attire).[49] Ever since the passage of
welfare reform in 1996, proponents of "family values" have demonstrated that some families are not valued the same as others.
Unmarried women with children must show they have a job or
are working hard to get one in order to get cash assistance. Prior
to welfare reform, millions of poor single mothers would have
had some financial help but must now somehow find a way to get
their kids into child care or make other arrangements so they can
take a job.[50] Supporters of welfare reform have not stepped up to
support the funding for child care that would allow mothers to
afford care for their children when they find a job. In fact, only
one in seven eligible mothers actually benefits from the programs

funded through the Child Care and Development Block Grant, which was supposed to add significant resources to enable women with children to work.[51] Currently at the Brookings Institution, Republican policy analyst Ron Haskins played a major role in developing welfare reform—but he now has qualms because the necessary funding has not materialized, saying, "We're going the wrong way. The direction public policy should move is to provide more of these mothers with subsidies. To tell people that the only way they can get day care is to go on welfare defeats the purpose of the whole thing."[52]

Perhaps, except for the very rich, no one is satisfied with the status quo. Ironically, the *New York Times* has published many of the pieces that state, based on sample sizes as small as three, that women are opting out by choice. But these articles ultimately prove the false nature of that choice—even apart from the fact that they tend to focus only on upper-income women who can forgo a salary. A recent article in the *New York Times Magazine*, profiling three women who had been the subject of a story when they left the workforce a decade ago, described their unhappiness and struggles to rejoin the workforce, especially after divorce, loss of self-esteem, and lack of respect from their husbands.[53] But our old tension between the view that some mothers should stay home with their children and the view that poor women should work has tied our policy making in knots, preventing us from adopting sensible policies that would ensure that all children actually have the care and attention they need to become adults who contribute to society and that mothers have the ability to work if they choose or must. Ironically, the fact that this overwhelming financial burden falls on so many Americans is one reason to hope we may make some progress in this area—with middle-class families also getting slammed by the costs, the issue has a broader political constituency.

PAY NOW OR PAY LATER

Other countries have marched ahead of the United States, recognizing the vital national interest in investing in children, as well as the value in women working outside the home. In fact, the United States ranks third to last among OECD countries in government-provided family programs.[54] Programs in those nations offer parents child care that is high quality, affordable, and universally available and have allowed women in families with two incomes to keep work hours near parity with those of men.[55] France has one of the best systems, providing free or low-cost care to all parents, with infants and toddlers starting in the *crèche*, or day care, which leads into the *école maternelle*, or preschool. The French require trained educators at every day care center and mental health professionals to be on call for children who might need special help. In the preschool, teachers are required to have an advanced degree and are paid as much as other public school teachers. While sending kids to early day care or preschool is optional for parents, most parents take advantage of the programs, especially at the preschool level. If they do opt to keep their children at home, French parents get tax benefits whether one of the parents stays home or they hire a nanny. In other words, women have a *choice*. As a result, 80 percent of French women work, versus only 60 percent of American women. While the government in France spends more than our government, French parents spend far less, between the tax subsidies and the low fees.[56] France may offer the most robust example of a successful child care program, but many other countries significantly outperform the United States in their investments in early education and have a very high participation rate. While in 1998 only 30 percent of children in developed countries attended preschool, today that number has grown to more than three-quarters of all children due to those countries' deep commitment to providing access to affordable early child care and education.[57]

While there is a vast disconnect between the European approach and the United States' laissez-faire "self-care" attitude toward child care, Americans are beginning to recognize how important investing in early education really is. After enjoying the advantages of having her children in France, journalist Pamela Druckerman discovered to her surprise that Americans are finally coming around to the value of public programs: "Something is changing in America. A new interest in early childhood is driven by studies showing how powerfully and permanently children's brains are shaped when they're young, and how the enormous gap between rich and poor children is already in place when they are in kindergarten." Addressing the discrepancy is much easier at an earlier age than when the children get older.[58] Many economists say that without critical investments, the American workforce of the future will be less competitive. Not only do adults who have benefited from good child care and early education end up achieving higher incomes, but they pay more in taxes and cause less social disruption than those adults who were shut out. When we fail to invest in the early years, we end up paying for it in the end: it is well documented that children without adequate care are more likely to have troubles in school, end up in jail or unemployed, or need urgent hospital care, all of which gets paid for by taxpayers. Recently, Ben Bernanke, the former chairman of the Federal Reserve, made the same argument, stating flatly that even more than the children, the rest of society gains the benefits.[59] Society also profits from parents being able to aim higher, seeking jobs that pay better or promotions that provide more benefits; women who might have stayed home because the cost of child care outweighed their earnings can pursue their dreams and perhaps achieve greater economic success in the long run. Child care is also good for companies' bottom lines, with studies showing that such benefits increase productivity and retention for employers.[60] And some politicians have grasped that we cannot continue to neglect the next generation. For example, the new mayor of New York, Bill de Blasio, campaigned on a platform of raising taxes on the wealthy to pay for early child care.[61]

One of the first U.S. institutions to acknowledge the value of child care was the American military. With more and more women serving in the armed forces and more wives of servicemen with jobs, the Department of Defense recognized it could not attract the requisite number of volunteers, particularly of the caliber it would like, without accommodating parents.[62] In a report to Congress, the Government Accountability Office stated that "about a million members of the United States' armed services are balancing the demands of serving our country and raising a family, and many need reliable, affordable child care. Deployments related to the wars in Iraq and Afghanistan have increased the demand for child care. Paying for high-quality child care can be challenging, so the Department of Defense subsidizes some child care costs for military families."[63] Currently, the Department of Defense provides both its own care centers on military bases at a low cost for parents and subsidies for private care where there is not a military care center, which is particularly relevant for members of the National Guard and Reserves. As with racial integration of the armed forces, sometimes (although not often) the military is steps ahead of the rest of society. We need to catch up.

Long ago, we recognized that public schooling was a necessary component of a true democracy, that an educated citizenry was vital for the system to function. With the many changes that have occurred over time in family structures and the composition of the workforce, we must now extend that public school concept to much younger children. The vital years of a child's early education cannot be neglected. We know that a child who is in a good facility with good caregivers reaps benefits that last for a lifetime; unfortunately, for the many who suffer in substandard facilities with poorly trained caregivers (or who are in "self-care"), the damage can be just as long lasting. President Barack Obama proposed a comprehensive program that could be the beginning of what we should adopt. He advocates universal pre-kindergarten, with states receiving federal grants to set up their own systems to serve three- and four-year-olds, with some subsidies for the care of younger children. Like Social Security, it would benefit all income levels and not stigmatize the poor for participating—and as we well know, programs designed solely for the poor often lack funding and quality control since true political backing is weak. Moreover, middle-class families are also struggling to cover the costs of child care. While there is not a great likelihood that this legislation will pass in the near term, we should see it as our moral duty to get this done as soon as we can. And if that doesn't persuade you, think about your tax dollars going to building more prisons, paying for more hospital visits, and subsidizing more dropouts.

Even in advance of a universal program, we can make the current programs work better. More families, including those in the middle class, should be able to afford quality child care. This could be accomplished through a combination of policy changes, including a commitment to capping child care expenses for families at 20 percent of what they earn over the poverty line; ensuring free child care services for families below the poverty level; making sure everyone who is eligible can actually get into the programs; and making sure the benefits are not dependent on the generosity or stinginess of specific states by having the federal government provide the bulk of funding.[64] In addition to increasing funding for the Earned Income Tax Credit and the Child and Dependent Care Credit, we should adopt a unified plan that would significantly help poorer families, by combining all the different subsidies and credits into one program.[65] Such a tax credit could include the Earned Income Tax Credit, the Child and Dependent Care Credit, and dependent exemptions in the tax code and could reduce marriage penalties as well as increase benefits with the number of children so that larger families are not penalized.[66] And if we truly think it is preferable for single parents to stay in the workforce to ensure that they remain employable later in life, we need to provide child care benefits so they will do so. For example, when the federal Earned Income Tax Credit was expanded from the late 1980s through the mid-1990s, single mothers increased their participation in the workforce and decreased the likelihood that they would be in poverty.[67] When child care is affordable and available, more women will work and rely on others to care for their children.

Lastly, to make this work, we cannot neglect the caregivers and teachers who need to be paid a decent salary and must have qualifications to care for young children. Unfortunately, we continue to undervalue the function of child care, holding the benighted attitude that because women have done this job uncompensated for generations, it need not be compensated at all, and certainly not compensated fairly. Currently, 97 percent of those providing child care are women and make very little money. Average earnings for someone working at a child care center are only barely over $21,000, with preschool teachers earning only around $30,000.[68] It is no wonder that the care is inadequate and the staff poorly trained.

When we were at war, policy makers provided child care facilities for the children of women working in war industries; our military continues this tradition by offering personnel affordable quality child care. In the rapidly changing demographics of the United States, we will either have children in larger numbers left to "self-care," with all the negative consequences, or we can admit that women are working in very high percentages and that they have children—and more and more of those women are the sole caregiver and not earning enough for private child care.

And this is of course also about women—child care is not just a way to ensure that children are properly cared for, but also a way to allow women to pursue whatever dreams they may have, or at a minimum allow them to have a greater choice about whether and how they will engage in the workforce. The unfortunate truth about motherhood in America is that it is one of the causes of lingering inequality between men's and women's wages. But public policy can make a real difference. In countries with publicly provided or funded child care, women pay a lesser penalty for motherhood. Countries that do little to assist with child care have a 9.5 percent wage penalty versus 4.3 percent in countries with more robust programs and only 2 percent in those countries with the highest enrollment in child care services.[69]

True choice means that women who want to stay home with children do that because they want to and not because lack of paid family leave and child care, unequal pay, and fewer job opportunities make staying in the workforce impossible.

7

LEANING TOGETHER

Patricia Francois came from Trinidad on her own and made her way in New York working as a nanny.[1] She took a job with a wealthy family, initially finding the couple not too difficult to work with since, at least at first, they came home when promised and she did not have to work unexpected overtime hours. That changed, as the parents began to stay out later without paying her the extra wages she should have earned. Apart from offering her old leftovers from the refrigerator, they did not provide food for her when she had to stay late. After six and a half years, she never had received a pay raise or a bonus. But Patricia stuck it out because she loved the little girl who was in her care.

In a voice tinged with grief and resentment, Patricia explained how she left that job: "What ended it was that he [the father] assaulted me. He crossed the line. Six and a half years I had dealt with every put-down and abuse, but what would keep me whole was love for the baby girl." When the father came home that day, Patricia did not expect a friendly—or even polite—greeting because he had always been rude to her. But things turned bad quickly. Hearing the little girl crying after he yelled at her for failing to learn her lines for a school play, Patricia tried to intervene. He became livid when she asked him to calm down, screaming at her that she was a "black bitch." She angrily described to me how he had slapped and then punched her, giving her black eyes and bruises. She ran out and a neighbor called the police and an ambulance.

Previously, on one of her frequent walks to Central Park with the little girl, Patricia had had the good luck to find a flyer on a park bench. She picked it up, she told me, because it "looked interesting." It was from Domestic Workers United, now part of the National Domestic Workers Alliance, and Patricia saw that its work focused on helping women like her, undocumented and often mistreated by their employers. Considering that at the time, she was "being underpaid, and working long hours with short pay," she began to attend the group's monthly meetings. "I saw women of different nationalities and different races but we all had one thing in common—being exploited, being invisible. We do our jobs so they can do theirs. We take care of the future generation and we take care of the elders. But we don't get any respect for what we do," she said. After that meeting, she "never turned back."

With the help of Domestic Workers United, she was able to file a lawsuit against her employers for assault and overtime violations. Her case went to trial and she prevailed on her claims for overtime and of assault and battery.[2] But she also joined with the other women in lobbying for legislation giving protections to New York's domestic workers, which has spurred other successes around the country. *That* is what leaning together looks like.

So many activists focus on Wall Street. Why not Main Street and K Street . . . Pennsylvania Avenue and Fifth Avenue? Groups focused on economic disparities challenge our acceptance of the rising inequality in America, and feminism demands an end to policies and practices that disadvantage women. This book proposes that neither can be successful without embracing the other. When more than 50 percent of the 99 percent are women and, increasingly, women of color, feminists and those fighting against inequality must come together to fuse a more powerful movement where our policies make the world fairer and our economy more responsive, without trading off the interests of the most vulnerable to ensure benefits for the few. At each turn, so many women, and now an increasing number of men, have been left out of the core protections for the American worker, from child care and family leave to flexible hours and a workplace free from discrimination. Our nation is in the midst of great change, with greater demographic diversity, where women, including mothers—from the most impoverished to the middle class and above—work in high percentages, and where more and more workers are falling into a legal wasteland of limited rights and contingent employment relationships. As the workplace changes, "their" suffering is increasingly becoming "our" suffering. Our safety net is in fact more like a sieve, letting more and more people slip through. It needs to be rewoven, so it will actually catch people when they fall.

There's a well-known Jain story about the blind men and the elephant. When each one grabbed a different part of the animal, he thought he knew what he was touching—the elephant's leg was a pillar, the belly was a wall, the trunk a pipe, the ear a fan. And each was right, but each understood the elephant only partially. So it is with women's lives. Credit Barbara Ehrenreich, who in her book *Nickle and Dimed* documented her transformation into a minimum-wage worker, living as they do, suffering the deprivations and humiliations they do, so she could more fully understand the three-dimensionality of the real challenges of surviving on much less than a living wage.[3] It wasn't just the wages; it was the lack of benefits and access to credit, child care,

paid sick days, and time off, and it was the indignities of harassment and misogyny. Those of us who are interested in addressing
economic inequality as well as the status of women need to step
back and examine the whole elephant to know what it really
looks like.

THE WHOLE ELEPHANT

As averse as we are as Americans to universal solutions, it is
clear that when we have adopted them, they have been our
greatest achievements: Social Security (as it is now, not as adopted), Medicare, and free public schooling. In the context of
legal reform, we need to follow these models and jettison the
idea of making critical rights dependent on employment status.
Only universal programs obviate the inevitable contortions used
by many companies to avoid financial liability. They are driven
to the low road even if they would prefer not to seek it because
of competitive pressures and profit motives. If they don't, their
competitors will.

A second-best option would be to make sure the rules from
the nineteenth century defining "employee" are modernized to
reflect the realities of the contemporary employment relationship. It is time to put an end to the shell games that enable firms
to avoid claiming responsibility for those working for them. With
more and more workers finding themselves locked out of traditional jobs and forced to work as temps and independent contractors, fewer of us are protected by the labor and employment
laws that guarantee a minimum wage and overtime, safe working
conditions, and the right to join a union.[4] If a worker is doing
work for a company, the law should apply whether she's called
an employee, a temp, an independent contractor, or a part-timer.
Twenty years after the Dunlop Commission's recognition that

the law is terribly out of date and leads directly to abuses, we need to put this right.

A more laborious route would be to attack each statute's flaws individually, eliminating the exclusion for certain types of jobs, such as domestic work and farm labor, and covering employers of all sizes. It is time we cleansed our laws of the legacy of racism and misogyny that sidelined these workers in the push for needed reforms. The New Deal statutes and our antidiscrimination laws gave new rights to many, but now it is time to fulfill those laws' goals of safeguarding those most in need. They should be applied to small businesses as well as large, and to a broader set of activities that harm women. As smaller companies proliferate and larger ones spin off branches, outsource, or franchise, more and more women face overt discrimination and harassment that cannot be legally challenged.

To address wages, in addition to stronger unions and an expanded right to organize, the most obvious and easiest step would be to raise the minimum wage and eliminate the tipped wage or, at the very least, set it at a percentage, 70 percent or higher, of the full wage. While Democrats have found political gold in periodically engaging in a fight to raise the minimum wage, the better policy would be to index the minimum wage so it regularly goes up with the cost of living. Too often, politicians have cut deals that make them heroes for lifting wages for some but that leave behind many others—a group that is almost always predominantly women of color, because they're the ones working the minimum- and subminimum-wage jobs.

With respect to women particularly, we need to develop legal tools to address occupational segregation and help women move into nontraditional fields. The Fair Pay Act, advanced by Senator Harkin, provides a beginning point, and the examples from Minnesota and Ontario show that forcing employers to evaluate the real value of a job and pay has a real impact. Moreover, these strategies will help bring attention to the need to place a higher societal value on certain professions where women are the majority. Professionalizing the care industry would help enormously—benefiting not just the workers, but children and elderly patients as well. It makes a good deal of sense to have trained teachers to work with young children and home health and nursing home aides who can provide a higher level of care for sick and elderly people.[5] But we should not limit ourselves to addressing the inequality in pay between male- and female-dominated job sectors; we also need to ensure that women have the ability to move into, and thrive in, nontraditional jobs. That means we need more funding for programs that encourage women to enter new occupations, in fields such as technology, construction, transportation, and finance, and train them to succeed. To do so, we need to make the law against discrimination truly enforceable. That means giving the Equal Employment Opportunity Commission adequate funding to do its job and dismantling the court-created barriers that make it harder and harder to bring, let alone win, a case alleging sex discrimination.

Moreover, we must finally accept that women work and that many of them also have caregiving responsibilities. We need to address the fact that not providing certain benefits—such as paid leave, or any leave at all—disproportionately harms women and thus should be seen as direct discrimination. Like other countries and more forward-thinking jurisdictions in the United States, we need family leave for all parents and child care for all children. It is not a luxury, but a necessity. Flexible workplaces should be the norm, where "flexibility" does not mean the employer can change a worker's hours without notice but means instead that a parent can request time for a parent-teacher conference or to attend a school play.[6] And we need to make sure that working does not actually lower the standard of living for poor families. Work supports that would enable low-income women to take care of themselves and their families should include earned income tax credits, child care assistance, health care, housing and food assistance, and transportation help.[7] Lastly, our Social Security system needs to reflect current family structures and not those of an idealized past, where mom stayed home and dad worked and they stayed married.

SHAMING—IN A GOOD WAY

And where the United States lags behind other countries, we should also focus the international lens on our failings. When we take these issues out of the domestic context and consider them in light of international human rights conventions and the laws of other countries, we see how far we fall short. Indeed, using shame as a tactic was one way domestic workers advanced their cause. American legislators hate having international bodies criticize the United States for our failings under human rights standards—all the more reason to invoke the standards. The oversight of an international entity and the treaty obligations undergirding their arguments give worker advocates greater credibility and status here at home and serve as useful fodder for organizing efforts.[8]

Several international covenants and treaties enumerate the rights due women and workers. Simply by virtue of their human dignity, these documents affirm, workers deserve and are entitled to a fair wage, working hours that are not overly long, time off for sickness, childbirth, and vacation, the right to associate with others and organize themselves as workers, and the right to be free of discrimination as women, minorities, and immigrants. The Universal Declaration of Human Rights enshrines the right to organize and join a trade union and the right to a just and fair workplace as fundamental human rights. Similarly, the International Covenant on Civil and Political Rights considers freedom of association and equality as essential to the protection of human rights, and the International Convention on the Elimination of all Forms of Racial Discrimination bans discrimination, protects associational rights, and requires affirmative efforts by nations to combat discrimination.[9]

And while American "exceptionalism" continues to rear its ugly head, that does not mean advocates cannot win some victories through shaming. Like our refusal to join other developed countries in providing child care and paid family leave, we have backed away from many pertinent international obligations. Despite our role in creating the United Nations and crafting the UN Charter, the Universal Declaration on Human Rights, as well as other central human rights documents, the United States has refused to ratify several of them. In addition, even where we have ratified them, our government argues that only if Congress passes implementing legislation can the treaties be considered in force in this country, thus limiting advocates' ability to invoke the International Covenant on Civil and Political Rights or the convention banning discrimination.[10]

Nonetheless, even their mere existence, reflecting the shared agreement among nations of basic human rights, can play a useful role in domestic advocacy. Founded in 2000, Domestic Workers United (now the National Domestic Workers Alliance) had organized by 2005 a Domestic Workers Human Rights Tribunal, where workers described their lives and the indignities they suffered in the workplace in front of human rights experts, including the UN special rapporteur on racial discrimination. While not the sole reason behind the successful 2010 effort to pass a Domestic Workers Bill of Rights in New York, the human rights framework helped to provide a unifying narrative and to publicize the abuses to a broader audience. Domestic workers also looked abroad to build relationships with the women who hold these jobs in other countries, creating the International Domestic Workers Network. In 2011, the network won further international protections, successfully pushing for the ILO Convention and Recommendation on Decent Work for Domestic Workers, which provides international recognition of the basic rights that should be accorded these workers, and, hopefully, the impetus for nations to provide statutory protections under their basic labor and employment laws.[11] This convention in turn has become one of the message points supporting the successful adoption of domestic workers' bills of rights here at home.

Similarly, fast-food workers have found critical allies overseas. They have made common cause with workers in other countries to gain leverage on non-U.S. companies doing business in America. In support of the American fight for better treatment, workers in the corporations' home countries have used domestic political power to pressure the firms not to block union drives in the United States. And to raise the profile of their fight for $15-per-hour wages, fast-food workers organized one-day strikes in eighty cities around the world and created a new federation, the International Union of Food, Agricultural, Hotel, Restaurant, Catering, Tobacco and Allied Workers' Associations, which counts among its members 12 million workers in 126 countries.[12]

We need to adopt similar tactics to challenge our pariah status on policies that help families deal with birth, sickness, and child care. The United States is a country that prides itself as leading the world in all things, but here is an area where we not only fall short but are among the worst. Look at Japan: discovering the graying of its workforce and the economic perils of a shortage of working women, it is instituting a radical increase in the available day care slots.[13] If that country, near the bottom of the rankings of the World Economic Forum for women's participation in the labor force, can outpace us on child care, we should be ashamed. If almost every country in the world does better than us on family leave, we should be ashamed. If the only people with paid family leave in this country are those at the top of the income scale, we should be ashamed.

This shame needs to become a rallying cry for more and more Americans. And it isn't just a matter of equality, dignity, or feminism, but an actual bottom-line concern for our economy.

Celebrating the victory for New York's domestic workers, Patricia exulted, saying, "My scars represent victory, strength, for other women. We set a precedent in New York so other states and other countries, so other workers could be in the labor laws and not exploited." These domestic workers, of different races and colors, some immigrants and some American-born, first met to give one another moral and emotional support. But they did more—they organized, protested, and lobbied, winning new rights for this exploited group of workers. Their victory was sweet but, being for just one profession in one state, is also a reminder of how much more there is to be done. Patricia Francois's words challenge us to keep fighting, just as those of President Roosevelt did in 1937, when he said, "Shall we pause now and turn our back upon the road that lies ahead? Shall we call this the promised land? Or, shall we continue on our way? For each age is a dream that is dying, or one that is coming to birth."[14]

We have definitely not reached the promised land. More and more of our jobs lack benefits; fewer of us are part of a union; almost none of us have decent or affordable child care; many are denied sick days or family leave and are forced to sign away their remaining protections to get or keep a job. So let's take up the challenge of giving birth to that new dream, where leaning in really means leaning together, where we face the reality that, except for a tiny elite, there's no "opting out."

NOTES

INTRODUCTION

1. Hannah Rubenstein, "LABOUR-US: Domestic Workers Unite for Their Rights," Inter Press Service News Agency, June 14, 2010, www.ipsnews.net/2010/06/labour-us-domestic-workers-unite-for-their-rights/.

2. Michelle Chen, "Massachusetts Nannies and Housekeepers Now Protected from Long Days, Abuse, Sexual Harassment," *The Nation*, June 23, 2014, www.thenation.com/blog/180372/massachusetts-nannies-and-housekeepers-now-protected-long-days-abuse-sexual-harassment.

3. "Employment Protections for Domestic Workers: An Overview of Federal Law," National Domestic Worker's Alliance, www.domesticworkers.org/sites/default/files/Domestic_Worker_Employment_Protections_Federal.pdf.

4. Arielle Kuperberg and Pamela Stone, "The Media Depiction of Women Who Opt Out," *Gender & Society* 22, no. 4 (August 2008): 497–517.

5. Saki Knafo, "Moms Working at Wal-Mart Earn Less than They Need to Feed Their Kids," *Huffington Post*, July 2, 2014, www.huffingtonpost.com/donna-p-hall/happy-mothers-day-to-the-workers_b_5285485.html.

6. Wal-Mart Stores Inc. v. Dukes, 131 S.Ct. 2541 (2011).

7. Rebecca Smith and Harmony Goldberg, *Unity for Dignity: Expanding the Right to Organize to Win Human Rights at Work* (New York: Excluded Workers Congress, 2010), 19, www.unitedworkerscongress.org/uploads/2/9/1/6/29166849/unity_for_dignity_report.pdf.

8. Dave Jamieson, "After Harris V. Quinn, SEIU Wants to Unionize 26,000 Home Care Workers in Minnesota," *Huffington Post*, July 8, 2014, www.huffingtonpost.com/2014/07/08/harris-v-quinn-seiu-minnesota_n_5568105.html.

9. Sumer Spika, "Home Care Workers Unionize to Bring Dignity to

Work We Love," *Twin Cities Daily Planet*, July 21, 2014, www.tcdailyplanet.net /news/2014/07/21/why-home-care-workers-are-forming-union.

10. Kim McGuire, "SEIU, Minnesota Home Health Care Workers File for Union Election," *Star Tribune*, July 8, 2014, www.startribune.com/local /west/266255171.html.

11. "SEIU Healthcare Minnesota Celebrates 80th Anniversary, Welcomes Home Care Workers," *Workday Minnesota*, September 22, 2013, www.work dayminnesota.org/articles/seiu-healthcare-minnesota-celebrates-80th -anniversary-welcomes-home-care-workers.

12. Mary Bauer and Mónica Ramírez, *Injustice on Our Plates: Immigrant Women in the U.S. Food Industry* (Montgomery, AL: Southern Poverty Law Center, 2010), 41–42, www.splcenter.org/sites/default/files/downloads/publica tion/Injustice_on_Our_Plates.pdf.

13. Danielle Shapiro, "For Working Moms, One Sick Kid Can Spell Disaster," *Daily Beast*, January 26, 2014, www.thedailybeast.com/articles/2014 /01/26/for-working-moms-one-sick-kid-can-spell-disaster.html.

14. Solvej Schou, "This Woman Lost Her Job Because Her Kid Got Sick—and She's Not Alone," *TakePart*, February 7, 2014, www.takepart.com /article/2014/02/07/federal-push-paid-leave-and-quality-child-care.

15. Alissa Quart, "Crushed by the Cost of Child Care," Opinionator blog, *New York Times*, August 17, 2013, opinionator.blogs.nytimes.com/2013/08/17 /crushed-by-the-cost-of-child-care/.

16. Jessica Dickler, "Moms: I Can't Afford to Work," CNN Money, April 20, 2012, money.cnn.com/2012/04/18/pf/moms-work/index.htm.

17. "The Low-Wage Recovery and Growing Inequality," National Employment Law Project Data Brief, August 2012, www.nelp.org/page/-/Job _Creation/LowWageRecovery2012.pdf. See also "The Low-Wage Recovery: Industry Employment and Wages Four Years into the Recovery," National Employment Law Project Data Brief, April 2014, www.nelp.org/page/-/Reports /Low-Wage-Recovery-Industry-Employment-Wages-2014-Report.pdf?nocdn=1.

18. Harold Meyerson, "The Forty-Year Slump," *American Prospect*, November 12, 2013, 24, 26, prospect.org/article/40-year-slump.

19. Many studies have demonstrated that mobility in America exists only in the history books, if there. Jason DeParle, "Harder for Americans to Rise from Lower Rungs," *New York Times*, January 4, 2012.

20. David K. Shipler, *The Working Poor: Invisible in America* (New York: Alfred A. Knopf, 2004), 6.

21. Peter Edelman, *So Rich, So Poor: Why It's So Hard to End Poverty in America* (New York: The New Press, 2012), xix.

22. White House Council on Women and Girls, *Women in America: Indicators of Social and Economic Well-Being* (Washington, DC: U.S. Department of Commerce and Executive Office of the President, 2011), 5.

23. Mitra Toossi, "Employment Outlook: 2010–2020," *Monthly Labor Review*, January 2012, 43, 61.

24. Edelman, *So Rich, So Poor*, 30.

25. See BLS, "A Profile of the Working Poor, 2011," U.S. Bureau of Labor Statistics Report 1041, April 2013, 2, www.bls.gov/cps/cpswp2011.pdf.

26. Heather Boushey and Alexandra Mitukiewicz, "Family and Medical Leave Insurance: A Basic Standard for Today's Workforce," Center for American Progress, April 2014, 4.

27. BLS, "Women in the Labor Force: A Databook," U.S. Bureau of Labor Statistics Report 1040, February 2013, 3, www.bls.gov/cps/wlf-databook-2012.pdf.

28. See U.S. Bureau of Labor Statistics, "Characteristics of Minimum Wage Workers: 2012," Labor Force Statistics from the Current Population Survey, www.bls.gov/cps/minwage2012.htm.

29. Information provided by Heidi Shierholtz, economist, Economic Policy Institute, July 2, 2014, on file with author.

30. Sylvia A. Allegretto and Kai Filion, "Waiting for Change: The $2.13 Federal Subminimum Wage," Economic Policy Institute, Briefing Paper #297, February 23, 2011, 2, www.epi.org/publication/waiting_for_change_the _213_federal_subminimum_wage/.

31. See U.S. Bureau of Labor Statistics, "Personal Care Aides," in Occupational Outlook Handbook, 2014–2015 ed. (Washington, DC: U.S. Department of Labor, 2014), www.bls.gov/ooh/healthcare/personal-care-aides .htm; U.S. Bureau of Labor Statistics, "Home Health Aides," in Occupational Outlook Handbook, 2014–2015 ed., www.bls.gov/ooh/healthcare/home-health -aides.htm; "Childcare Workers," in Occupational Outlook Handbook, 2014– 2015 ed., www.bls.gov/ooh/personal-care-and-service/childcare-workers.htm.

32. See U.S. Bureau of Labor Statistics, "Independent Contractors in 2005," TED: The Editors Desk, July 29, 2005, U.S. Department of Labor, www .bls.gov/opub/ted/2005/jul/wk4/art05.htm.

33. BLS, "Highlights of Women's Earnings in 2012," U.S. Bureau of Labor Statistics Report 1045, issued October 2013, 6, tables 4 and 5, www.bls.gov/cps /cpswom2012.pdf.

34. Meyerson, "Forty-Year Slump," 26.

35. Stephanie Coontz, "How Can We Help Men? By Helping Women," New York Times, January 11, 2014, 6.

36. Heather Boushey, "The New Breadwinners," in The Shriver Report: A Woman's Nation Changes Everything: A Study by Maria Shriver and the Center for American Progress, ed. Heather Boushey and Ann O'Leary (Washington, DC: Center for American Progress, 2009), 37.

37. Ellen Galinsky, James T. Bond, and Eve Tahmincioglu, "What If Employers Put Women at the Center of Their Workplace Policies?," in The Shriver Report: A Woman's Nation Pushes Back from the Brink: A Study by Maria Shriver and the Center for American Progress, ed. Olivia Morgan and Karen Skelton (Washington, DC: Center for American Progress, 2014), loc. 4342, citing the 2008 National Study of the Changing Workforce.

38. White House Council on Women and Girls, Women in America, 14.

39. Boushey, "New Breadwinners," 36.

40. Edelman, *So Rich, So Poor*, 36.

41. White House Council on Women and Girls, *Women in America*, 14.

42. Quart, "Crushed by the Cost of Child Care."

43. Smith and Goldberg, "Unity for Dignity," 3.

44. Juan F. Perea, "The Echoes of Slavery: Recognizing the Racist Origins of the Agricultural and Domestic Worker Exclusion from the National Labor Relations Act," *Ohio State Law Journal* 72, no. 1 (2001): 118, citing Raymond Wolters, "The New Deal and the Negro," in *The New Deal: The National Level*, ed. John Braeman, Robert H. Bremner, and David Brody (Columbus: Ohio State University Press, 1975), 194.

45. Heidi Hartmann and Jeffrey Hayes, *Equal Pay for Working Women and Their Families: National Data on the Pay Gap and Its Costs* (Washington, DC: Institute for Women's Policy Research, forthcoming), cited in Heather Boushey, "A Woman's Place Is in the Middle Class," in Morgan and Skelton, *Shriver Report*, loc. 799–812, 815–16.

1: THE TEST OF OUR PROGRESS: A BRIEF HISTORY OF RACE, GENDER, AND WORKER PROTECTIONS IN THE TWENTIETH CENTURY

1. Harvard Sitkoff, *A New Deal for Blacks: The Emergence of Civil Rights as a National Issue* (New York: Oxford University Press, 1978), 46, citing Walter White, *A Man Called White: The Autobiography of Walter White* (New York: Viking, 1948), 69–70.

2. See National Women's History Museum, "Understanding the Criticism of Working Women During the Depression," Exhibit: A History of Women in Industry, 2007, www.nwhm.org/online-exhibits/industry/critiqueofwomen .htm. See also Alice Kessler-Harris, *Out to Work: A History of Wage-Earning Women in the United States* (New York: Oxford University Press, 1982), 253.

3. Kessler-Harris, *Out to Work*, 253, quoting Frank L. Hopkins, "Should Wives Work?," *American Mercury*, December 1936, 411.

4. Kessler-Harris, *Out to Work*, 253–54.

5. Jacqueline Jones, *Labor of Love, Labor of Sorrow: Black Women, Work and the Family, from Slavery to the Present* (New York: Basic Books, 1985), 200.

6. Susan Ware, "Women in the Great Depression," Gilder Lehrman Institute of American History, www.gilderlehrman.org/history-by-era/great -depression/essays/women-and-great-depression.

7. See National Women's History Museum, "The Depression and World War II (1930–1945)," Exhibit: A History of Women in Industry, 2007, www .nwhm.org/online-exhibits/industry/12.htm, citing Susan Ware, *Holding Their Own: American Women in the 1930s* (Boston: Twayne Publishers, 1982), 32.

8. Philip Foner, *Women and the American Labor Movement: From the First Trade Unions to the Present* (New York: The Free Press, 1979), 297–98.

9. Ibid.

10. See "Depression and World War II (1930–1945)," citing Ware, *Holding Their Own*, 28.

11. Kessler-Harris, *Out to Work*, 271.

12. Ella Baker and Marvel Cooke, "The Slave Market," *The Crisis*, November 1935, 330–31.

13. Jones, *Labor of Love, Labor of Sorrow*, 206–7.

14. Marc Linder, "Farm Workers and the Fair Labor Standards Act: Racial Discrimination and the New Deal," *Texas Law Review* 65 (1987): 1335, 1348–49. See Bailey v. Alabama, 219 U.S. 219, 227–28, 245 (1911).

15. See Hina Shah and Marci Seville, "Domestic Worker Organizing: Building a Contemporary Movement for Dignity and Power," *Albany Law Review* 75, no. 1 (2011–12): 416, citing Daniel E. Sutherland, *Americans and Their Servants: Domestic Servants in the United States from 1800 to 1920* (Baton Rouge: Louisiana State University Press, 1981), 4–5.

16. Ware, *Holding Their Own*, 37.

17. Kessler-Harris, *Out to Work*, 258.

18. Ibid., 269.

19. Jones, *Labor of Love, Labor of Sorrow*, 217.

20. Ibid., 218.

21. Kessler-Harris, *Out to Work*, 262–63.

22. Juan F. Perea, "The Echoes of Slavery: Recognizing the Racist Origins of the Agricultural and Domestic Worker Exclusion from the National Labor Relations Act," *Ohio State Law Journal* 72, no. 1 (2001): 104–5.

23. Jones, *Labor of Love, Labor of Sorrow*, 210. The National Recovery Administration was established by the National Industrial Recovery Act.

24. Perea, "Echoes of Slavery," 109.

25. Jones, *Labor of Love, Labor of Sorrow*, 220.

26. Economic Security Act: Hearings on H.R. 4120 Before the House Comm. on Ways & Means, 74th Cong. 108 (1935) , 796–97, 976–77.

27. Kessler-Harris, *Out to Work*, 270.

28. Perea, "Echoes of Slavery," 119.

29. "Employee Rights Under the National Labor Relations Act," National Labor Relations Board, www.nlrb.gov/sites/default/files/attachments/basic-page/node-3788/employeerightsposter-8-5x11.pdf.

30. Ira Katznelson, *Fear Itself: The New Deal and the Origins of Our Time* (New York: Liveright, 2013), 260.

31. See National Labor Relations Act, 49 Stat. 449, 450 (1935). Southern Democrats are credited with drafting the amendment. Perea, "Echoes of Slavery," 120.

32. Perea, "Echoes of Slavery," 122. The NLRA also did not include a provision to bar unions from discriminating on the basis of race. Ibid., 123.

33. See 29 U.S.C. 152(2) (1970) (repealed, 1974).

34. Foner, *Women and the American Labor Movement*, 402. Despite this sad history, Local 1199 did believe these workers deserved fair wages and working conditions and helped to get them protections under state and federal law.

Ibid., 396–416. This story of 1199's successful multiracial efforts is inspiring, especially in advancing the rights of low-wage women workers, the majority of whom were African American or Puerto Rican. Ibid., 399.

35. See Senate Subcommittee on Labor of the Committee on Labor and Public Welfare, 93rd Cong., Legislative History of the Coverage of Nonprofit Hospitals Under the National Labor Relations Act, 1974, 10.

36. Ibid.; Health Care Amendments of 1974, Pub. L. No. 93-360 (codified as amended at 29 U.S.C. §§ 151–69 [2000]).

37. Kessler-Harris, *Out to Work*, 268–69.

38. National Women's History Museum, "Understanding the Criticism of Working Women During the Depression."

39. Shah and Seville, "Domestic Worker Organizing," 417.

40. Ibid., 419n38.

41. "Inventory of Farmworker Issues and Protections in the United States," Bon Appétit Management Company Foundation and United Farm Workers, March 2011, www.ufw.org/pdf/farmworkerinventory_0401_2011.pdf.

42. See Section 152(3) of the National Labor Relations Act, 29 U.S.C. @ 152 (3).

43. Frances Perkins, *The Roosevelt I Knew* (New York: Viking, 1946), 266.

44. See Arianne Renan Barzilay, "Women at Work: Towards an Inclusive Narrative of the Rise of the Regulatory State," *Harvard Journal of Law and Gender* 31, no. 1 (2008): 169, 206, weblaw.haifa.ac.il/he/Faculty/RenanBarzilay/Publications/Women%20at%20Work.pdf.

45. Jonathan Grossman, "Fair Labor Standards Act of 1938: Maximum Struggle for a Minimum Wage," Office of the Assistant Secretary for Administration and Management, U.S. Department of Labor, www.dol.gov/oasam/programs/history/flsa1938.htm.

46. "New Deal legislation, including the FLSA, became infected with unconstitutional racial motivation." Linder, "Farm Workers and the Fair Labor Standards Act," 1336.

47. 82 Cong. Rec. 1404 (1937).

48. 81 Cong. Rec. 7881–82 (1937).

49. 82 Cong. Rec. App. 442 (1937).

50. Grossman, "Fair Labor Standards Act of 1938."

51. Farmworkers "were excluded from nearly all legislation that guarantees the rights of workers." Foner, *Women and the American Labor Movement*, 417.

52. Katznelson, *Fear Itself*, 268 (citing the FLSA), 271.

53. Jennifer Gonnerman, "The Nanny Uprising: In the Struggle Over Rights for Household Workers, the Political Is Very Personal," *New York*, June 6, 2010, nymag.com/news/features/66471/index3.html.

54. Katznelson, *Fear Itself*, 272.

55. Jones, *Labor of Love, Labor of Sorrow*, 199, 221.

56. See 29 U.S.C. @ 152(3); Perea, "Echoes of Slavery," 127.

57. FLSA was amended to include domestic workers in 1974. "However, domestic workers who reside in an employer's home are not covered by overtime

law, though they are still covered by the federal minimum wage law. 29 U.S.C. § 213(b)(21)." Employment Protections for Domestic Workers: An Overview of Federal Law," National Domestic Worker's Alliance, www.domesticworkers .org/sites/default/files/Domestic_Worker_Employment_Protections_Federal .pdf. Agricultural workers were also added to those workers entitled to a minimum wage—but not overtime. See Fair Labor Standards Amendments of 1966, Pub. L. No. 89-601, § 203(a), 80 Stat. 833, 833–34 (1966).

58. Richard Carlson, "The Small Firm Exemption and the Single Employer Doctrine in Employment Discrimination Law," *St. John's Law Review* 80, no. 4 (2006): 1197, 1199, scholarship.law.stjohns.edu/lawreview/vol80/iss4/2.

59. Marc Linder, "The Small-Business Exemption Under the Fair Labor Standards Act: The 'Original' Accumulation of Capital and the Inversion of Industrial Policy," *Journal of Law and Policy* 6 (1998): 421.

60. Carlson, "Small Firm Exemption," 1262.

61. 110 Cong. Rec. S 13086 (June 9, 1964) (statement of Senator Cotton).

62. Carlson, "Small Firm Exemption," 1269.

63. See 110 Cong. Rec. 13089 (1964).

64. Carlson, "Small Firm Exemption," 1261.

65. James D. Walsh, "Reaching Mrs. Murphy: A Call for Repeal of the Mrs. Murphy Exemption to the Fair Housing Act," *Harvard Civil Rights-Civil Liberties Law Review* 34, no. 2 (Summer 1999): 605, 609, citing 114 Cong. Rec. 2495 (1968).

66. See Equal Employment Opportunity Act of 1972, Pub. L. No. 92-261, @2, 86 Stat. 103, 103 (1972) (codified as amended at 42 U.S.C. @ 2000e[b] [1994]).

67. Pam Jenoff, "As Equal as Others? Rethinking Access to Discrimination Law," *University of Cincinnati Law Review* 81, no. 1 (2013): 85, 104–5 (citing multiple studies).

68. Genetic Justice Act, S. 1045, introduced by Senator Thomas A. Daschle, July 22, 1997.

2: THE WAGES OF DISCRIMINATION: PAYCHECK UNFAIRNESS

1. Plus ça change. Philip Foner describes this same phenomenon after World War I. As he puts it, "Women workers were shut out of the work they had done so effectively during the war." Foner, *Women and the American Labor Movement* (New York: The Free Press, 1979), 266.

2. Jacqueline Jones, *Labor of Love, Labor of Sorrow: Black Women, Work and the Family, from Slavery to the Present* (New York: Basic Books, 1985), 234–35, 256.

3. Alice Kessler-Harris, *Out to Work: A History of Wage-Earning Women in the United States* (New York: Oxford University Press, 1982), 295.

4. African American women have always worked outside the home in higher percentages than other women. Heather Boushey, "The New

Breadwinners," in *The Shriver Report: A Woman's Nation Changes Everything: A Study by Maria Shriver and the Center for American Progress*, ed. Heather Boushey and Ann O'Leary (Washington, DC: Center for American Progress, 2009), 49.

5. Heidi Shierholz, "The Wrong Route to Equality: Men's Declining Wages," in *Equal Pay Symposium: 50 Years Since the Equal Pay Act of 1963*, ed. Stephanie Coontz (Miami: Council on Contemporary Families, 2013), 18, contemporaryfamilies.org/wp-content/uploads/2014/06/2013_Symposium _Equal-Pay.pdf.

6. Ibid., 18.

7. Heather Boushey, "A Woman's Place Is in the Middle Class," in *The Shriver Report: A Woman's Nation Pushes Back from the Brink: A Study by Maria Shriver and the Center for American Progress*, ed. Olivia Morgan and Karen Skelton (Washington, DC: Center for American Progress, 2014), loc. 798–99.

8. White House Council on Women and Girls, *Women in America: Indicators of Social and Economic Well-Being* (Washington, DC: U.S. Department of Commerce and Executive Office of the President, 2011), 32. "Compared to their direct male counterparts, however, White women earned 79 percent as much as White men in 2009, while Asian women earned 82 percent as much as Asian men. For Blacks and Hispanics, the figures were 94 percent and 90 percent, respectively." Ibid.

9. Boushey, "New Breadwinners," 58.

10. Ibid., 59.

11. Ledbetter v. Goodyear Tire & Rubber Co., Inc., 127 S.Ct. 2162 (2007).

12. "Fact Sheet: Lily Ledbetter Fair Pay Act," National Women's Law Center, January 29, 2013, www.nwlc.org/resource/lilly-ledbetter-fair-pay-act-0.

13. 1 Public Law No. 111-2, 123 Stat. 5 (2009).

14. Boushey, "New Breadwinners," 58.

15. See "Equal Pay Act Frequently Asked Questions," American Association of University Women, www.aauw.org/resource/equal-pay-act-faq/.

16. Dina Bakst, "Pregnant and Pushed Out of a Job," *New York Times*, January 31, 2012.

17. Spivey v. Beverly Enter., Inc., 196 F.3d 1309, 1312, 1313 (11th Cir. 1999).

18. Wiseman v. Wal-Mart Stores, Inc., No. 08-1244-EFM, 2009 WL 1617669 (D. Kan. June 9, 2009).

19. Young v. UPS, Inc., 707 F.3d 437, 116 FEP Cases 1569, 27 AD Cases 560 (4th Cir. 2013) [2013 BL 9231]. This case will be in front of the Supreme Court during the 2014–15 term.

20. Brigid Schulte and Nia-Malika Henderson, "EEOC to Employers: Stop Discriminating Against Pregnant Workers," She the People blog, *Washington Post*, July 15, 2014, www.washingtonpost.com/blogs/she-the-people/wp/2014/07/15 /eeoc-to-employers-stop-discriminating-against-pregnant-workers/.

21. Bridgid Schulte, "For Some, Pregnancy Is Heavy-Duty Work," *Washington Post*, August 5, 2014, E1, E4.

22. Rachel L. Swarns, "Placed on Unpaid Leave, a Pregnant Employee Finds Hope in a New Law," *New York Times*, February 3, 2014, A14.

23. Emily Werth, "Keeping Pregnant Workers on the Job Unanimously Carries the Day in Delaware," National Women's Law Center Blog, July 1, 2014, www.nwlc.org/our-blog/keeping-pregnant-workers-job-unanimously-carries-day-delaware.

24. The Pregnant Workers Fairness Act (PWFA), H.R. 1975 and S. 942, 113th Cong., 1st sess.

25. Boushey, "New Breadwinners," 60.

26. Ann O'Leary and Karen Kornbluh, "Family Friendly for All Families," in *The Shriver Report: A Woman's Nation Changes Everything: A Study by Maria Shriver and the Center for American Progress*, ed. Heather Boushey and Ann O'Leary (Washington, DC: Center for American Progress, 2009), 84.

27. See FAQs on Family Responsibility Discrimination, Center for WorkLife Law, UC Hastings College of the Law, worklifelaw.org/frd/faqs/.

28. Virginia Rutter, "Executive Summary," in Coontz, *Equal Pay Symposium*, 4.

29. *Sarah Crawford*, "The Equal Employment Opportunity Restoration Act: Ensuring Access to Justice After 'Wal-Mart v. Dukes,'" ACSblog, American Constitution Society, June 20, 2012, www.acslaw.org/acsblog/the-equal-employment-opportunity-restoration-act-ensuring-access-to-justice-after-wal-mart-v.

30. Paul Elias, "Betty Dukes, Wal-Mart Greeter, Leads Class Action," *Huffington Post*, May 1, 2010, www.huffingtonpost.com/2010/05/01/betty-dukes-Wal-Mart-greet_n_559892.html.

31. Monee Fields-White, "Meet Betty Dukes, the Black Woman Who's Taking on Wal-Mart," *The Root*, December 13, 2010, newamericamedia.org/2010/12/meet-betty-dukes-the-black-woman-whos-taking-on-Wal-Mart.php.

32. Wal-Mart Stores Inc. v. Dukes, 131 S.Ct. 2541 (2011).

33. Lyle Denniston, "Opinion Analysis: *Wal-Mart's* Two Messages," SCOTUSblog, June 20, 2011, www.scotusblog.com/2011/06/opinion-analysis-wal-marts-two-messages/.

34. Tara Siegel Bernard, "Allstate Case Shows Risk of Signing Away the Right to Sue," *New York Times*, April 29, 2014.

35. Steven Davidoff Solomon, "Arbitration Clauses Let American Apparel Hide Misconduct," *New York Times*, July 16, 2014, B10.

36. Ashcroft v. Iqbal, 556 U.S. 662 (2009).

37. Bell Atlantic Corp. v. Twombly, 550 U.S. 544 (2007).

38. Arthur R. Miller, "Simplified Pleading, Meaningful Days in Court, and Trials on the Merits: Reflections on the Deformation of Federal Procedure," *NYU Law Review* 88, no. 1 (April 2013): 286, 331.

39. Joshua Civin and Debo P. Adegbile, "Restoring Access to Justice: The Impact of *Iqbal* and *Twombly* on Federal Civil Rights Litigation," American

Constitution Society Issue Brief, September 2010, www.acslaw.org/sites/default /files/Civin_Adegbile_Iqbal_Twombly.pdf. (Internal citation omitted.)

40. See "Changing the Rules: Will Limiting the Scope of Civil Discovery Diminish Accountability and Leave Americans Without Access to Justice?," testimony of Arthur Miller Before the Subcommittee on Bankruptcy and the Courts of the United States Senate Judiciary Committee, November 5, 2013, www.judiciary.senate.gov/imo/media/doc/11-5-13MillerTestimony.pdf. See also David L. Franklin, "Why Does Business (Usually) Win in the Roberts Court?," American Constitution Society Issue Brief, February 22, 2011, www.acslaw .org/files/Franklin%20Issue%20Brief%20Final.pdf.

41. P.G. Barnes, "The EEOC's New Gameplan," When the Abuser Goes to Work blog, September 8, 2012, http://abusergoestowork.com/the-eeocs -new-gameplan/.

42. Barbara Ehrenreich, foreword to Linda Burnham and Nik Theodore, *Home Economics: The Invisible and Unregulated World of Domestic Work* (New York: National Domestic Workers Alliance, 2012), vii.

43. Kessler-Harris, *Out to Work*, 314.

44. See "1099'd: Misclassification of Employees as 'Independent Contractors,'" National Employment Law Project Fact Sheet, April 2010.

45. See the Unfair Immigration-Related Employment Practices Act, 15 U.S.C. @ 1324b(a)(3), which bars discrimination based on national origin or citizenship, but does not cover those who are in the United States without proper documentation—a large category of workers, some of whom came illegally but many of whom came legally but overstayed their visas. A better approach would be to allow immigrants who are victims of serious labor violations to apply for U.S. visas, which would provide them with the legal status they need in order to advocate for their rights in the workplace. See "The Power Act: An Essential Component of Immigration Reform," National Immigration Law Center, March 2013, www.nilc.org/powerir.html.

46. Richard Carlson, "The Small Firm Exemption and the Single Employer Doctrine in Employment Discrimination Law," *St. John's Law Review* 80, no. 4 (2006): 1197, 1204, scholarship.law.stjohns.edu/lawreview/vol80/iss4/2.

47. Stone v. Indiana Postal & Federal Employees Credit Union, U.S. District Court for the Northern District of Indiana, No. 1:05-CV-114 (09/26/05).

48. Lauren Feeney, "Nannies to Get New Protections in New York, But Is More Needed?," *Need to Know*, PBS, August 26, 2010, www.pbs.org/wnet/need-to -know/culture/nannies-to-get-new-protections-in-new-york-but-is-more -needed/3083/.

49. New York City adopted, subsequent to this news story, a law expanding protections against pregnancy discrimination to nannies and other employees in small firms and families.

50. Firms use a variety of arguments in court to argue they are too small to be covered: they argue that they are not liable because employees were independent contractors (see Holland v. Gee, 719 F. Supp. 2d 1361 [M.D. Fla. 2010]); because the sued entity is a separate legal entity from the employer

(see St. Jean v. Orient-Express Hotels Inc., 119 Fair Empl.Prac.Cas. [BNA] 923); because "shareholders" of a law firm are not employees (see Johnson v. Cooper, Deans & Cargill, P.A., 884 F. Supp. 43 [D.N.H. 1994]); because family members were not employees of the company (see Smith v. Castaways Family Diner, 453 F.3d 971 [7th Cir. 2006]).

51. See more at Joelle Emerson, "Missing from the Women's Agenda: The Threat of Sexual Violence at Work," Speaking Out: The ERA Blog, February 4, 2014, www.equalrights.org/missing-from-the-womens-agenda-the -threat-of-sexual-violence-at-work/.

52. Jane Slaughter, "Sexual Harassment Still 'Normal' in Low-Wage Jobs," *Labor Notes*, March 5, 2014, labornotes.org/blogs/2014/03/sexual -harassment-still-normal-low-wage-jobs.

53. See Irma Morales Waugh, "Examining the Sexual Harassment Experiences of Mexican Immigrant Farmworking Women," *Violence Against Women* 16, no. 3 (March 2010): 237–61; *Injustice on Our Plates: Immigrant Women in the U.S. Food Industry* (Montgomery, AL: Southern Poverty Law Center, 2010), www.splcenter.org/sites/default/files/downloads/publication /Injustice_on_Our_Plates.pdf. Because so many farmworkers are immigrants, and many do not have legal documents, they have little recourse.

54. Slaughter, "Sexual Harassment Still 'Normal.'"

55. "Violence in the Fields: One Rape Victim Won in Court. But How Many Silent Victims Are There Among Female Farmworkers?," editorial, *Los Angeles Times*, May 20, 2008.

56. *Injustice on Our Plates*, 41–42, 46–48.

57. Testimony of Andrea, in favor of California Domestic Worker Bill of Rights, provided to author by Mujeres Unidas.

58. Interviews done by author with organizers of Latino Union, Chicago, on file with author.

59. Indeed, New York City just amended its human rights law to cover interns because of the prevalence of harassment. They had not been covered because they were not considered "employees." Michael M. Grynbaum, "Unpaid Interns Gain the Right to Sue," *New York Times*, April 15, 2014.

60. Slaughter, "Sexual Harassment Still 'Normal.'"

61. Carlson, "Small Firm Exemption," 1249.

62. Stephanie Bornstein and Robert J. Rathmell, "Caregivers as a Protected Class? The Growth of State and Local Laws Prohibiting Family Responsibilities Discrimination," Center for WorkLife Law, UC Hastings College of the Law, December 2009, www.worklifelaw.org/pubs/LocalFRDLawsReport.pdf.

63. "The Impact of Raising the Minimum Wage on Women," White House Report, March 2014, 3, citing Census Bureau, Historical Table.

64. White House Council on Women and Girls, *Women in America*, 33.

65. "Separate and Not Equal? Gender Segregation in the Labor Market and the Gender Wage Gap," Institute for Women's Policy Research Briefing Paper, September 2010, 2.

66. Boushey, "Woman's Place Is in the Middle Class," loc. 881–82.

67. "Separate and Not Equal?," 1.

68. Carlos Gradín, Coral del Río, and Olga Alonso-Villar, "Occupational Segregation by Race and Ethnicity in the U.S.: Differences Across States," Society for the Study of Economic Inequality Working Paper, ECINEQ 2011-190, January 2011, 3, www.ecineq.org/milano/WP/ECINEQ2011-190.pdf.

69. "Separate and Not Equal?," 13.

70. Ibid., 11.

71. Boushey, "Woman's Place Is in the Middle Class," loc. 895, citing Christine Williams, "The Glass Escalator: Hidden Advantages for Men in the 'Female' Professions,'" *Social Problems* 39, no. 3 (1992).

72. "Separate and Not Equal?," 1–2.

73. *Women in Construction: Still Breaking Ground* (Washington, DC: National Women's Law Center, 2014), 2, www.nwlc.org/sites/default/files/pdfs/final_nwlc_womeninconstruction_report.pdf.

74. Ibid., 4.

75. Emily Gurnon, "St. Paul to Settle Police Officer's Sexual Harassment Lawsuit for $60,000," *Pioneer Press*, July 10, 2014, www.twincities.com/crime/ci_26126013/st-paul-pay-decorated-female-cop-60k-settle.

76. Pennsylvania State Police v. Suders, 542 U.S. 129, 134–35 (2004).

77. Burlington Northern & Santa Fe Railway Co. v. White, 548 U.S. 53 (2006).

78. ROC-United, "Tipped Over the Edge: Gender Inequity in the Restaurant Industry," February 13, 2012, 2.

79. ROC-NY, *The Great Service Divide: Occupational Segregation & Inequality in the New York City Restaurant Industry* (New York: Restaurant Opportunities Center [ROC-NY] and the New York Restaurant Industry Coalition, 2009), 2, 11, rocunited.org/the-great-service-divide.

80. ROC-United, "Tipped Over the Edge," 2; ROC-NY, *Great Service Divide*, 39.

81. Ibid.

82. Arlene Dohm and Lynn Shniper, "Occupational Employment Projections to 2016," *Monthly Labor Review*, November 2007, 97–98, Table 3, www.bls.gov/opub/mlr/2007/11/art5full.pdf.

83. Jones, *Labor of Love, Labor of Sorrow*, 302.

84. Ruth Milkman, "From the Folks Who Brought You the Weekend: What Unions Do for Women," in Coontz, *Equal Pay Symposium*, 10.

85. H.R. 377, S. 84, 113th Cong.

86. "On Fourth Anniversary of Lilly Ledbetter Act, Harkin Introduces the Fair Pay Act to Ensure Equal Pay for Equal Work," press release, January 29, 2013, www.harkin.senate.gov/press/release.cfm?i=339442.

87. See, e.g., Fair Pay Act of 2011, S.788 § 6(b), 112th Cong. (2011–12), 1st sess., April 12, 2011, thomas.loc.gov/cgi-bin/query/z?c112:S.788:.

88. MN ST § 43A.01(3).

89. MN ST § 43A.02(14a); MN ST § 471.992(1).

90. Instead, Minnesota's wage discrimination provisions are modeled on the Fair Pay Act. MN ST § 181.67(1).

91. Ibid., 12.

92. "Two Progressive Models on Pay Equity: Minnesota and Ontario," National Committee on Pay Equity, 1, www.pay-equity.org/ PDFs/Progressive Models.pdf.

93. Ibid., 2.

94. Pay Equity Act, R.S.O. 1990, P.7, Preamble.

95. Ibid., P.5.1(1). See also "Summary of Requirements: Part I: Requirement for ALL Employers to Achieve Pay Equity: Achievement of Pay Equity," Pay Equity Commission, August 15, 2012, www.payequity.gov.on.ca/en/resources /guide/ope/ope_4.php.

96. "Ratifications of C111–Discrimination (Employment and Occupation) Convention, 1958 (No. 111)," International Labour Organization, www.ilo.org/dyn/normlex/en/f?p=1000:11300:0::NO:11300:P11300_INSTRU MENT_ID:312256.

97. Marie-Thérèse Chicha, "A Comparative Analysis of Promoting Pay Equity: Models and Impacts," International Labour Organization Working Paper, September 2006, iii, www.ilo.org/wcmsp5/groups/public/—-ed _norm/—-declaration/documents/publication/wcms_decl_wp_27_en.pdf.

98. "Guiding Principles for Interpreting the Act," Pay Equity Commission, August 15, 2012, www.payequity.gov.on.ca/en/resources/guide/ope/ope_3.php.

99. "Two Progressive Models on Pay Equity," 2.

100. "Separate and Not Equal?," 13.

101. ROC-United, "Tipped Over the Edge," 14.

102. Ibid., 15.

103. ROC-United, *The Third Shift: Child Care Needs and Access for Working Mothers in Restaurants* (New York: Restaurant Opportunities Centers United, 2013), 7.

104. David Cooper, "Raising the Minimum Wage to $10.10 Would Lift Wages for Millions and Provide a Modest Economic Boost," EPI Briefing Paper #371, December 19, 2013, 8.

105. Ibid., 8. See also Benjamin H. Harris and Melissa S. Kearney, "The 'Ripple Effect' of a Minimum Wage Increase on American Workers," Up Front blog, Brookings Institution, January 10, 2014, brookings.edu/blogs/up-front /posts/2014/01/10-ripple-effect-of-increasing-the-minimum-wage-kearney -harris.

106. Cooper, "Raising the Minimum Wage," 3.

107. Ibid., 4, 10–11.

108. Ibid., 5.

109. Robert Kuttner, "The Task Rabbit Economy," *American Prospect*, September–October 2013, 52. See also "Impact of Raising the Minimum Wage on Women," 13–14, citing Sylvia Allegretto, "Waiting for Change: Is It Time to Increase the $2.13 Minimum Wage?," Institute for Research on Labor and Employment, Working Paper No. 155-13, December 16, 2013.

110. Wage and Hour Division, "Fact Sheet #15: Tipped Employees Under the Fair Labor Standards Act (FLSA)," U.S. Department of Labor, revised July 2013, www.dol.gov/whd/regs/compliance/whdfs15.pdf.

111. Rebecca Smith and Harmony Goldberg, *Unity for Dignity: Expanding the Right to Organize to Win Human Rights at Work* (New York: Excluded Workers Congress, 2010), 32, www.unitedworkerscongress.org/uploads/2/9/1/6/29166849/unity_for_dignity_report.pdf.

112. ROC-United, "Tipped Over the Edge," 10; Colette Irving, "75 Years of Fair Labor Standards: Happy 75th Birthday to the FLSA!," National Women's Law Center blog, June 25, 2013, www.nwlc.org/our-blog/75-years-fair-labor-standards-happy-75th-birthday-flsa.

113. Tipped workers were not even covered by the FLSA until 1966, when Congress amended the law to establish a tipped minimum wage at 50 percent of the full minimum wage because of the "great need for extending the present coverage of the act to large groups of workers whose earnings today are unjustifiably and disproportionately low." Senate Report (Labor and Public Welfare Committee) No. 8901487 on HR 13712, 1966 U.S.C.C.A.N. 3002, 3004 (1966).

114. ROC-United, "Tipped Over the Edge," 12.

115. Mary Bottari, "The National Restaurant Industry Spends Big to Keep Wages Low," *The Progressive*, May 15, 2014, www.progressive.org/news/2014/05/187690/national-restaurant-association-spends-big-keep-wages-low.

116. Ned Resnikoff, "Big Business Gets Creative in Minimum Wage Fight," MSNBC.com, May 23, 2014, www.msnbc.com/msnbc/minimum-wage-fight-takes-another-turn.

117. Steven Greenhouse, "Proposal to Raise Tip Wages Resisted," *New York Times*, January 27, 2014, B1.

118. ROC-United, "Tipped Over the Edge," 1, 12.

119. ROC-United, *Third Shift*, 7 (second set of dashes omitted in original).

120. ROC-NY, *Great Service Divide*, 20. Of course, getting a front-of-the-house job is hard enough based on evidence that restaurants strongly prefer white men for these positions, especially those with a European accent. Ibid., 24–29.

121. ROC-United, "Tipped Over the Edge," 9.

122. ROC-United, *Third Shift*, 5. See also Greenhouse, "Proposal to Raise Tip Wages Resisted," B2.

123. Smith and Goldberg, *Unity for Dignity*, 32.

124. "The Impact of Raising the Minimum Wage on Women: And the Importance of Ensuring a Robust Tipped Minimum Wage," White House Report, March 2014, 7, www.whitehouse.gov/sites/default/files/docs/20140325minimumwageandwomenreportfinal.pdf.

125. Steven Greenhouse, "McDonald's Workers File Wage Suits in 3 States," *New York Times*, March 13, 2014.

126. Steven Greenhouse, "Sports Bar Chain Agrees to Pay $6.8 Million for Violating Wage Laws," *New York Times*, February 21, 2014, B3.

127. Kuttner, "Task Rabbit Economy," 51.

128. Gregory K. McGillivary and Megan K. Mechak, "Current Trends in Pursuit and Defense of Hybrid FLSA and State Wage and Hour Litigation," 2006, 2, apps.americanbar.org/labor/annualconference/2007/materials/data/pa pers/v1/029.pdf. "Notably, the low opt-in rate is not true, however, when FLSA claims are brought on behalf of a unionized workforce." Ibid., 2.

129. "Impact of Raising the Minimum Wage on Women," 9.

130. ROC-United, "Tipped Over the Edge," 2.

131. Ibid., 22.

132. Steven Greenhouse, "Advocates for Workers Raise the Ire of Business," *New York Times*, January 16, 2014.

133. Laurie Woolever, "High-End Food, Low-Wage Labor," *Dissent*, Spring 2012, www.dissentmagazine.org/article/high-end-food-low-wage-labor.

134. Bottari, "National Restaurant Industry Spends Big."

135. Michael A. Fletcher and Peyton M. Craighill, "Majority of Americans Want Minimum Wage to Be Increased," *Washington Post*, December 18, 2013.

136. "Impact of Raising the Minimum Wage on Women," 3. See also Harris and Kearney, "The 'Ripple Effect' of a Minimum Wage Increase," 7.

137. See Massachusetts Institute of Technology (MIT)'s website, Poverty in America: Living Wage Calculator, livingwage.mit.edu.

138. Stephanie Luce and Naoki Fujita, *Discounted Jobs: How Retailers Sell Workers Short* (New York: Retail Action Project/CUNY Murphy Institute, 2012), 22.

139. Lawrence Mishel, "The Right to Organize, Freedom and the Middle Class Squeeze," testimony before the U.S. Senate Committee on Health, Education, Labor, and Pensions, March 27, 2007, www.epi.org/publication /webfeatures_efca_testimony_20070326/.

140. John Schmitt, "Unions and Upward Mobility for Women Workers," Center for Economic and Policy Research, December 2008, www.cepr.net /index.php/publications/reports/unions-and-upward-mobility-for-women -workers/; Heather Boushey, Jane Farrell, and John Schmitt, *Job Protection Isn't Enough: Why America Needs Paid Parental Leave* (Washington, DC: Center for American Progress and the Center for Economic and Policy Research, 2013), 10.

141. Milkman, "From the Folks," 10–11.

142. Katherine V.W. Stone, "Legal Protections for Atypical Employees: Employment Law for Workers Without Workplaces and Employees Without Employers," *Berkeley Journal of Employment and Labor Law* 27, no. 2 (2006): 251, 268, scholarship.law.berkeley.edu/bjell/vol27/iss2/1.

143. Benjamin I. Sachs, "Employment Law as Labor Law," *Cardozo Law Review* 29, no. 6 (2008): 2698–700.

144. Labor Innovations for the 21st Century, internal AFL-CIO document, November 2013, 1, on file with author.

145. National Day Laborers Organizing Network, National Domestic Work-ers Alliance, Restaurant Opportunities Center United, National Guestworker

Alliance, Food Chain Workers Alliance, and National Taxi Workers Alliance. Victor Narro, "Perspectives: Worker Centers and the AFL-CIO National Convention," Law at the Margins, August 21, 2013, lawatthemargins.com /perspectives-worker-centers-and-the-afl-cio-national-convention/. I think his list actually understates the number of networks.

146. Narro, "Perspectives."

147. Janice Fine, "Worker Centers: Organizing Communities at the Edge of the Dream," Economic Policy Institute Briefing Paper, December 13, 2005, www.epi.org/publication/bp159/.

148. Labor Innovations for the 21st Century, 2.

149. "The Rise of Worker Centers and the Fight for a Fair Economy," United Workers Congress Briefing Paper #1, April 2014, 6–10, www.unitedworkers congress.org/uploads/2/4/6/6/24662736/_uwc_rise_of_worker_centers-_sm.pdf.

150. Labor Innovations for the 21st Century, 3; conversation with Bill Lurye, general counsel, AFSCME, May 6, 2014.

151. "Domestic Workers' Bill of Rights," New York State Department of Labor: Legal, www.labor.ny.gov/legal/domestic-workers-bill-of-rights.shtm. See also Irin Carmon, "Fighting Our New Nanny Economy," Salon, November 29, 2012, www.salon.com/2012/11/29/fighting_our_new_nanny_economy/.

152. Amy B. Dean, "How Domestic Workers Won Their Rights: Five Big Lessons," Yes! Magazine, October 9, 2013, www.yesmagazine.org/people-power /how-domestic-workers-won-their-rights-five-big-lessons.

153. CCH-HRMCGD P 32398 (C.C.H.), 2013 WL 3465777; SB535 C.D. 1., www.capitol.hawaii.gov/session2013/bills/SB535_CD1_.htm.

154. Kirk Semple, "A Boon for Nannies," New York Times, April 14, 2011.

155. Sharon Lerner, "'The Help' Gets Its Due," DoubleX blog, Slate, February 22, 2012, www.slate.com/articles/double_x/doublex/2012/02/domestic_workers _bill_of_rights_and_other_new_laws_protecting_nannies_housekeepers _and_other_in_home_employees_.html.

156. Carmon, "Fighting Our New Nanny Economy."

157. Interview with Andrea Lee, Mujeres Unidas, February 21, 2014, on file with author.

158. Smith and Goldberg, Unity for Dignity, 48.

159. "On Fourth Anniversary of Lilly Ledbetter Act."

160. Public Law No. 111-2, 123 Stat. 5 (2009).

161. Ashley Soley-Cerro, "Lilly Ledbetter Shares Her Story of Overcoming the Wage Gap," The Sundial, March 6, 2013, sundial.csun.edu/2013/03/lilly -ledbetter-shares-her-story-of-overcoming-the-wage-gap/.

162. eXtina, "Lilly Ledbetter, Women's Equality Icon, Struggling in Retirement," Daily Kos, March 15, 2012, www.dailykos.com/story/2012/03 /15/1074062/-Lilly-Ledbetter-Women-s-Equality-Icon-Struggling-in -Retirement.

163. Ibid.

164. O'Leary and Kornbluh, "Family Friendly for All Families," 98.

165. Ibid., 98–99. Similar to the other New Deal laws, the congressional

record on the Social Security Act is replete with assumptions about the lesser economic needs of women, who could cook for themselves if widowed, unlike a man, who would need to pay for restaurant food. Ibid., citing Eugene Steuerle, Christopher Spiro, and Adam Carasso, "Does Social Security Treat Spouses Fairly?," Urban Institute, November 30, 1999, www.urban.org/UploadedPDF/Straight12.pdf.

166. Gene B. Sperling, "A 401(k) for All," *New York Times*, July 23, 2014, A25.

3: PUNCHING THE CLOCK: PART-TIME, JUST-IN-TIME, AND OVERTIME

1. Ginger Adams Otis, "NYPD Forcing 911 Operators Working on Mother's Day to Stay Four Hours of Mandatory Overtime," *New York Daily News*, May 12, 2013.

2. In 1940, Congress lowered the maximum number of hours to forty. Gerald Mayer, Benjamin Collins, and David H. Bradley, "The Fair Labor Standards Act (FLSA): An Overview," Congressional Research Service, June 4, 2013, 1, fas.org/sgp/crs/misc/R42713.pdf.

3. Brooklyn Sav. Bank v. O'Neill, 324 U.S. 697, 707n18 (1945).

4. Jonathan Grossman, "Fair Labor Standards Act of 1938: Maximum Struggle for a Minimum Wage," www.dol.gov/oasam/programs/history/flsa1938.htm.

5. Colin Gordon, "The Bare Minimum: Labor Standards and American Inequality," in *Growing Apart: A Political History of American Inequality* (Washington, DC: Inequality.org, 2014), scalar.usc.edu/works/growing-apart-a-political-history-of-american-inequality/the-minimum-wage.

6. Richard D. Lipman, Allison Plesur, and Joel Katz, "A Call for Bright-Lines to Fix the Fair Labor Standards Act," *Hofstra Labor and Employment Law Journal* 11, no. 2 (1994): 378–79.

7. The original draft of the legislation did include a specific carve out of small businesses but left it to administrators to determine the size of the business to be covered through regulation. See John Forsythe, "Legislative History of the Fair Labor Standards Act," *Law and Contemporary Problems* 6, no. 3 (Summer 1939): 483, scholarship.law.duke.edu/lcp/vol6/iss3/14. See also Marc Linder, "The Small-Business Exemption Under the Fair Labor Standards Act: The 'Original' Accumulation of Capital and the Inversion of Industrial Policy," *Journal of Law and Policy* 6 (1998): 418.

8. See testimony of Mr. James A. Emery, general counsel of the National Association of Manufacturers, *Joint Hearings Before the Senate Committee on Education and Labor and the House Committee on Labor on S. 2475 and H.R. 2700*, 75th Cong., 1st sess. (1937), 623–45.

9. See 81 Cong. Rec. 7648 (1937).

10. Heather Boushey and Chris Tilly, "The Limits of Work-Based Social Support in the United States," *Challenge* 52, no. 2 (March–April 2009): 90.

11. This is not to suggest that the law has not been updated to some extent. See, for example, Colette Irving, "75 Years of Fair Labor Standards: Happy 75th Birthday to the FLSA!," National Women's Law Center blog, June 25, 2013, www.nwlc.org/our-blog/75-years-fair-labor-standards-happy-75th-birthday -flsa, discussing 1961 amendments adding enterprises engaged in interstate commerce, as opposed to requiring each worker individually to be involved in interstate commerce; the 1966 amendments adding a wider variety of institutions (but also creating the distinction for tipped employees); and the 1974 amendments that added some domestic workers.

12. Testimony of Myrla Baldonado, a certified nursing assistant and caregiver for the elderly in Chicago, for Secretary of Labor Thomas Perez, supplied to author by Ms. Baldonado.

13. Lonnie Goldman and Helene Jorgensen, "Time After Time: Mandatory Overtime in the U.S. Economy," Economic Policy Institute Briefing Paper, January 2002, 1.

14. Youngjoo Cha, "Overwork and the Persistence of Gender Segregation in Occupations," *Gender & Society* 27, no. 2 (April 2013): 159, 164, doi:10.1177/0891243212470510. Women make up more than 90 percent of registered nurses and more than half of state and local government employees; both job categories face unpredictable work hours and unplanned overtime. Ann O'Leary and Karen Kornbluh, "Family Friendly for All Families," in *The Shriver Report: A Woman's Nation Changes Everything: A Study by Maria Shriver and the Center for American Progress*, ed. Heather Boushey and Ann O'Leary (Washington, DC: Center for American Progress, 2009), 92, citing U.S. Bureau of Labor Statistics, "Table 11. Employed Persons by Detailed Occupation and Sex, 2007 Annual Averages," Labor Force Statistics from the Current Population Survey, 2008, www.bls.gov/cps/wlf-table11-2008.pdf; U.S. Bureau of Labor Statistics, "Table 16. Employed and Unemployed Full- and Part-Time Workers by Class of Workers, Sex, Race and Hispanic or Latino Ethnicity, Annual Average 2008," Labor Force Statistics from the Current Population Survey, 2009. See also Katherine Kany, "Mandatory Overtime: New Developments in the Campaign," *American Journal of Nursing* 101, no. 5 (2001): 67–70, journals.lww.com/ajnonline/Fulltext/2001/05000/Mandatory _Overtime_New_Developments_in_the.26.aspx.

15. Kany, "Mandatory Overtime," 67–70.

16. Cha, "Overwork and the Persistence of Gender Segregation," 160.

17. Goldman and Jorgensen, "Time After Time," 1.

18. Anonymous, quoted in *We Can't Wait! Americans Speak Out for Fair Pay for Home Care Workers* (Bronx, NY: Paraprofessional Healthcare Institute, 2013), 34.

19. See Fair Labor Standards Act Amendments of 1974, Pub. L. No. 93-259, 88 Stat. 53, explicitly noting that nannies are engaged "in commerce." See also "Fact Sheet: Proposed Rule Changes Concerning In-Home Care Industry Under the Fair Labor Standards Act (FLSA)," U.S. Department of Labor,

Wage and Labor Division, www.dol.gov/whd/flsa/whdfs-NPRM-companion
ship.htm.

20. See "Fact Sheet: Proposed Rule Changes."

21. Steven L. Dawson, founder and past president of the Paraprofessional
Healthcare Institute, in *We Can't Wait!*, 60.

22. Dorie Seavey and Abby Marquand, *Caring in America: A Comprehensive
Analysis of the Nation's Fastest Growing Jobs: Home Health and Personal Care
Aides* (Bronx, NY: Paraprofessional Healthcare Institute, 2011), 16, phina
tional.org/sites/phinational.org/files/clearinghouse/caringinamerica-20111212
.pdf.

23. Paul K. Sonn, Catherine K. Ruckelshaus, and Sarah Leberstein,
*Fair Pay for Home Care Workers: Reforming the U.S. Department of Labor's
Companionship Regulations Under the Fair Labor Standards Act* (New
York: National Employment Law Project, 2011), 10, www.nelp.org/page
/-/Justice/2011/FairPayforHomeCareWorkers.pdf?nocdn=1.

24. Long Island Care at Home, Ltd., et al. v. Coke, 551 U.S. 158, 167 (2007).

25. See "Fact Sheet: Proposed Rule Changes." See also Fair Labor Standards
Act Amendments of 1974, Pub. L. No. 93-259, 88 Stat. 53, explicitly noting
that nannies are engaged "in commerce."

26. U.S. Department of Labor, "Minimum Wage, Overtime Protections
Extended to Direct Care Workers by US Labor Department," press release, September 17, 2013, www.dol.gov/whd/media/press/whdpressVB3.asp
?pressdoc=national/20130917.xml.

27. Kelly Kennedy, "Home Health Industry Fights Minimum Wage Rule,"
USA Today, February 16, 2012, usatoday30.usatoday.com/news/washington
/story/2012-02-15/home-health-care-minimum-wage/53110228/1.

28. Lipman et al., "Call for Bright-Lines," 361, 363–64.

29. "Fact Sheet #17G: Salary Basis Requirement and the Part 541
Exemptions Under the Fair Labor Standards Act (FLSA)," U.S. Department
of Labor, Wage and Labor Division, revised July 2008, www.dol.gov/whd/regs
/compliance/fairpay/fs17g_salary.htm.

30. Lisa Girion, "White-Collar Employees Winning Overtime Redress,"
Los Angeles Times, June 8, 2001, A1, A9.

31. "W.D.Va.: Dollar General 'Store Manager' May Have Been Misclassified
as Executive Exempt; Defendant's Motion for SJ Denied," Overtime Law Blog:
FLSA Decisions, July 11, 2010, flsaovertimelaw.com/2010/07/11/w-d-va-dollar
-general-%E2%80%9Cstore-manager%E2%80%9D-may-have-been
-misclassified-as-executive-exempt-defendant%E2%80%99s-motion-for-sj
-denied/.

32. Gayle Cinquegrani and Chris Opfer, "Obama to Direct FLSA Overtime
Expansion to Promote Administration's Wage Agenda," *Daily Labor Report*,
March 13, 2014, www.bna.com/obama-direct-flsa-n17179882912/.

33. Ross Eisenbrey and Jared Bernstein, "Eliminating the Right to
Overtime Pay: Department of Labor Proposal Means Lower Pay, Longer Hours

for Millions of Workers," Economic Policy Institute Briefing Paper, June 2003, www.epi.org/files/page/-/old/briefingpapers/flsa_jun03.pdf.

34. Michael D. Shear and Steven Greenhouse, "Obama Will Seek Broad Expansion of Overtime Pay," *New York Times*, March 12, 2014, A1, A17, quoting Ross Eisenbrey, a vice president at the Economic Policy Institute.

35. "These salary requirements do not apply to outside sales employees, teachers, and employees practicing law or medicine." "Fact Sheet #17G: Salary Basis Requirement."

36. Cinquegrani and Opfer, "Obama to Direct FLSA Overtime Expansion." See also Jared Bernstein and Ross Eisenbrey, "New Inflation-Adjusted Salary Test Would Bring Needed Clarity to FLSA Overtime Rules," Economic Policy Institute Report, March 13, 2014, www.epi.org/publication /inflation-adjusted-salary-test-bring-needed/.

37. Aspen Institute Economic Opportunities Program, "Working in America," fact sheet, www.aspenwsi.org/wordpress/wp-content/uploads/minimum -wage-background.pdf.

38. Ross Eisenbrey, "It's Time to Update Overtime," *New York Times*, January 10, 2014. Eisenbrey suggests raising the threshold to $970, which would reflect where it was in 1975 in today's dollars.

39. Shear and Greenhouse, "Obama Will Seek Broad Expansion."

40. Data provided by the Economic Policy Institute, on file with author.

41. U.S. Bureau of Labor Statistics, cited in Brad Plumer, "How Worrisome Is the Rise of Involuntary Part-Time Workers?," Wonkblog, *Washington Post*, October 9, 2012, www.washingtonpost.com/blogs/wonkblog/wp/2012/10/09 /who-are-americas-part-time-workers.

42. Interview with Dolly Martinez, March 17, 2014, on file with author.

43. Joe Maniscalco, "Artists in Revolt: Supply Store Workers Vote to Unionize," *LaborPress*, March 6, 2014, laborpress.org/sectors/union-retail/3388 -artists-in-revolt-supply-store-workers-vote-to-unionize.

44. Whitney Kimball, "Update: Utrecht Workers Call for Living Wage," Art F City, July 7, 2014, artfcity.com/2014/07/07/utrecht-workers-call-for-living-wage/.

45. See Rebecca Glauber, "Wanting More but Working Less: Involuntary Part-Time Employment and Economic Vulnerability," Carsey Institute Issue Brief No. 64, Summer 2013, 4.

46. Jonathan P. Hiatt, "Policy Issues Concerning the Contingent Work Force," *Washington and Lee Law Review* 52, no. 3 (1995): 739, 741, scholarly commons.law.wlu.edu/wlulr/vol52/iss3/5.

47. BLS, "Highlights of Women's Earnings in 2012," U.S. Bureau of Labor Statistics Report 1045, October 2013, 38–41, Tables 4 and 5, www.bls.gov/cps /cpswom2012.pdf.

48. Glauber, "Wanting More but Working Less," 2.

49. Stephanie Luce and Naoki Fujita, *Discounted Jobs: How Retailers Sell Workers Short* (New York: Retail Action Project/CUNY Murphy Institute, 2012), 12.

50. Glauber, "Wanting More but Working Less," 2, 5.

51. Steven Greenhouse, "Gap to Raise Minimum Hourly Pay," *New York Times*, February 20, 2014, B1–2.

52. Interview with Nala Toussaint, March 17, 2014, on file with author.

53. Joseph Williams, "My Life as a Retail Worker: Nasty, Brutish, and Poor," *The Atlantic*, March 11, 2014, www.theatlantic.com/business/archive/2014/03/my-life-as-a-retail-worker-nasty-brutish-and-poor/284332.

54. See "Questions and Answers on Employer Shared Responsibility Provisions Under the Affordable Care Act," last updated May 13, 2014, www.irs.gov/uac/Newsroom/Questions-and-Answers-on-Employer-Shared-Responsibility-Provisions-Under-the-Affordable-Care-Act.

55. Luce and Fujita, *Discounted Jobs*, 19.

56. Sandhya Somashekhar, "Businesses Gear Up for Employer Mandate," *Washington Post*, June 24, 2014, A2.

57. UC Berkeley Labor Center, "Which Workers Are Most at Risk of Reduced Work Hours Under the Affordable Care Act?," Data Brief, February 2013, 1.

58. Robert Pear, "Public Sector Capping Part-Time Hours to Skirt Health Care Law," *New York Times*, February 21, 2014, A12, A15.

59. Luce and Fujita, *Discounted Jobs*, 6.

60. ROC-United, *The Third Shift: Child Care Needs and Access for Working Mothers in Restaurants* (New York: Restaurant Opportunities Centers United, 2013), 11.

61. Interview with Rebekah Christie, March 17, 2014, on file with author.

62. Luce and Fujita, *Discounted Jobs*, 13.

63. Herb Weisbaum, "How 'On-Call' Hours Are Hurting Part-Time Workers," CNBC.com, December 4, 2013, www.cnbc.com/id/101244403.

64. Steven Greenhouse, "A Push to Give Steadier Shifts to Part-Timers," *New York Times*, July 16, 2014, A1, B4.

65. Luce and Fujita, *Discounted Jobs*, 25.

66. Goldman and Jorgensen, "Time After Time," 15.

67. New York is one of fourteen states to have such legislation. "Mandatory Overtime," Nursing World, American Nurses Association, nursingworld.org/MainMenuCategories/Policy-Advocacy/State/Legislative-Agenda-Reports/MandatoryOvertime.

68. Greenhouse, "Push to Give Steadier Shifts," A1, B4.

69. Carrie Gleason, "Part-Time Workers' Cut-Rate Deal," *New York Times*, December 4, 2013.

70. Greenhouse, "Push to Give Steadier Shifts."

71. Luce and Fujita, *Discounted Jobs*, 26.

72. See Karen Kornbluh, "The Joy of Flex," *Washington Monthly*, December 2005, www.washingtonmonthly.com/features/2005/0512.kornbluh.html.

73. Lipman et al., "Call for Bright-Lines," 377.

74. Eileen Appelbaum, Heather Boushey, and John Schmitt, *The Economic Importance of Women's Rising Hours of Work: Time to Update Employment Standards* (Washington, DC: Center for American Progress and the Center

for Economic and Policy Research, 2014), 18, cdn.americanprogress.org/wp-content/uploads/2014/04/WomensRisingWorkv2.pdf.

75. Work in America Institute, *New Work Schedules for a Changing Society* (Scarsdale, NY: Work in America Institute, 1981), 3, quoted in Lipman et al., "Call for Bright-Lines," 380.

76. O'Leary and Kornbluh, "Family Friendly for All Families," 93.

77. Appelbaum et al., *Economic Importance of Women's Rising Hours of Work*, 19.

78. Kornbluh, "Joy of Flex."

79. Working Families Flexibility Act, H.Rept. 1274, 111th Cong., 1st sess., 2009.

80. Appelbaum et al., *Economic Importance of Women's Rising Hours of Work*, 19.

81. "Part-Time Workers Bill of Rights," United Food and Commercial Workers Union Action, www.ufcwaction.org/part-time-workers/.

82. Glauber, "Wanting More but Working Less," 5.

83. Robert Kuttner, "The Task Rabbit Economy," *American Prospect*, September–October 2013, 51.

84. Luce and Fujita, Discounted Jobs, 24.

4: THE WILD WEST: THE LAWLESS WORLD OF THE CONTINGENT WORKFORCE

1. Gabriel Thompson, "The Workers Who Bring You Black Friday," *The Nation*, November 26, 2013, www.thenation.com/article/177377/holiday-crush.

2. Jonathan P. Hiatt, "Policy Issues Concerning the Contingent Work Force," *Washington and Lee Law Review* 52, no. 3 (1995): 739, 742, scholarly commons.law.wlu.edu/wlulr/vol52/iss3/5.

3. "In addition to meeting the test of 'employee,' an employer is only covered by the FLSA if the employer is an enterprise engaged in interstate commerce and has a gross volume of business of at least $500,000 per year." Katherine V.W. Stone, "Legal Protections for Atypical Employees: Employment Law for Workers Without Workplaces and Employees Without Employers," *Berkeley Journal of Employment and Labor Law* 27, no. 2 (2006): 251, 259, scholarship.law.berkeley.edu/bjell/vol27/iss2/1.

4. Marc Linder, "The Small Business Exemption Under the Fair Labor Standards Act: The 'Original' Accumulation of Capital and the Inversion of Industrial Policy," *Journal of Law and Policy* 6 (1997–98): 498. See also Stone, "Legal Protections for Atypical Employees," 253–55.

5. Hiatt, "Policy Issues Concerning the Contingent Work Force," 739, 743.

6. Commission on the Future of Worker-Management Relations, "V. Contingent Workers," in U.S. Department of Labor, Fact Finding Report, May 1994, www.dol.gov/_sec/media/reports/dunlop/section5.htm.

7. Hiatt, "Policy Issues Concerning the Contingent Work Force."

8. Stone, "Legal Protections for Atypical Employees," 254, referencing U.S. Bureau of Labor Statistics, "Contingent and Alternative Employment Arrangements, February 2005," U.S. Department of Labor, press release, July 27, 2005, www.bls.gov/news.release/pdf/conemp.pdf.

9. Hiatt, "Policy Issues Concerning the Contingent Work Force."

10. Stone, "Legal Protections for Atypical Employees," 259.

11. Richard Carlson, "The Small Firm Exemption and the Single Employer Doctrine in Employment Discrimination Law," *St. John's Law Review* 80, no. 4 (2006): 1197, 1200–1201, scholarship.law.stjohns.edu/lawreview/vol80/iss4/2.

12. Harold Meyerson, "The Forty-Year Slump," *American Prospect*, November 12, 2013, 29, prospect.org/article/40-year-slump. This trend is steadily increasing in the manufacturing sector, going from 2.3 percent of manufacturing workers in 1989 to almost 9 percent in 2004. Ibid.

13. Lydia DePillis, "This Is What a U.S. Manufacturing Job Looks Like," *Washington Post*, March 16, 2014, G1, G5.

14. Thompson, "Workers Who Bring You Black Friday."

15. Max Ehrenfreund, "It's Been a Really Bad Week for Hummus," Wonkblog, *Washington Post*, May 23, 2014, www.washingtonpost.com/blogs/wonkblog/wp/2014/05/23/its-been-a-really-bad-week-for-hummus/.

16. Stone, "Legal Protections for Atypical Employees," 259.

17. Hiatt, "Policy Issues Concerning the Contingent Work Force."

18. Stone, "Legal Protections for Atypical Employees," 264–65. Some states have attempted to address this problem through statute. Ibid.

19. Bill Raden and Gary Cohn, "Ten Years a Temp: California Food Giant Highlights National Rise in Exploited Labor," *Capital and Main*, May 27, 2014, capitalandmain.com/ten-years-a-temp-california-food-giant-highlights-national-rise-in-exploited-labor/.

20. Steven Greenhouse, "Ruling Says McDonald's Is Liable for Workers," *New York Times*, July 30, 2014, B1.

21. William Shakespeare, *Romeo and Juliet*, Act II, Scene ii, 1–2.

22. By contrast, I happened to be chatting with the woman who cleans the building I work in, who said she only did that job for five hours per day and that she also worked another job. I asked if she got any benefits, assuming that she, too, was an "independent contractor" and thus without any job protections. "Oh no," she said, "I have a union. I get health care—in fact, I just had a cap on a tooth that would have cost me $900." Thank goodness for unions.

23. Stone, "Legal Protections for Atypical Employees," citing U.S. Bureau of Labor Statistics, "Contingent and Alternative Employment Arrangements," 254.

24. Stone, "Legal Protections for Atypical Employees," 279–80. See also Hiatt, "Policy Issues Concerning the Contingent Work Force."

25. David Bensman, "Workers on the Edge," *American Prospect*, April 7, 2014, prospect.org/article/workers-edge.

26. Moshe Z. Marvit, "How Crowdworkers Became the Ghosts in the

Digital Machine," *The Nation*, February 2, 2014, www.thenation.com/article /178241/how-crowdworkers-became-ghosts-digital-machine.

27. Ibid.

28. Hiatt, "Policy Issues Concerning the Contingent Work Force."

29. Peggie R. Smith, "The Future of Family Caregiving: The Value of Work-Family Strategies that Benefit Both Care Consumers and Paid Care Workers," in *Women Who Opt Out: The Debate over Working Mothers and Work-Family Balance*, ed. Bernie D. Jones (New York: New York University Press, 2012), 126.

30. Harris v. Quinn, 573 U.S. ___ (2014).

31. Dave Jamieson, "After Harris v. Quinn, SEIU Wants to Unionize 26,000 Home Care Workers in Minnesota," *Huffington Post*, July 8, 2014, www .huffingtonpost.com/2014/07/08/harris-v-quinn-seiu-minnesota_n_5568105 .html.

32. Tamar Lewin, "More College Adjuncts See Strength in Union Numbers," *New York Times*, December 4, 2013, A18.

33. Tara Siegel Bernard, "Allstate Case Shows Risk of Signing Away the Right to Sue," *New York Times*, April 29, 2014.

34. Ibid.

35. Rebecca Smith and Harmony Goldberg, *Unity for Dignity: Expanding the Right to Organize to Win Human Rights at Work* (New York: Excluded Worker Congress, 2010), 13, www.unitedworkerscongress.org/uploads/2/9/1/6/29166849 /unity_for_dignity_report.pdf. See also GAO, *Employment Arrangements: Improved Outreach Could Help Ensure Proper Worker Classification*, GAO-06 -656 11 (Washington, DC: U.S. Government Accountability Office, 2006), 11 (finding that "independent contractors" constitute 7.4 percent of employees). According to Smith and Goldberg, this number includes many workers who have been inappropriately categorized as independent contractors, and thus the percentage of the workforce should actually be smaller than the GAO reports. Smith and Goldberg, *Unity for Dignity*, 50n21.

36. Siegel Bernard, "Allstate Case Shows Risk."

37. Philip S. Foner, *Women and the American Labor Movement: From the First Trade Unions to the Present* (New York: The Free Press, 1979), 1.

38. Carlson, "Small Firm Exemption," 1209.

39. Holland v. Gee, 719 F.Supp.2d 1361, 1365 (S.D.Fla. 2010) (quoting Santelices v. Cable Wiring, 147 F.Supp.2d 1313,1319 [S.D.Fla. 2001]). In the case of Lisa Holland, her employer tried unsuccessfully to describe her as an independent contractor to get out from under a pregnancy discrimination charge.

40. Bensman, "Workers on the Edge."

41. Commission on the Future of Worker-Management Relations, "V. Contingent Workers."

42. S. 2504, 103d Cong., 2d sess. (1994); H.R. 2188, 103d Cong., 1st sess. (1993).

43. In summary, the commission recommended the following: "(1) The

definition of employee in labor, employment, and tax law should be modernized, simplified, and standardized. Instead of the control test borrowed from the old common law of master and servant, the definition should be based on the economic realities underlying the relationship between the worker and the party benefiting from the worker's services. (2) The definition of employer should also be standardized and grounded in the economic realities of the employment relationship. Congress and the NLRB should remove the incentives that now exist for firms to use variations in corporate form to avoid responsibility for the people who do their work." Commission on the Future of Worker-Management Relations, "V. Contingent Workers."

44. Commission on the Future of Worker-Management Relations, "V. Contingent Workers."

45. Gertrude Stein, "Sacred Emily," in *Writings: 1903–1932*, ed. Catharine R. Stimpson and Harriet Chessman (New York: Library of America, 1998), 387–96.

5: BYE-BYE, BABY: GIVING BIRTH AND BACK TO WORK

1. Janet Walsh, *Failing Its Families: Lack of Paid Leave and Work-Family Supports in the US* (New York: Human Rights Watch, 2011), 5, www.hrw.org /reports/2011/02/23/failing-its-families-0.

2. Office of the Assistant Secretary for Planning and Evaluation, *Indicators of Welfare Dependence*, Annual Report to Congress (Washington, DC: U.S. Department of Health and Human Services, 1998), aspe.hhs.gov/hsp/indica tors98/indicators98.htm.

3. Walsh, *Failing Its Families*, 47, internal citations omitted.

4. Heather Boushey and Alexandra Mitukiewicz, *Family and Medical Leave Insurance: A Basic Standard for Today's Workforce* (Washington, DC: Center for American Progress, 2014), www.americanprogress.org/issues/labor /report/2014/04/15/87652/family-and-medical-leave-insurance/. See also Jane Waldfogel, "International Policies Toward Parental Leave and Child Care," *Caring for Infants and Toddlers* 11, no. 1 (2001): 101, futureofchildren.org /futureofchildren/publications/docs/11_01_06.pdf.

5. Sarah Fass, "Paid Leave in the States: A Critical Support for Low-Wage Workers and Their Families," National Center for Children in Poverty, Mailman School of Public Health, Columbia University, March 2009, 5, hdl .handle.net/10022/AC:P:8888.

6. Heather Boushey and John Schmitt, "Job Tenure and Firm Size Provisions Exclude Many Young Parents from Family and Medical Leave," Center for Economic and Policy Research Issue Brief, June 2007, www.cepr .net/documents/publications/firmsize_2008_02.pdf.

7. Boushey and Mitukiewicz, *Family and Medical Leave Insurance*, 14.

8. Waldfogel, "International Policies Toward Parental Leave," 101.

9. Jacob Alex Klerman, Kelly Daley, and Alyssa Pozniak, *Family and*

Medical Leave in 2012: Technical Report (Cambridge, MA: Abt Associates, 2012), www.dol.gov/asp/evaluation/fmla/FMLA-2012-Technical-Report.pdf.

10. Heather Boushey, Jane Farrell, and John Schmitt, *Job Protection Isn't Enough: Why America Needs Paid Parental Leave* (Washington, DC: Center for American Progress and the Center for Economic and Policy Research, 2013), 4.

11. Ibid., 3.

12. Eileen Appelbaum, Heather Boushey, and John Schmitt, *The Economic Importance of Women's Rising Hours of Work: Time to Update Employment Standards* (Washington, DC: Center for American Progress and Center for Economic and Policy Research, 2014), 4, cdn.americanprogress.org/wp-content/uploads/2014/04/WomensRisingWorkv2.pdf.

13. Fass, "Paid Leave in the States," 5 (internal citations omitted).

14. Walsh, *Failing Its Families*, 31.

15. The Affordable Care Act does require that nursing mothers have access to break time and a nursing room but allows employers with fifty or fewer employees to opt out in case of "undue hardship." Section 4207 of the Patient Protection and Affordable Care Act (P.L. 111-148) amending Section 7 of The Fair Labor Standards Act. This provision also protects only women who are not otherwise exempted from FLSA's overtime protections.

16. Walsh, *Failing Its Families*, 4–6.

17. Katherine V.W. Stone, "Legal Protections for Atypical Employees: Employment Law for Workers Without Workplaces and Employees Without Employers," 27 *Berkeley Journal of Employment and Labor Law* 27, no. 2 (2006): 251, 268, scholarship.law.berkeley.edu/bjell/vol27/iss2/1.

18. Boushey et al., *Job Protection Isn't Enough*, 1–2.

19. Ibid.

20. U.S. Bureau of Labor Statistics, *National Compensation Survey: Employee Benefits in the United States, March 2009* (Washington, DC: U.S. Department of Labor, 2009), Appendix Table 1 and Table 2, www.bls.gov/ncs/ebs/benefits/2009/ebbl0044.pdf; U.S. Bureau of Labor Statistics, "Table 21: Leave Benefits, Access Civilian Workers, National Compensation Survey, March 2008," Employee Benefits Survey, U.S. Department of Labor, March 2008, www.bls.gov/ebs/benefits/2008/ownership/civilian/table21a.htm.

21. Walsh, *Failing Its Families*, 5.

22. Ibid., 18. See also Boushey and Mitukiewicz, *Family and Medical Leave Insurance*, 10.

23. Walsh, *Failing Its Families*, 24–25.

24. Karen Kornbluh, "The Joy of Flex," *Washington Monthly*, December 2005, www.washingtonmonthly.com/features/2005/0512.kornbluh.html.

25. Lake Research Partners and Chesapeake Beach Consulting, "Work-Family Strategy Council Poll," 2013, cited in Boushey and Mitukiewicz, *Family and Medical Leave Insurance*, 4.

26. Fass, "Paid Leave in the States," 5 (internal citations omitted).

27. Netsy Firestein, Ann O'Leary, and Zoe Savitsky, *A Guide to Implementing*

Paid Leave: Lessons from California (Berkeley: Report of the Labor Project for Working Families and the Berkeley Center on Health, Economics & Family Security, 2011), paidfamilyleave.org/pdf/pfl_guide.pdf.

28. Brigid Schulte, "States Make Moves Toward Paying for Family Leave," *Washington Post*, December 30, 2013, A3.

29. Fass, "Paid Leave in the States," 7.

30. Ibid. (internal citations omitted).

31. Boushey and Mitukiewicz, *Family and Medical Leave Insurance*, 21.

32. Schulte, "States Make Moves."

33. Walsh, *Failing Its Families*, 20–21.

34. Curtis Skinner and Susan Ochshorn, "Paid Family Leave: Strengthening Families and Our Future," National Center for Children in Poverty Brief, April 2012, 8, www.nccp.org/publications/pdf/text_1059.pdf.

35. Schulte, "States Make Moves."

36. Walsh, *Failing Its Families*, 21.

37. Boushey et al., *Job Protection Isn't Enough*, 4.

38. Boushey and Mitukiewicz, *Family and Medical Leave Insurance*, 27.

39. Walsh, *Failing Its Families*, 23, citing Andrea Bassanini and Danielle Venn, "The Impact of Labour Market Policies on Productivity in OECD Countries," *International Productivity Monitor* 17 (Fall 2008): 11. "Multifactor productivity is the measure of changes in output per unit of combined inputs." Walsh, *Failing Its Families*, 28n69.

40. Walsh, *Failing Its Families*, 29–30.

41. Rebecca Ray, Janet Gornick, and John Schmitt, "Parental Leave Policies in 21 Countries: Assessing Generosity and Gender Equality," Center for Economic and Policy Research report, September 2008, 2, www.cepr.net /documents/publications/parental_2008_09.pdf.

42. Walsh, *Failing Its Families*, 3.

43. Schulte, "States Make Moves."

44. Boushey and Mitukiewicz, *Family and Medical Leave Insurance*, 25.

45. Ray et al., "Parental Leave Policies in 21 Countries," 10n19.

46. Jens Hansegard, "For Paternity Leave, Sweden Asks if Two Months Is Enough," *Wall Street Journal*, July 31, 2012.

47. Sharon Lerner, "Daddy's Home," *American Prospect*, September–October 2013, 15.

48. Walsh, *Failing Its Families*, 29–30.

49. Ray et al., "Parental Leave Policies in 21 Countries," 5, 10.

50. Boushey and Mitukiewicz, *Family and Medical Leave Insurance*, 26.

51. Isabelle de Pommereau, "German Powerhouse Leaves Working Mothers Behind," *Christian Science Monitor*, April 4, 2012, www.csmonitor.com/World /Europe/2012/0404/German-powerhouse-leaves-working-mothers-behind.

52. Bee Rowlatt, "The Reluctant Hausfrau: Being a German Mother," *The Telegraph*, August 3, 2013, www.telegraph.co.uk/culture/tvandradio/10216510 /The-reluctant-hausfrau-being-a-German-mother.html.

53. Suzanne Daley and Nicholas Kulish, "Germany Fights Population Drop," *New York Times*, August 13, 2013.

54. Population replacement is considered to be 2.1 for Europe. "Eurostat—2004 figures," cited in "Norway's Welfare Model 'Helps Birth Rate,'" BBC News, March 28, 2006, news.bbc.co.uk/go/pr/fr/-/2/hi/europe/4786160.stm.

55. Shira Schoenberg, "Massachusetts Nannies, Housecleaners, Domestic Workers Visit State House in Boston to Push for 'Bill of Rights,'" MassLive.com, November 12, 2013, www.masslive.com/politics/index.ssf/2013/11/massachusetts_domestic_workers.html.

56. Elise Gould, Kai Filion, and Andrew Green, "The Need for Paid Sick Days: The Lack of a Federal Policy Further Erodes Family Economic Security," Economic Policy Institute Briefing Paper #319, June 29, 2011, 2, 6, www.epi.org/files/temp2011/BriefingPaper319-2.pdf.

57. Boushey and Mitukiewicz, *Family and Medical Leave Insurance*, 13.

58. Gould et al., "Need for Paid Sick Days," 5.

59. Ibid., 6.

60. Emily Friedman, "Dena Lockwood Was Fired When She Called in Sick to Care for Her Daughter," ABC News, January 29, 2010, abcnews.go.com/Business/SmallBiz/single-mother-wins-court-losing-job-care-sick/story?id=9689779.

61. Gordon Lafer, "One by One, States Are Pushing Bans on Sick Leave Legislation," Economic Policy Institute, November 6, 2013, www.epi.org/publication/states-pushing-bans-sick-leave-legislation/.

62. Sharon Lerner, "Get Sick, Get Fired: America's Low-Wage Workers Push Back," *American Prospect*, June 23, 2014, prospect.org/article/working-families-take-white-house-stage-paid-sick-leave-battle-continues.

63. Appelbaum et al., *Economic Importance of Women's Rising Hours of Work*, 23.

64. Healthy Families Act, H.R. 1876, S. 984, 112th Cong., 1st Sess. (2011).

65. Appelbaum et al., *Economic Importance of Women's Rising Hours of Work*, 23.

66. Lerner, "Daddy's Home."

6: DID MARY POPPINS HAVE KIDS? CHILD CARE AND THE WORKING MOTHER

1. Peter S. Goodman, "Cuts to Child Care Subsidy Thwart More Job Seekers," *New York Times*, May 23, 2010.

2. BLS, "Women in the Labor Force: A Databook," U.S. Bureau of Labor Statistics Report 1040, February 2013, 1, www.bls.gov/cps/wlf-databook-2012.pdf.

3. The Census Bureau quaintly refers to this as "self-care."

4. Jonathan Cohn, "The Hell of American Day Care: An Investigation into the Barely Regulated, Unsafe Business of Looking After Our Children,"

New Republic, April 15, 2013, quoting Jane Addams, *Twenty Years at Hull House*, 9.

5. It is estimated that close to 11 million children under age five are in some type of child care arrangement. *Child Care in America: 2012 Fact Sheets* (Arlington, VA: Child Care Aware of America, 2012), 5, www.naccrra.org /public-policy/resources/child-care-state-fact-sheets-0.

6. *Child Care in America*, 5.

7. Lisa Dodson and Randy Albelda with Diana Salas Coronado and Marya Mtshali, *How Youth Are Put at Risk by Parents' Low-Wage Jobs* (Boston: Center for Social Policy, 2012), 6, cdn.umb.edu/images/centers_institutes /center_social_policy/Youth_at_RiskParents_Low_Wage_Jobs_Fall_121.pdf.

8. Michele Friedman, "Child Care," Almanac of Policy Issues, www .policyalmanac.org/social_welfare/childcare.shtml.

9. Sarah Minton and Christin Durham, *Low-Income Families and the Cost of Child Care: State Child Care Subsidies, Out-of-Pocket Expenses, and the Cliff Effect* (Washington, DC: Urban Institute, 2013), www.urban.org /UploadedPDF/412982-low-income-families.pdf.

10. Ann O'Leary and Karen Kornbluh, "Family Friendly for All Families," in *The Shriver Report: A Woman's Nation Changes Everything: A Study by Maria Shriver and the Center for American Progress*, ed. Heather Boushey and Ann O'Leary (Washington, DC: Center for American Progress, 2009), 103.

11. Office of the Assistant Secretary for Planning and Evaluation, "ASPE Issue Brief: Estimates of Child Care Eligibility and Receipt for Fiscal Year 2009," Office of Human Services Policy, U.S. Department of Health and Human Services, December 2012.

12. Karen Schulman and Helen Blank, *Downward Slide: State Child Care Assistance Policies 2012* (Washington, DC: National Women's Law Center, 2012), 1, www.nwlc.org/sites/default/files/pdfs/NWLC2012_StateChild CareAssistanceReport.pdf. These authors suggest the possible reason for the backsliding may be the end of funding provided to states by the American Recovery and Reinvestment Act, which sought to mitigate the effects of the recent severe recession.

13. Ibid.

14. ROC-United, *The Third Shift: Child Care Needs and Access for Working Mothers in Restaurants* (New York: Restaurant Opportunities Centers United, 2013), 8.

15. Eduardo Porter, "In the War on Poverty, a Dogged Adversary," *New York Times*, December 18, 2013, B1, B3.

16. Minton and Durham, *Low-Income Families*, 1–2.

17. Dodson and Albelda, *How Youth Are Put at Risk*, 8; Minton and Durham, *Low-Income Families*, 1–2.

18. Goodman, "Cuts to Child Care Subsidy."

19. Dodson and Albelda, *How Youth Are Put at Risk*, 6.

20. ROC-United, *Third Shift*, 1, 12–13.

21. Stephanie Schmitt, Hannah Matthews, Sheila Smith, and Taylor

Robbins, "Investing in Young Children: A Fact Sheet on Early Care and Education Participation, Access, and Quality," National Center for Law and Social Policy, November 2013, 9, www.nccp.org/publications/pdf/text_1085 .pdf.

22. *Child Care in America*, 6.

23. Cohn, "Hell of American Day Care."

24. Katharine Mieszkowski, "California's Lack of Online Child Care Records Leaves Parents in Dark," Center for Investigative Reporting, January 30, 2014, cironline.org/reports/california's-lack-online-child-care-records -leaves-parents-dark-5819.

25. Courtney E. Martin, "Child Care and the Overwhelmed Parent," Opinionator blog, *New York Times*, July 24, 2014, opinionator.blogs.nytimes .com/2014/07/24/child-care-and-the-overwhelmed-parent/.

26. Mark Lino, *Expenditures on Children by Families, 2006* (Alexandria, VA: Center for Nutrition Policy and Promotion, U.S. Department of Agriculture, 2007), 18, cnpp.usda.gov/Publications/CRC/crc2006.pdf.

27. Alissa Quart, "Crushed by the Cost of Child Care," Opinionator blog, *New York Times*, August 17, 2013, opinionator.blogs.nytimes.com/2013/08/17 /crushed-by-the-cost-of-child-care/.

28. Lynda Laughlin, "Who's Minding the Kids? Child Care Arrangements: Spring 2011," U.S. Census Bureau, April 2013, 17, www.census.gov/prod /2013pubs/p70-135.pdf.

29. Tara Siegel Bernard, "Choosing Child Care When You Go Back to Work," *New York Times*, November 23, 2013, B1.

30. *Child Care in America*, 5.

31. Siegel Bernard, "Choosing Child Care."

32. O'Leary and Kornbluh, "Family Friendly for All Families," 102–3.

33. Schmitt et al., "Investing in Young Children," 1.

34. Dodson and Albelda, *How Youth Are Put at Risk*, 9–15.

35. Schmitt et al., "Investing in Young Children," 2.

36. Motoko Rich, "Language-Gap Study Bolsters a Push for Pre-K," *New York Times*, October 22, 2013, 1.

37. OECD data shows that disadvantaged children do better over the long term when they are enrolled in day care early in life. OECD, *Education at a Glance 2012: Highlights* (Paris: OECD Publishing, 2012), dx.doi.org/10.1787 /eag_highlights-2012-en.

38. Rich, "Language-Gap Study."

39. Philp S. Foner, *Women and the American Labor Movement: From the First Trade Unions to the Present* (New York: The Free Press, 1979), 352.

40. Alice Kessler-Harris, *Out to Work: A History of Wage-Earning Women in the United States* (New York: Oxford University Press, 1982), 294–95, quoting Florence Kerr.

41. Cohn, "Hell of American Day Care," 10.

42. Ibid., 11.

43. Nancy L. Cohen, "Why America Never Had Universal Child

Care," *New Republic*, April 24, 2013, www.newrepublic.com/article/113009 /child-care-america-was-very-close-universal-day-care.

44. Kessler-Harris, *Out to Work*, 317.

45. See generally Bernie D. Jones, ed., *Women Who Opt Out: The Debate over Working Mothers and Work-Family Balance* (New York: New York University Press, 2012).

46. Stephanie Coontz, "Why Gender Equality Stalled," op-ed, *New York Times*, February 16, 2013.

47. Ibid.

48. Jason Furman, "Poverty and the Tax Code," *Democracy: A Journal of Ideas*, Spring 2014, 8, 13.

49. Heather Boushey, "The New Breadwinners," in *The Shriver Report: A Woman's Nation Changes Everything: A Study by Maria Shriver and the Center for American Progress*, ed. Heather Boushey and Ann O'Leary (Washington, DC: Center for American Progress, 2009), 55–56.

50. Cohn, "Hell of American Day Care," 12.

51. Peter Edelman, *So Rich, So Poor: Why It's So Hard to End Poverty in America* (New York: The New Press, 2012), 74–75.

52. Goodman, "Cuts to Child Care Subsidy."

53. Judith Warner, "Ready to Rejoin the Rat Race," *New York Times Magazine*, August 11, 2013.

54. Cohen, "Why America Never Had Universal Child Care," 1.

55. Eileen Appelbaum, Heather Boushey, and John Schmitt, *The Economic Importance of Women's Rising Hours of Work: Time to Update Employment Standards* (Washington, DC: Center for American Progress and Center for Economic and Policy Research, 2014), 4, cdn.americanprogress.org/wp -content/uploads/2014/04/WomensRisingWorkv2.pdf.

56. Cohn, "Hell of American Day Care," 17–18.

57. Pamela Druckerman, "Catching Up with France on Day Care," *New York Times*, September 1, 2013, 12.

58. Ibid.

59. Cohn, "Hell of American Day Care," 19.

60. ROC-United, *Third Shift*, 11.

61. Rich, "Language-Gap Study."

62. Cohn, "Hell of American Day Care," 18.

63. GAO, *Military Child Care: DOD Is Taking Actions to Address Awareness and Availability Barriers* GAO-12-21 (Washington, DC: U.S. Government Accountability Office, 2012), 1, www.gao.gov/assets/590/588188.pdf.

64. Nancy K. Cauthen, "Improving Work Supports: Closing the Financial Gap for Low-Wage Workers and Their Families," Economic Policy Institute Briefing Paper #198, October 2, 2007, 19, www.gpn.org/bp198.html, citing the recommendations of Suzanne W. Helburn and Barbara R. Bergmann, *America's Child Care Problem: The Way Out* (New York: Palgrave Macmillan, 2002), 215.

65. Cauthen, "Improving Work Supports," 16. The current Child and

Dependent Care Credit is not refundable, meaning that low-income families can make little use of it. Ibid., 17, 27, Table A2.

66. Ibid., 17. The Earned Income Tax Credit, say these advocates, should also be increased for those parents who do not have custody and for workers without children.

67. Ibid.

68. *Child Care in America*, 10.

69. Joya Misra, "Which Policies Promote Gender Pay Equality?," in *Equal Pay Symposium: 50 Years Since the Equal Pay Act of 1963*, ed. Stephanie Coontz (Miami: Council on Contemporary Families, 2013), 12, contemporaryfamilies .org/wp-content/uploads/2014/06/2013_Symposium_Equal-Pay.pdf.

7: LEANING TOGETHER

1. The following section is based on an interview with Patricia Francois on February 4, 2014.

2. See Francois v. Mazer, 523 Fed. Appx. 28, June 25, 2013 (affirming judgment of District Court awarding attorney's fees to Francois). The Mazers attempted to introduce evidence of Francois's immigration status into the case to raise questions about her credibility. The court properly found the evidence prejudicial and excluded it. 2012 WL 1506054 (S.D.N.Y.). Though unsuccessful in this court case, the Mazers were attempting to use a tactic often employed to intimidate undocumented workers into accepting unfair or illegal treatment.

3. Barbara Ehrenreich, *Nickle and Dimed: On (Not) Getting By in America* (New York: Metropolitan Books, 2001).

4. Katherine V.W. Stone, "Legal Protections for Atypical Employees: Employment Law for Workers Without Workplaces and Employees Without Employers," *Berkeley Journal of Employment and Labor Law* 27, no. 2 (2006): 251, 253–55, scholarship.law.berkeley.edu/bjell/vol27/iss2/1.

5. Robert Kuttner, "The Task Rabbit Economy," *American Prospect*, September–October 2013, 53.

6. See Karen Kornbluh, "The Joy of Flex," *Washington Monthly*, December 2005, washingtonmonthly.com/features/2005/0512.kornbluh.html.

7. Nancy K. Cauthen, "Improving Work Supports: Closing the Financial Gap for Low-Wage Workers and Their Families," Economic Policy Institute Briefing Paper #198, October 2, 2007, 4, www.gpn.org/bp198.html.

8. Rebecca Smith and Harmony Goldberg, *Unity for Dignity: Expanding the Right to Organize to Win Human Rights at Work* (New York: Excluded Workers Congress, 2010), 39, www.unitedworkerscongress.org/uploads/2/9/1 /6/29166849/unity_for_dignity_report.pdf. The report describes numerous other campaigns that resulted in legal or legislative victories for excluded workers, built on a foundation of human rights and often invoking international norms and bringing in international organizations to support and validate the efforts.

9. Ibid., 35.

10. Human Rights Network, "United States: Summary Submission to the UN Universal Periodic Review," Ninth Session of the UPR Working Group of the Human Rights Council, April 2010, 2, 3, www.prrac.org/pdf/USHRN _Overarching_UPR_Report.pdf.

11. Smith and Goldberg, *Unity for Dignity*, 35.

12. Steven Greenhouse, "Fast Food Protests Spread Overseas," *New York Times*, May 14, 2014.

13. Anna Fifield, "Japan's Economic Plan: More Day Care," *Washington Post*, August 2, 2104, A1, A9.

14. Franklin D. Roosevelt, Inaugural Address, January 20, 1937.

INDEX

ABOUT THE AUTHOR

Caroline Fredrickson is the president of the American Constitution Society (ACS) and a senior fellow at Demos. She has been widely published on a range of legal and constitutional issues and is a frequent guest on television and radio shows. Before joining ACS, Fredrickson served as the director of the ACLU's Washington legislative office and as general counsel and legal director of NARAL Pro-Choice America. In addition, Caroline was chief of staff to Senator Maria Cantwell and deputy chief of staff to the then Senate Democratic Leader Tom Daschle. During the Clinton administration, she served as special assistant to the president for legislative affairs. She lives in Silver Spring, Maryland.

PUBLISHING IN THE PUBLIC INTEREST

Thank you for reading this book published by The New Press. The New Press is a nonprofit, public interest publisher. New Press books and authors play a crucial role in sparking conversations about the key political and social issues of our day.

We hope you enjoyed this book and that you will stay in touch with The New Press. Here are a few ways to stay up to date with our books, events, and the issues we cover:

- Sign up at www.thenewpress.com/subscribe to receive updates on New Press authors and issues and to be notified about local events
- Like us on Facebook: www.facebook.com/newpressbooks
- Follow us on Twitter: www.twitter.com/thenewpress

Please consider buying New Press books for yourself; for friends and family; or to donate to schools, libraries, community centers, prison libraries, and other organizations involved with the issues our authors write about.

The New Press is a 501(c)(3) nonprofit organization. You can also support our work with a tax-deductible gift by visiting www.thenewpress.com/donate.